"THE CRACK IN THE COSMIC EGG is the Phoenix rising from the ashes."

—Alan Watts

"The book itself is impossible to pin down and analyze; it allows only for being experienced and absorbed through the skin of eyes and intuition. . . . If you are game for some creative, inventive thinking, this book can provide the spark for many upsetting controversies."

—*The Critic*

"A uniquely challenging brain-cracker, one that offers a constant interplay among the ideas of Blake, Bruner, Jesus, Laing, Polanyi, Teilhard, Tillich, and Castaneda." —*Publishers Weekly*

"The most disturbing and stimulating book I have read in many years." —*Parapsychology Review*

Selected by Psychology Today Book Club

Books by Joseph Chilton Pearce

The Crack in the Cosmic Egg
Exploring the Crack in the Cosmic Egg

Published by POCKET BOOKS

The Crack in the Cosmic Egg

Challenging constructs of mind and reality

Joseph Chilton Pearce

PUBLISHED BY POCKET BOOKS

POCKET BOOKS, a Simon & Schuster division of
GULF & WESTERN CORPORATION
1230 Avenue of the Americas, New York, N.Y. 10020

Published by arrangement with Julian Press, Inc.

ISBN: 0-671-80621-1

First Pocket Books printing January, 1973

9th printing

to the memory of my wife
Patricia Ann
mother of our five

There was a child went forth every day,
And the first object he looked upon, that object he became,
And that object became part of him for the day or a certain part of the day,
Or for many years or stretching cycles of years.

—WALT WHITMAN

contents

introduction *xi*
1. *circles and lines* *1*
2. *valves and solvents* *19*
3. *blueprints and viewpoints* *49*
4. *questions and answers* *63*
5. *mirror to mirror* *84*
6. *fire-burn* *104*
7. *behold and become* *116*
8. *mythos and logos* *141*
9. *don Juan and Jesus* *162*
10. *vision and reflection* *190*
references and notes *199*
bibliography *213*

introduction

Almost a decade has passed since I first experienced *the crack* in my own cosmic egg, and made tentative attempts to translate it into communicable form. A certain urgency underlay my efforts, for I felt frustrated by a lack of both technique and background, and outpaced by a growing social outrage and general collapse of cultural logic.

In spite of the radical, fundamental, and shattering effect of the crack personally, it simply would not translate into the common domain. My concern was social, and I hoped for some charismatic formula for altering the broad stream leading to destruction. But the crack remained, and still remains, a fragile, lonely way of nonstatistical balance in a rough statistical world.

I searched for that explosive translation that would magically halt the grinding forces of war, ease our ideological hatreds, and abate our wholesale battenings on our brothers' blood. I longed to find some clever cosmic sign, signalling abroad the way for mass exodus from a Naked Ape despair, and leading to that ecstasy of being fully human. I have ended, at best, with the hope that I might be heard by two or three suffering our common concern, recognizing the dilemma of logical demise, and willing to gather together to explore the crack as a mutual way down and out.

When logic bankrupts it empties the coffers of possibility. And now, as Orwell's *1984* shapes its fantasy about us, our need for alternatives is acute—but alternatives are absent from the scene.

Here in this crack alternatives *abound*—but only for that lone reader, driven, perhaps, to hate a world of instant death, shifting enemy symbols, perpetually stimulated fears and hatreds, economic servitude, psychological enslavement, and general absence of joy; a world where alternatives polarize into equally abhorrent either-ors; a world of logic that at its best has conceived the antiballistic missile—that combatting of direct death with an equally-sure death once removed; a world where leaders tend to become that very thing they behold and declare most intolerable; where Pentagons and CIA's, assuming the role of problem-solvers, tend to bring about the very events which make necessary, verify the assumptions of, and justify the existence and techniques of, Pentagons and CIA's; where the only known underground railway is run by an opposition leading back into the common circles of despair.

My generation boasts its accomplishments, and wonders that our young might spurn the splendors offered. Yet there are those who read the price tag, and find the cost of psyche, life, and hope to be too high. And so I write for that reader who cannot stand where he is and has no place to go. I write of an alternative that is a kind of excluded middle in this logical impasse.

There *is* a third alternative in this world of exclusive either-ors, but the way out is a way *beyond,* not a rehashing of ruined ingredients. The delusion of problem-solving is the first false hope that must be abandoned, for problem-solving tends to be circular. The techniques used to solve a problem determine the nature of the solutions with which we must then live. Problem-solving is like patching holes in a rotten boat; for each patch applied, two more leaks spring up. There are times when a way out is needed that is not available to logical patching techniques. There are times when we need a way beyond rotten hulks, a way not for restructuring a new boat or even a serviceable life jacket, but rather some submariner's way through a sea of confusion to new terrain.

I can only approach the crack obliquely, using ordinary language that includes those unknown but highly charged "trigger-words" we all carry, words that block hearing, words having overtones drowning out the fundamental intended. Further, my alternative suffers the old dilemma of "don't go near the water until you can swim." For I must question archaic assumptions that not only underlie science and religion equally, but which go to the very roots of our culture and are accepted unconsciously. To question such concepts is to question the very ground on which we stand. So I can only plunge the reader in immediately, asking him for a bit of faith and water-treading through these first pages, until, hopefully, more tangible grounds for understanding form.

Mind over matter is a misleading notion, and not the issue here. I have, however, traced the *relation* of mind and reality, as complementary poles of a continuum, and have found, for instance, that a spontaneous healing in a terminal patient occurs in the same way that a discovery forms in science, an illumination in religion, or that change of concept which turns the student into the mature physicist.

When the Hindu walks through a pit of white-hot charcoal, or the scientist experiences his *Eureka!* that opens new levels of reality, each uses the same reality-shaping function of mind. This book traces the pattern of development underlying this function, paying particular attention to the formation of answers to passionate questions, or the filling of empty categories proposed by creative imagination. The empty category proposed by a scientist, for instance, brings about its own fulfillment in the same way, and for the same reasons, that a popular disease is entertained, promoted by publicity, feared by all, and watched for in the contemporary form of physician-priest and patient-supplicant, until if fulfills itself on a statistically predictable and self-verifying basis.

While my book explores this mirroring of thinking and experience, I avoid philosophical arguments, such as the "reality" of the world. What I have explored, in this personal search, is the way we experience a world, and, more importantly, the way this relation influences that world so experienced.

Our reality is influenced by our notions *about* reality,

regardless of the nature of those notions. No notion can arise in isolation from, or stand outside, the current fabric of all our notions. My book has been shaped within the context of cultural beliefs in which I find myself, so I must consider some of the many current influences, even though these conflict and my aim is to go beyond them.

Peter McKellar writes that: "Dislike of the models that have become the symbols of an opposing school of thought may partially or completely seal off the work of one thinker from another, until some third thinker notices that they are both saying something worthy of impartial attention."

My attention is hardly impartial, but I think I can sketch a third-man theme by drawing the similarities between apparently unrelated fields. I hope to show that many recent developments, though insulated one from the other, are lines pointing toward the same functional "crack in the cosmic egg."

Our *cosmic egg* is the sum total of our notions of what the world is, notions which define what reality *can be* for us. The crack, then, is a mode of thinking through which imagination can escape the mundane shell and create a new cosmic egg. The crack is that "twilight between the worlds" found by the young anthropologist, Carlos Castaneda, in his study of the Yaqui Indian sorcerer, don Juan, and his "Way of Knowledge." The crack is found as well in that "narrow gate" of Jesus' Way of Truth. The crack is an open end, going beyond the broad, statistical way of the world.

Readers will think of many pros and cons which I should have acknowledged, but to keep my work within bounds I have selectively chosen my supporting material, and selectively ignored arguments not fitting my purpose. The implications of the crack have expanded exponentially, and I have had to limit those past notions and current studies which point up the growing awareness of an unbroken continuum between mind and reality. I have used these sources in the hope of both clarifying and verifying my translation, but I must state clearly that I cannot claim *their* sanction for *my* efforts, though I do not think I have used others against their own purposes or too reductively.

The last portion of my book is theological in intent, though hardly calculated to win applause from the pulpit. Readers looking for divine absolutes, closed systems of security, or neat formulas and directives, may find these last chapters inconclusive. The crack contains an enormous, indeed romantic, optimism, however, by which I hope to counter our current passion for nihilistic self-doubt.

An awareness of the creative force of mind is springing up increasingly, after a gestation of nearly two millennia. If the dark forces of the Pentagon or the technician mentality do not destroy us in their death throes of naïve realism, the childhood of Man could well draw to a close within our own time. Then it may be that we shall "seize the tiller of the world," as Teilhard de Chardin dreamed. This seizure can only take place as a "crack in the egg," whatever shape the egg might have by then. The reality-shaping function operates automatically in spite of us, but this breath of life that structures all things is also the deepest level of our very minds, and available to any of us, even now. The technique for making this function consciously available will be clarified, hopefully, in the following pages—for that reader with perseverance and an open mind.

J.C.P.

Williamstown, Massachusetts
June 1970

The Crack in the Cosmic Egg

1

circles and lines

There is a relationship between what we *think* is out there in the world and what we experience as being out there. There is a way in which the energy of thought and the energy of matter modify each other and interrelate. A kind of rough mirroring takes place between our mind and our reality.

We cannot stand outside this mirroring process and examine it, though, for we *are* the process, to an unknowable extent. Any technique we might use to 'look objectively' at our reality becomes a part of the event in question. We are an indeterminately large part of the function that shapes the reality from which we do our looking. Our looking enters as one of the determinants in the reality event that we see.

This mirroring between mind and reality can be analyzed, and more actively directed, if we can suspend some of our ordinary assumptions. For instance, the *procedure* of mirroring must be considered the only fixed element, while the *products* of the procedure must be considered relative. William Blake claimed that perception was the universal, the perceived object was the particular. *What* is discovered by man is never the "universal" or cosmic "truth." Rather, the *process* by which the mind brings about a "discovery" is itself the "universal."

Jerome Bruner,* of Harvard's Center for Cognitive

* The reader is referred to the author's "Guide to the References and Bibliography System" described on page 197.

Studies, doubts that there is a world available for "direct touch." We are not in a subjective trap of our own making, either. Rather, we *represent* the world to ourselves and *respond* to our representations. There is, I would add, a subtle and random way in which "the world" responds to our representations too. Naive realism and naive idealism must be equally dismissed if we are to grasp the mirroring function of mind and reality toward which Bruner points.

We used to believe that our perceptions, our seeing, hearing, feeling and so on, were reactions to active impingements on them by the "world out there," We thought our perceptions then sent these outside messages to the brain where we put together a reasonable facsimile of what *was* out there. We know now that our concepts, our notions or basic assumptions, *actively direct* our percepts. We see, feel, and hear according to what Bruner calls a "selective program of the mind." Our mind *directs* our sensory apparatus every bit as much as our sensory apparatus *informs* the mind.

It used to be thought that the physical was a fixed entity "out there," unaffected by anything our transient, incidental thoughts might make of it. Holding to this idea today are the "tough-minded," whose boastful posturing of a "realistic, no-nonsense objectivity" cloaks a narrow and pedantic selective-blindness, a "realism" that sees only what has been established as safe to see. Yet there *is* a way in which physical and mental events merge and influence each other. A change of world view can change the world viewed. And I am not referring to such parlor games as influencing the roll of dice. The stakes are higher, the relationships more subtle and far-reaching.

For instance, as a young man I once found myself in a certain somnambulistic, trance-like state of mind which I will later in this book define as autistic. In the peculiarities of this frame of reference I suddenly knew myself to be impervious to pain or injury. With upwards of a dozen witnesses I held the glowing tips of cigarettes against my palms, cheeks, eyelids, grinding them out on those sensitive areas. Finally, I held the tips of several cigarettes tightly between my lips and blew sparks over my amazed companions. To the real consternation of my dormitory fellows, there were *no* after-effects, no blisters, no later signs of my folly. This stimulated the physics majors to test the temperature of a cigarette tip, which they found to be around 1380° F. My contact with such heat had been quite genuine, steady, and prolonged.

Later, when I did a bit of research on Hindu firewalking, I understood quite well the state of mind involved, though I never again achieved it myself. It was apparent to me, however, that I had suspended my ordinary thinking, and was using a mode of mind strongly suggestive of early childhood. At the same time I was *aware* of myself though experiencing some dissociation within, rather as though I were sitting and watching myself.

Several things intrigued me about this venture. First, of course, why were the ordinary reactions of live flesh to extreme heat not operative under that strange state of mind? What *was* the state of mind? Could the reality of this state be different from the reality of ordinary thinking, and if so, was there a relative and arbitrary quality to *any* reality state? What were the possibilities of this kind of thinking, particularly if it could be controlled by a fully operational, conscious person? (I had surely *not* been fully operational, and the cigarette trick was the only expression of imperviousness my imagination could seize on.)

Last but not least, certain of my tough-minded colleagues of later years were so unnecessarily hostile to my accounts of this and similar personal experiences. Why did they refuse to believe the experience had taken place? Why did they insist that I had hallucinated, simply misinterpreted my data, or was, perhaps, just lying? This threw another aspect into my search, in addition to trying to determine the role our concept-percept interaction plays in our reality: why is our ordinary, logical thinking so hostile to these rifts in the common fabric?

Reality is not a fixed entity. It is a contingent interlocking of moving events. And events do not just happen to us. We are an integral part of every event. We enter into the shape of events, even as we long for an absolute in which to rest. It may be just this longing for an absolute in which our concepts might *not* have to be responsible for our percepts, and so indirectly our reality, that explains the hostility of our ordinary intellect to these shadowy modes of mind.

Later I will try to summarize how an infant's mind is shaped into a "reality-adjusted" personality, and show how this representation helps determine the reality in which the adult then moves. By analyzing how our representations of the world come about we may be able to grasp the arbitrary, and thus flexible, nature of our reality. The way we represent the world arises, though, from our whole social fabric, as Bruner put it. There is no escaping this rich web of language, myth, history, ways of doing things, unconsciously-accepted attitudes, notions, and so on, for these make up our only reality. If this social fabric tends to become our shroud, the only way out is by the same weaving process, for there is only the one. So we need to find out all we can about the loom involved, and weave with imagination and vision rather than allow the process to happen as a random fate.

Our inherited representation, our world view, is a language-made affair. It varies from culture to culture. Edward Sapir, the linguist, called this idea of ours that we adjust to reality without the use of language an *illusion.* He claimed that the "real world" is to a large extent built up on the language habits of the group.

None of us exercises our logical, social thinking as a blank slate, or as a photographic plate, seeing what is "actually there." We focus on the world through an esthetic prism from which we can never be free except by exchanging prisms. There is no pure looking with a naked, innocent eye. When I found myself in that peculiar twilight world in which fire no longer burned me, I had not found "the true reality" or "the truth." I had simply skipped over some syllogisms of our ordinary logical world and restructured an event not dependent on ordinary criteria. Even our most critical, analytical, scientific, or "detached" looking is a verification search, sifting through possibilities for a synthesis that will strengthen the hypotheses that generate the search.

Our world view is a cultural pattern that shapes our

mind from birth. It happens to us as fate. We speak of a child becoming "reality-adjusted" as he responds and becomes a cooperating strand in the social web. We are shaped by this web; it determines the way we think, the way we see what we see. It is our pattern of representation and our response sustains the pattern.

Yet any world view is arbitrary to an indeterminable extent. This arbitrariness is difficult to recognize since our world to *view* is determined by our world view. To consider our world view arbitrary and flexible automatically places our world of reality in the same questionable position. And yet we are always changing this world view. We represent such changes as discoveries of absolutes in order to protect ourselves *from* our arbitrary status, and to avoid the implication that human thinking is a creative process. We deny that disciplines of mind synthetically create; we insist we are but discovering "nature's truths." We possess an open-ended potential at considerable variance with contemporary nihilisms, but we must recognize and accept the dynamic interplay of representation-response if we are not to be acted on rather than fully acting.

For instance, years after my little fireburn experience, my world faced dissolution when two massive "radical surgeries" and other macabre manipulations on my wife failed to check a malignancy wildly stimulated by the growth hormones of pregnancy. Finally, having had everything cut off or out, she offered little for further experimentation. The priests of the scalpel passed judgment and gave her but a few short weeks to live. Surely the evidence was in their favor.

Nevertheless, I remembered that strange world in which fire could not burn, and entered into a crash program to find that crack in the egg that we might restructure events more in our favor. During five- and six-day fasts, I subjected her to a total "brainwash" day and night, never letting her mind alone. Through all her waking hours I read her literature related to healing, and while she slept I endlessly repeated suggestions of hope and strength. I had no thought of how the restructuring would take place, but in a few hours, some three weeks later, she was suddenly healed and quite well.

We traipsed back to the temple, I with misgivings over such a risk of the new structure, to have the priests declare us clean. And that we were duly declared and recorded, with the reaction pattern among the many doctors of that research center running the gamut. From emotional talk about miracles, the brass-tack realists soon rebounded with dire warnings that some fluke had occurred and that we should present ourselves regularly for constant watches for the "inevitable reoccurrence;" just the sort of doubt-category I would have avoided at all costs.

True, a year or so later our carefully-balanced private world fell apart. This began when it became obvious that our last child, born in the midst of all that carnage, was in serious trouble. When the trouble proved to be severe cerebral palsy, our bubble burst, the dragon roared back, and within weeks my world was in ruins.

Nevertheless, by a change of concept concerning possibilities, we beat the broad way of the statistical world, if only for a while. The social fabric is sustained by agreement on which phenomena are currently acceptable. Susanne Langer referred to nature as a language-made affair, subject to "collapse into chaos" should ideation fail. Threat of this chaos proves sufficient stimulus to insure a ready granting of validity to the current ideas. And strangely, even when this ideation decrees that a particular event must end in death, most people would rather accept the sentence than risk the chaos.

To be "realistic" is the high mark of intellect, and assures the strengthening of those acceptances that make up the reality and so determine what thoughts are "realistic." Our representation-response interplay is self-verifying, and circular. We are always in the process of laying our cosmic egg.

The way by which our reality picture is changed provides a clue to the whole process. A change of concept changes one's reality to some degree, since concepts direct percepts as much as percepts impinge on concepts. There are peculiarities and exceptions, such as my no-

fireburn venture, by which our inherited fabric is bypassed temporarily in small private ways. These are linear thrusts that break through the circles of acceptancy making up our reality.

Metanoia is the Greek word for conversion: a "fundamental transformation of mind." It is the process by which concepts are reorganized. *Metanoia* is a specialized, intensified adult form of the same world-view development found shaping the mind of the infant. Formerly associated with religion, *metanoia* proves to be the way by which all genuine education takes place. Michael Polanyi points out that a "conversion" shapes the mind of the student into the physicist. *Metanoia* is a seizure by the discipline given total attention, and a restructuring of the attending mind. This reshaping of the mind is the principal key to the reality function.

The same procedure found in world view development of the child, the *metanoia* of the advanced student, or the conversion to a religion, can be traced as well in the question-answer process, or the proposing and eventual filling of an "empty category" in science. The asking of an ultimately serious question, which means to be seized in turn by an ultimately serious quest, reshapes our concepts *in favor of* the kinds of perceptions needed to "see" the desired answer. To be given ears to hear and eyes to see is to have one's concepts changed in favor of the discipline. A question determines and brings about its answer just as the desired end shapes the nature of the kind of question asked. This is the way by which science synthetically creates that which it then "discovers" out there in nature.

Exploring this reality function shows how and why we reap as we sow, individually and collectively—but no simple one-to-one correspondence is implied. The success or failure of any idea is subject to an enormous web of contingencies. Any idea seriously entertained, however, tends to bring about the realization of itself, and will, regardless of the nature of the idea, to the extent it can be free of ambiguities. The "empty category" of science as an example will be explored later and the same function is triggered by any set of expectancies, as, for instance, a disease.

For instance, in my wife's case, a grandmother who had died of cancer was the family legend, and all the females scrupulously avoided all the maneuvers rumored to have possibly caused the horror. Then, in neat, diabolical two-year intervals, my wife's favorite aunt died of cancer; her mother developed cancer but survived the radical-surgery mutilations; her father then followed and died in spite of extensive medical machinations. Naturally, two years after burying her father, my wife's own debacle occurred, in spite of her constant submissions to the high priests for inspections, tests, and, no doubt, full confessionals. The fact that all these carcinomas were of different sorts, and on opposite sides of the family, was incidental. Few people understood my fury when the medical center that had attended my wife requested that I bring my just-then-budding teenage daughter for regular six-monthly check-ups for ever thereafter, since they had found—and thoroughly advertised—that mammary malignancies in a mother tended to be duplicated in the daughter many hundred percent above average. And surely such tragic duplications *do* occur, in a clear example of the circularity of expectancy verification, the mirroring by reality of a passionate or basic fear.

The "empty category" is no passive pipe dream—it is an active, shaping force in the making of events. There are not as many hard line, brass tack qualifications to the mirroring procedure to be outlined in this book as one might think. For instance, the Ceylonese Hindu undergoes a transformation of mind that temporarily bypasses the ordinary cause-effect relationships—even those we must have for the kind of world we know. Seized by his god and changed, the Hindu can walk with impunity through pits of white-hot charcoal that will melt aluminum on contact. Recently, in our own country, hypnotically-induced trance states have replaced chemical anaesthesias, allowing bloodless, painless, quickly-healing operations to be performed.

These are "mutations" in the metaphoric fabric of our "semantic universe," as Lévi-Strauss has called our word-built world. The cults seized these novelties previously, and, in their longing for magic, alluded to shadowy cosmic mysteries. Rather, trance states prove to be forms of *metanoia,* temporary restructurings of reality orientation. Some fundamental restructuring of mind underlies all disciplines and pursuits. Mathematician and physicist follow the same mirroring of idea and fact, just on a wider scope, from a different set of metaphors, with a different set of expectancies, and from a different esthetic.

My neighbor was "seized and changed" somewhere in his final year of doctoral studies in topology. The structure of his mind, and his resulting world, were never again the same as that of non-mathematicians. He lived in a world of mathematical spaces. He loved to figure the spaces of *knots,* the kind you tie, though I could not relate his marvelous figurings to *my* shoelace world. He tried to show me, in beautifully-diagrammed hieroglyphics, how he could remove an egg from an intact shell through mathematical four-space. In my naive concreteness, frustrated that I had no ears to hear or eyes to see, I wanted him to apply his four-space miracle to a common hen's egg. But my friend's world was cerebral, his eggs those rare cosmic ones found in the inner land of thought, and his frustration at my blindness was as great as my own.

There is an eloquent madness in topology, but from that strange brotherhood's abstractions lunar modules have been built. From their four-spaced absurdities have come real ships for spaces other than our own. The mythos leads the logos. The language of fantasy goes before the language of fact.

The physicist, David Bohm, computed the "zero-point energy" due to quantum-mechanical fluctuations in a single cubic centimeter of space, and arrived at the energy of 10^{38} ergs. A cubic centimeter of space is next to nothing at all, and yet Bohm translates his ergs into the energy equivalent of about *ten billion tons of uranium.* That is a lot of fireworks to come from nothing at all.

It was proposed once that if we had the "faith of a grain of mustard seed" we could say to the mountain:

"Be removed to the sea"—and it would be. Is this not an oddly similar proposal to physicist Bohm's?

Bohm wrote that under present conditions this energy he hypothesized is inaccessible, but as conditions change we will get our hands on some of it. The techniques of getting will reside in the remote recesses of those minds seized by Bohm's kind of faith. When finally brought about, that enormous energy will be hailed as a "discovery of nature's secrets." It will have been, instead, the filling by life of an empty category. It is not just that nature abhors a vacuum. This will be an example of the way "Eternity is in love with the productions of time," as William Blake put it.

Physicist Gerald Feinberg frets at a universe where Einstein's light speed is the maximum allowed for our reality, so Feinberg has substituted "imaginary numbers" for Einstein's "real ones" that created the limitation involved. Feinberg sees no way of repealing Einstein's law, and so tries to use the whole abstraction against itself for a new era of freedom—at least freedom for imaginative thinking. Physicist Feinberg has been seized too, and no longer lives in a world of common breakfast eggs, but in that cosmic one where aberrations of thinking bring new realities into play. So great is Feinberg's faith that he has already given a fitting Greek name, *tachyon,* or speed, to his as yet undiscovered faster-than-light bits of energy. And already there is confidence in Feinberg's minus-mathematics. Universities have started building the kinds of machines that might respond to the new representation and "find" those speedy little minus-number things that might hurry other things along.

Once found, the rest of us will then presume that God built *tachyons* into the universe way back there. We have automatically assumed that about atoms, molecules, and the rest of our new marvels. Who would doubt that these were *a priori* facts awaiting discovery by a slowly awakening man?

Nevertheless, this assumption has outlived its usefulness. It is probably the most basic "fact" we accept, too self-evident even to dwell on as in any way questionable.

Yet this assumption keeps us subject to fate, blind to our potential, and ignorant of God.

The history of the scientific discipline shows that after a certain discreet courtship, the proper passion to implant the mathematical gamete into the cosmic egg currently in season, a new idea, "indwelled" by the brotherhood as Polanyi might say, will finally gestate and eventually be born into the world of the common domain.

First comes The Word, the cabalistic sign, the representation of possibility in a way that can be believed by the brotherhood of believers. After that comes the discovery. The relation of fact and idea is not quite magic, and it is not quite of the same reality as hens' eggs either. Rather, thinking is a shaping force in reality.

William Blake claimed that "anything capable of being believed is an image of truth." Our capacity for belief is highly conditioned however, and "truth" always proves to be a synthesis of current possibilities. Physicist Feinberg, frustrated by the limits of the Einsteinian universe, has, nevertheless, no other materials to work with—certainly not if he is to be a physicist. The very idea of great speeds came about only with that metaphoric framework resulting in Einstein. Any possibilities *beyond* Einstein's restrictions exist only because of the necessary defintions of the system itself.

Our imaginations cannot set out to find the cracks in the cosmic egg until someone lays the egg. New representations for reality, new ideas, new fabrications of fantasy searching for supporting logic, must precede the final "discovery" by which verification of the notion is achieved.

It has been claimed that our minds screen out far more than we accept, else we would live in a world of chaos. Our screening process may be essential, but it is also arbitrary and changeable. We pick and choose, ignore or magnify, illuminate or dampen, expand upon or obscure, affirm or deny, as our inheritance, adopted discipline, or passionate pursuit dictate. At root is an esthetic response, and we invest our esthetic responses with sacred overtones.

Value, as Whitehead said, is limitation. Limitation involves faith, faith that an exclusive interest is worth life investment, worth the sacrifice of every other possibility. I like to think of our "open-ended potential," but potential is always limited to the sum total of the images that can be conjured up by the mind, and this ties us down immediately to syntheses of things already realized—although, as we will find later with the sorcerer don Juan, such syntheses can grow exponentially, like a tree at every tip.

Among the potentials of resyntheses of our current reality, one possibility must be selected, heard as a question one might answer, seen as a goal one might achieve. Every choice involves such a commitment. Once we have made an investment and corresponding sacrifice of other possibilities, our life is at stake. Feinberg has made such a choice and risked his professional life on the possibility that his *tachyons* might come about. The excluded possibilities will act as counterpoints of discord until his notion sufficiently reorients the concepts of his brotherhood. Then the overall selectivity will rule out the contradictory notions altogether, and for a generation or two or more, the new "discovery" might shape reality—until replaced in turn.

Most people respond automatically to their given circle of representation, and strengthen it by their unconscious allegiance. Since their cultural circle is made of many conflicting drives *for* their allegiance, their lives are fragmented and ambiguous.

To be *converted* is to be seized by an idea that orients us around a single focal point of possibility. The point of focus groups into orderly sequence the myriad necessities for choice we face continually. Given a central thesis for orientation, all the energies and interests of personal or group life can reinforce and amplify each other, rather than now-here, now-there attempts at tending to fragmenting demands.

The power of Freudian thought was in its metaphoric simplicity. A few dramatic images stabilized and organized all the data of a world in flux. Its simplicity made it readily available to anyone for whom the imagery was esthetically satisfying. Hans Sachs read Freud's *Interpre-*

tation of Dreams and found in it "the one thing worth living for." He was caught up in an imagery by which he too could interpret the universe and give it meaning. He was seized by the material he had seized, and saw his life as meaningful in serving the new construct.

This centering of mind fills a person with power and conviction. It creates mathematicians, saints, or Nazis with equal and impartial ease.

A mind divided by choices, confused by alternatives, is a mind robbed of power. The body reflects this. The ambiguous person is a machine out of phase, working against itself and tearing itself up. That person is an engine with sand in its crankcase, broken piston rods, water in its fuel lines. In spite of great effort and noise, nothing much happens.

Metanoia tunes the engine, gets it running on all cylinders, functioning with power and efficiency. Conversion is like a laser; it centers the diffusing and fragmented energy into a tight, potent focus. But where the beam *goes,* the direction it takes, while germane to its structure, is incidental to the function. This questions those religious justifications each system inwardly grants itself in the struggle for superiority among conflicting and competing drives.

Yet the nature of the imagery by which any conversion occurs, if incidental to the process, is closely related to the product. Direction and end will always be in keeping with the centered notion by which the organization takes place. The end is in the beginning. Heaven or hell is contained in the choice for center, not in the function of centering. Single-minded devotion to any point tends to give power—for that point's use. All gods are jealous, but all are equally productive if they can take over completely and run the machine.

Metanoia restructures, to varying degrees and even for varying lengths of time, those basic representations of reality inherited from the past. On those representations we base our notions or concepts of what is real. In turn, our notions of what is real direct our perceptual apparatus, that network of senses that tells us what we feel, hear, see, and so on. This is not a simple subjective maneuver, but a reality-shaping procedure.

We are taught to believe that only the "out there" is real. We are taught to consider our perception of reality to be transient, accidental, and insignificant, arising from and oriented only to economic biological necessities. This becomes an enormous inner contradiction, as Jung would call it, splitting our reality in half. The inner conflict is reflected outwardly, and the world happens to us as fate.

We look on archetypal world views, those held by "primitive" tribes, and consider them archaic "survival" mechanisms. We have been taught that the real "out there" has been seen only dimly before, but with a progressively more realistic, aware, civilized eye, culminating in *our* viewpoint. (Alien world views can thus be exploited or even removed as threats to our true one, lending a religious sanctification to our culture destructions.)

Lévi-Strauss, the French anthropologist, challenges our smug chauvinisms. He claims that archaic thought patterns were highly disciplined, intellectual structures, designed to give the world coherence, shape, and meaning. This is, in fact, just what all world views do. Primitive man "sacralized" his intellectual structure no more than we do ours. Neither system is any more true than the other. Ours is more esthetically desirable to us, but is bought at the same price all selective systems are, the price of those possibilities sacrificed to keep a limited structure intact. The difference between Einstein's relative universe and the Dream-Time cosmology of the Australian aborigine is not a matter of truth or falsehood, realism or illusion, progression or regression, intelligence or stupidity, as the naive realists have claimed. It is a matter of esthetic choice. Each system produces results unobtainable to the other; each is closed and exclusive.

Robert Frost saw civilization as a small clearing in a great forest. We have hewn our space at no small cost, and the dark "out there" seems ever ready to close in again—a collapse into chaos should our ideation fail. In my book I shall consider Frost's clearing to be the disciplines of mind, reality-adjusted thinking, reason, logic, civilization, society, culture. I shall consider the dark forest to be the primal stuff, the unconscious, the unknown potential—perhaps just an "empty category." In my next chapter I will define the psychological term *autistic-thinking* and refer to it as the borderline between clearing and forest. Then I will try to outline the interaction between these aspects of the reality function.

Our archaic background was concerned with keeping stable our small clearing in the forest. Our clearing is a world view, a cosmic egg structured by the mind's drive for a logical ordering of its universe. The clearing is an organization imposed by us on a random possibility. It is a circle of reason won from meaninglessness. Each person is a potential line capable of breaking through the circle of reason. Yet the circle is an accomplishment of no small order. An enormous force bends all lines into circles. Each new mind threatens the structure but ages of pressure weigh on the infant to win from him agreement with, modification to, and help in sustaining his cultural circle.

Teilhard de Chardin saw human destiny spreading the light from our small clearing out into the dark beyond. In archaic times we feared lest the dark engulf our fragile construction of reason, and all actions were oriented toward keeping the cultural circle intact. Teilhard and the "new nominalists" of physics speak with a new and bold confidence that dares move beyond stability.

We have been passionately involved in strengthening our ideation, cataloging and indexing our clearing in the forest. Some unanimity of opinion has begun to form. But the nature of the *dark forest* is the real problem. For our attitude toward the forest influences sharply the way we look upon our clearing, and affects the kind of new clearing we can make.

The Platonists and Stoics have always assumed the forest to be ready planted. Corresponding ideas of what was "out there" were planted also in our minds, leading us by heuristic devices until we finally stumbled our way to various discoveries and conclusions. The gods and fates looked on, rather as we would watch rats in a maze.

Consider, however, that the kind of trees we succeed in

felling at the clearing's edge need not have always *been.* Indeed, there may be no trees at all in the depths of that dark. Rather, the forest may shape, the trees may grow, according to the kind of light our reason throws.

Scientists speak of the dark forest of nature as essentially simple. Nature is a category, however, a label, a concept shot through and through with man's thought. And man's thought is designed to simplify from an endless possibility. Scientists are never really talking about the unknown nature of the forest beyond their circle of reason and logic. They talk about their garden within it, the forest converted, the trees labeled, the plants and shrubs cataloged, selected, arranged in orderly patterns. When the scientists look at the forest, they look for additions to their garden, and they look with a gardener's eye.

The nature "discovered" is determined, to an indeterminable degree, by the mind that sets out to discover. We can never know the full extent we play in this reality formation. It will never be computable or reducible to formula. An ultimately serious commitment of mind, however, can be the determinate in any issue, overriding randomness and chance.

In the following chapters I hope, by showing what I have found about this reality play, to suggest a way by which we may take a more active part in shaping our events. I will explore the formation of world view, which determines our adult world-to-view, and this will require some exploration of different phenomena of mind, particularly from that shadow-side of thinking called *autistic.* Then I will explore the way a passionate pursuit or commitment of mind shapes its own fulfillment—the way a question can bring about its answer, a belief its illumination, a desire its gratification, by reshaping, as needed, those concepts shaped from birth, and so reshaping perceptual patterns.

I have traced this mirroring of mind and reality in scientific pursuits, the postulate, the *Eureka!,* the new notion that changes the actual tangibles for a civilization. Then I have tried to show how this same relation between idea and fact found in science equally underlies such a cultic affair as fire not burning a person under certain circumstances.

Mind over matter is a misnomer, and even to speak of a *mirroring* between the two probably implies a false dualism. I will try to trace the function by which events are shaped, and avoid those comfortable categories, those idolatries, those easy psychological clichés that act as stopping-places before the goal is reached. And the goal is nothing less than the very ontological underpinnings of things, the reality-shaping way by which events come about.

In this opening chapter I have given a rough survey of the kinds of questions, and the kinds of answers, I will deal with in the rest of the book. Our clearing in the forest is all there appears for us to go on. I have no *deus ex machina* to introduce skilfully at the last. There is no magic for us—and no outside interference. The game is ours. Our responsibility is ultimately serious, yet there is often only one way really to serve our cultural circle, and that is by breaking through its tight logic, and plunging into that empty category, the dark forest beyond. I attempted to do this when disaster struck at my own little world. I failed in the last analysis—though of course in retrospect I see my failure as needless.

The high priests of the disciplines controlling our cultural circle try to tell us that logic and reason are the sum total of things, or, if more is possible, that it is only so through *their* controls, which are their own logical rules. Logic and reason are surely the stuff of which the clearing is made, and the high point of life's thrust. Yet these techniques of mind tend to become destructive and to trap us in deadlocks of despair.

Logic and reason are like the tip of an iceberg. The naive realists, the biogenetic psychologists, the rats-in-the-maze watchers, claim the tip is all there is. Yet life becomes demonic when sentenced to so small an area. There are times when we need to open the threshold of mind to that unknown subterranean depth—and we always need to believe in its existence.

And so, though our cosmic egg is the only reality we have, and is not to be treated lightly, what I hope to show is that there is available to us a crack in this egg. For there are times when the shell no longer protects but suffocates and destroys. The crack must be approached with care, however, lest the egg itself be destroyed. There is a story in the Codez Bezae, a fifth-century manuscript of the Gospel According to St. Luke, that illustrates this circle-line problem. Jesus and his disciples were cutting across a field one Sabbath morning when they came across a man gathering in his grain. The Sabbath was a strictly no-work day, of course, and Jesus had been censured by the Establishment for just this kind of infringement. He knew that only by agreed upon criteria for acceptable acts can a civilization exist, and so he looked at the man and said: "Man, if you *know* what you are doing, you are blest. If you do *not* know what you are doing, you are accurst and a transgressor of the law."

The mirroring of mind and reality finds its best expression in a comment by Jesus almost universally ignored. Those who claim to have heard him insist that *supplication* is the way out. They cry that we should look to heaven for our answers. But Jesus, that harsh realist, recognized the play of mirrors, and pointed out that: "What you loose on earth is loosed in heaven."

2

valves and solvents

Our clearing in the forest is the form by which content is shaped, a content which in turn helps determine the form of the clearing. Our clearing is ancient and archetypal, of infinitely contingent formative lines, but there are experiences in which a crack forms in this egg, when nonordinary things are possible, or nonordinary solutions occur to mind.

This crack formation is the key to reality formation, and involves an exploration of our modes of thinking. We need a broader look at "mind" than the biogenetically indoctrinated psychologists have given. We are aware of our reality-adjusted thinking, our ordinary, socially-oriented, logical, rational thinking. We are less aware of another mode of thinking with which we are continually but more peripherally involved.

The god Odin, discovering the secret spring of wisdom and poetry, asked the guardian of the spring for a drink. He was told: "The price is your right eye." Jerome Bruner writes of "thinking for the left hand." Michael Polanyi wrote of a primary process thinking that is typical of the thinking of children and animals. Psychologists refer to *autistic* thinking, and it is this last term that I have found most descriptive of and useful in talking about the shadow-side of thinking.

Autistic thinking (or A-thinking) is an unstructured, non-logical (but not necessarily illogical), whimsical thinking that is the key to creativity. It involves "unconscious processes" but is not necessarily unconscious. Autistic thinking is indulged in, or in some cases *happens* to one, in ordinary conscious states. The autistic is a kind of dream-world mode of thinking. This left-handed thinking is nevertheless a functional part of reality formation. It is the connecting link between our "clearing" and "forest." It is the pearl of great price. It is the way by which potential unfolds.

Later I will suggest how this primary process of mind is structured and modified into an adult world view. This structuring process that we call *maturing* is a modifying procedure that represses and largely eliminates, by the very act of maturation, the open-ended potential which thinking encompasses.

Michael Polanyi wrote that creative thinking was thinking as a child with the tools of logical structuring given by maturity. This is the key. Most logical structuring is bought at the price of this child-thinking. There remains a certain feyness, a childlike quality, in all great creative people. In them, somehow, a thread remains intact between their modes of thought. It is a return to this primary-process thinking which brings about *metanoia,* conversion, the *Eureka!* illumination of creative thinking, the seizure by the gods which restructures an event to allow fire-walking, the transfer of hypnotism which allows non-ordinary structurings of events, and so on.

It was this re-entrance into primary-process thinking by the adult, matured, reality-adjusted mind that brought about Jesus' Kingdom. The structuring process by which the world is born and shaped anew in a mind is the way by which the mind and its world may be reborn and reshaped.

Whether this re-entry and reshaping process gives a Kingdom of Heaven, the illumination of $E=MC^2$, or the double-helix postulate as an "empty category" to be eventually filled with content, is incidental to the process. All leavenings raise the flour. There is no logical, rational, prestructured criterion "out there" with a divine plan. There is no truth "out there" which our weak minds or souls eventually run across. There is this casual, haphazard, amoral process that leaps the logical gaps and brings about newness. And the procedure's only demand is that given talents be invested, risked, doubled, the possibilities explored.

World view development in a child modifies his primary process thinking, that archetypal mode that melts out into a continuum. This structuring modifies, but also gives the child's world-to-view the form in which, and only in which growth, expansion, and possibility can unfold. World view development limits and thwarts, but there is no other way to have a world-to-view.

Metanoia changes, to varying extents, this fundamental structure built since infancy. The change of concept is brought about by a *retracing* of the original formative process of world view development, and a reshaping of the concepts originally formed.

When the postulate arrives out of the blue, and a person suddenly "sees" a long desired answer to a problem, when "illumination" or understanding is suddenly achieved, this re-formation process has taken place in relation to some specific possibility. All creative mental phenomena involve this autistic thinking and follow a similar pattern of development in the mind. All such phenomena are reality-influencing, or capable of influencing reality. In each case there is a change of concept that changes some aspect of the logical world view and introduces a new "seeing," which itself may eventually bring about new things to be seen within the broad, statistical mode of reality-adjusted, social thinking.

One cannot induce creative autistic thinking *ad lib.*, however. It is bought at a price. The creative aspect of A-thinking is not controllable, and cannot be duplicated by a computer, for the autistic mode *adds something* not in the given context. There is a catalystic quality in A-thinking that gives *more than* the sum of the parts suggesting and bringing about the new possibility.

This A-thinking catalyst is not one's *personal* thinking. Rather, it happens to a person. It *happens* to a person, though, only after the person has achieved a certain saturation point of his controlled, directed reasoning. The creative will-o'-the-wisp occurs only *after* rigorous logical thinking. It is the Spirit that is found only when one has exceeded and gone beyond the lawyers and Pharisees.

Autistic thinking can only be defined in a roundabout way. For instance, a pianist friend told me of the following experience, the most impressive of his life. His favorite work, one he had lived with for years, was Mozart's last sonata, K576, the one written after the composer's late discovery of Bach. My friend was giving a concert one evening, and was scheduled to play this sonata. Just before commencing, he leaned back for a moment to sense the mood of that contrapuntal texture, and was struck anew by its exquisiteness and his love of it. At that moment, in a single frozen instant out of time, he "experienced" the sonata. It happened to him, rather as Susanne Langer's volume-filled time. Every note, phrase, nuance, shadow and line formed in an ethereal circle of perfection for him. He described it as a volume, a sort of universal whole, perfect, far more than human, and *happening* to him as something unique and totally outside of himself. Though it had occupied only a second, the occurrence was immeasurable by any kind of time, and was numinous and profound.

This autistic experience, a kind of esthetic illumination, gives the pattern of all creative formations. Even my own small "illumination" which triggered the search leading to this book, happened in this way. I had spent more than two years reading, corresponding, thinking, struggling with the relation of thought and reality in general, and with the mechanics of *metanoia* in particular, for a form of this had dramatically altered my own life.

One day, following an exciting connection of ideas that had unfolded over several weeks and seemed tantalizingly close to "jelling," I grew stale and unable to go further. I went out to relax with my children and dutifully climbed an apple tree at their insistence that it gave a lovely view. And there, in my own little suspended moment out of mind, I "saw." The connecting link between the fragmented parts of my search fused. There was a great wash of understanding, powerful, total. I had my answer. Nothing was specific or articulate. It just *was,* in a perfectly clear kind of ultimate certainty. The answer seemed utterly remote from *my* thinking, however, far larger than the sum total of my insignificant bits of material gathered over the years, and far exceeding the scope of my own ideas or capacity of thought. I knew the "translating" of that experience, making it articulate, structuring the answer into a logical, communicable shape, would involve me for a long time.

Let me add now that in my experience what was understood to be the "answer" was the very *function* by which I had achieved my "seeing." My answer was a turning in on the process of questioning. That is, the answer to my passionate pursuit was insight into how the answers to passionate questions are formed in the mind. I saw that this was but an extension of the very ontological function by which "things were." I saw that this was the way the "empty category" of science was shaped and filled. For me no "universal out-there truth" was given. Rather, I saw that the only "truth" for us is the process of questioning what truth might be, and receiving answers in keeping with the nature of our questions.

I will return to this question-answer procedure in some detail. For now I want to explore the state of mind involved in the moment of answer itself. The state is brought on by a *chance suspension* of ordinary thinking, following a rigorous exercise of normal logic. Both the Sonata and apple tree experiences show how the autistic mode breaks into mind with "universals," but universals in keeping with the mundane nature of the suggestions triggering the experience, suggestions drawing on ordinary life and its materials.

An unconscious synthesis is involved in the formation of this answering experience. *Unconscious,* though, carries too many limiting connotations. For instance, imagination (creating images not present to the senses,) is surely one of the active ingredients of creative thinking, and the prime ingredient of the "empty category." But imagination is our *conscious* play with potential, just not hampered with modifications or adjustments to other things or other thinkers. A sonata-type experience, or apple tree illumination, the finally-arriving scientific *Eureka!,* or for that matter: Higamous, Hogamous, Women are Monogamous, etc., *happens* to a person. The synthesis is other to him, even as it is wholly within him, and he is within it.

Yet it should not be overlooked that the great postulate-illumination-answer happens only to a mind that has been deeply immersed in the proper materials for its genesis, and has passionately asked the question for a prolonged period. The *Eureka!* arrives out of the blue, but from a well-prepared and primed one. The spirit bloweth where it listeth, but inevitably the direction it finally takes is determined by hard work and true commitment.

Autistic thinking, then, refers to an autonomous, self-contained kind of thinking that makes no adjustment to the world of other things or other thinkers, but it must have its materials *from* this other source. A-thinking includes conscious imagination and apparently unconscious processes and so offers a label for a wide range of similar phenomena.

The *hypnagogic state,* a jargon term you do not have to know to experience, is a common form of autistic thinking that "happens" to a person. Have you ever spent a day in some rare, new venture, such as picking wild strawberries, and that night, just as you start to drift off to sleep, found yourself suddenly "looking" at the most real strawberries of your life? In fact, they are more than real; they are the most fragrant, beautiful, green-leafed, red-fruited berries conceivable to mind, occurring in a vital and sensual immediacy more real than any *actual* occurrence of your life.

Consider the similarity between this "strawberry hypnagogery," my friend's Mozart Sonata, and my apple tree experience, and you will see the basic outline by which life moves randomly from possibility to possibility. This kind of thinking acts on some exceptional, dramatic, emotional, ultimately serious, or even just repetitive, involvement from actual experience. It synthesizes this into something larger and more perfect than the original. Then the autistic synthesis breaks into the mind, at some odd off-guard moment, when the logical processes have been suspended. The autistic mode then presents this streamlined, utterly superior version, as something unique, larger than life, and unavailable to previously accepted logical manipulations.

Hans Selye wrote that every really important scientific idea he knew of had occurred in the twilight moments between sleep and waking, that state called hypnagogic, a point to which I will return.

The hypnagogic's strawberry vision is free of half-ripe, bird-pecked, imperfect berries; free of gnats, dirt, sore knees, or aching back. The sonata-illumination was beyond all mechanical frailties; beyond the limitations of instrument, muscle and bone, the small errors, the (adventurous) possibility of serious failure of productions that makes precarious and tenuous a living music, or living things. My apple tree experience showed a living unity of all things, in a tranquil simplicity free of all the logical problems its translation would involve, and that the "translated world" surely entails. The autistic version is free of the excluded possibilities that stand as possible static in the standard broadcast. This is the key issue. Autistic thinking is unambiguous—a point to which I will return time and again. To the mind in this state all things are possible, all postulates are true. To the mind *seized* by this mode, fire need not burn, affliction cripple, or disease kill.

There is, then, this freely-synthesizing aspect of mind, self-contained, untrammeled by harsh realities, abstracting and idealizing certain isolated phenomena from the world of realized events, and breaking into the conscious mind with this idealization. Such breakthroughs may be numinous, awesome, universal, with a feeling of sureness that gives the person involved the confidence to push his translation of the experience in spite of all outward evidence to the contrary. Polanyi believes an esthetic appreciation of the beauty of a discovery gives its bearer his sense of rightness and conviction. This is surely an element, for the autistic non-ambiguity is highly colored with esthetic sanction and absoluteness.

Bearing this in mind, consider again William Blake's claim that: "Eternity is in love with the productions of time." And add to this Jesus' postulate that: "What you loose on earth is loosed in Heaven."

The hypnagogic form of the autistic state, though happening as a rare and fleeting otherness to most of us, can be developed by care and discipline. The price is suspension of the ordinary world view. If the ordinary categories which hold our world together can be bypassed, anything capable of being thought of can be "true." Sometimes the hypnagogic state happens to a person as a kind of "empty category." There are rare half-sleep moments when we suddenly realize that we are in this pseudo-dream state. At those times the first flicker of thought can be instantly "made real" in the dream state and directed by conscious desire and volition. The erotic dream is occasionally a form of this.

The "little lizard" divination rite of the Yaqui Indian sorcerer, don Juan (of whom more later), created a form of this "empty category." And the divination would answer the first question asked. It would succeed, however, only if the question were presented without confusion or ambiguity. Paul Tillich wrote that the "hidden content" of prayer was always the decisive factor, which is another expression of the same function, and a point to which I will return. The real assumption of our underlying beliefs is the determinant in our lives. Surface verbal plays of mind are often only forms of wishful thinking posited against the deep strata of a belief to the contrary. But the deep strata are the determinant in the reality event because of the nonambiguous nature of this level of thought. Jesus' "prayer in the secret place" refers to this level of certainty that underlies all the contingencies of any reality.

Ambiguous confusion, lack of an "ultimate desire" or basic motivation, fragments and dissolves the autistic-hypnagogic possibilities, should they occur to a person's mind. Seven centuries ago, Roger Bacon recognized that mathematics would be the gateway to the sciences. This is because of the non-ambiguous nature of mathematics. An idea that can be expressed mathematically is one that can be represented unambiguously, and anything which can be represented and believed in non-ambiguously tends to be expressed in reality. Mathematics serves as a projection device giving objective certainly, just as the god Kataragama does for the Hindu, for instance.

The Tibetan Yoga spends years developing a state of mind that bears, from written reports, direct relation to the hypnagogic. The Yoga cultivated, practiced, and finally "entered into" the potential of his autistic mode of thinking. The state he brought about was a subset of his ordinary reality, organized along specific and controlled lines, as found in hypnotism. By a subset I mean that he drew on his background experience in selective ways, setting up a world within a world, the equivalent of a concretized dream state under direct conscious control. (Later, the similarities between this Hindu activity and the Path of Knowledge outlined by the sorcerer, don Juan, will become apparent.)

One Yogic activity was the production of a *tulpa,* a phantasm, or imaginary person. The production was a slow development which could itself only be undertaken in a mature stage of training. Eventually the *tulpa* creation would begin to form and take on aspects of reality for the subject-creator. Fleeting glimpses, peripheral and insubstantial, would become more stable, until a full and permanent image could be brought to focus. A *tulpa* became responsive to speech and the whole sensory range of the subject. *Tulpas* developed definite personality traits and full capacities for ordinary human response. Occasionally a *tulpa* would take on strong enough reality aspects to be glimpsed by other people, people who had no knowledge of the production-project itself. *Tulpas* were known to display the same passionate adherences to their developed personalities as would a real person (bringing to mind the strange tenacity of the personality, Eve Black, in Thigpen's case of the "Three Faces of Eve").

The Tibetan monk used this technique to create a form of the local goddess, voluptuous creature, as a consort with whom connubial bliss could be indulged at whim. This might seem only a cultic freak of subjectivity, but several aspects of it are indicative of both *metanoia,* that creates physicists from students, and the *Eureka!* postulate that brings about reality-changing concepts and "discoveries."

First, the process of mind takes its idea and its material from the real world. The goddess is a well-established and familiar part of the culture. Further, experience with a real woman must be undergone by the novice, followed by a complete mastery of all sexual desire. That is, the novice not only experiences a real woman, he then must gain complete mental control over his actual glandular reactions (and it is a medical fact that the Yoga can control all "old-brain" autonomous activities, such as heart beat, body heat, glandular output, and so on), as well as psychological reactions, until he can turn desire on or off at will, without ambiguous double-thinking.

These are the "given materials," then, that are acted upon by the catalyzing synthesis within the autistic mode of thinking. The materials are synthesized and "given back" to ordinary thinking in a unified image, larger and greater than life. True to all autistic creations, the goddess achieved proves superior to frail woman, though some plain Tibetan girl was part of the raw material for the "divine synthesis." To achieve a state of non-ambiguity is the final goal of Yogic training. Then when a specific desire is singled out, as for instance *tulpa* creation, the attention of mind, the passionate pursuit, brings about a slow *metanoia* of the necessary concepts, tranforming them to direct the percepts in the needed ways. Finally the Yoga's senses respond according to the dictates of his "editorial hierarchy" of mind, and the goddess materializes and becomes real for him.

The superiority of autistic creations suggest an additive unavailable from the ordinary ambiguous processes of mind. Autistic thinking can apparently synthesize out of the sum total of the context of the ultimate desire triggering the process. But it also adds that maddening quality of perfection, larger and more real than any of the elements in the triggering background. The autistic experience is felt as a wholeness that lies beyond all mundane reality, a numinous quality that makes us feel we have received lightning from the hand of God.

There are other ramifications of autistic thinking. In our

town lived a child called autistic by the psychologists. For some reason ordinary reality adjustments were never made by the child. At age seven she could perform prodigious intellectual feats, whenever the world was randomly tuned in. Certain blocks seemed operative; tight channelings allowed in only a few selected perceptions. Perhaps the rewards of reality adjustment, with its self-modification, demands for choice, exclusion of other potential, damping of archaic thought-processes, risk of self to a world of other selves, and so on, were never as strong for her as the lure of the autonomous, inner synthesis. Perhaps the bits and pieces of reality perceived were put together in a free synthesis similar to a Yogic wonderland, though a frightful construct is apparently more often the case with these unfortunates.

My own small son gave insight into autistic-reality tensions. For his birthday he was given a vicious little soldier-doll; complete with scarred face, movable limbs, and murderous paraphernalia of war, it captivated my boy. For close to two years he was absorbed with the "G.I. Joe" and played with nothing else.

One summer day, he became even more fey than usual, withdrawn, faraway and quiet. He ate little, looking at us with the strange pitying look of one possessed of universal secrets. He would not leave the house but sat quietly with his soldier-doll, no longer playing or speaking. The spell lasted four days, when he was suddenly himself again.

Later he voluntarily, if haltingly, explained to me why he had been "so rude" those four days. It had occurred to him, in a burst of insight, that his G.I. Joe could become *alive* for him, as he had passionately wished and daydreamed about so long, and that they could play together for ever and ever. But, and here he groped his way carefully, G.I. Joe would have been alive only for him, not for anyone else, and then he, my son, could no longer have been a part of us, his family, or take part in things we did.

The issues were clear-cut, equally real, and equally rewarding. His decision had been no light thing, weighed those silent days. Why *we* happened to win I will never know. Perhaps we rather lost. Life should be a venture of liberty, with a safe harbor for return. Perhaps my son would only have entered on an adventurous path, as don Juan the sorcerer might say, and probably that path might have been traversed more freely than we can imagine. Ronald Laing, the Scotch psychiatrist, would have understood and sympathized with my boy. Laing knows the social structure to be every bit as much as exercise in madness as these opposites. He considers escape from our world a fairly rational maneuver, if rather an exchange of chains.

Back to the autistic procedures. A-thinking is not reality adjusted, and so not hinged about by modifications to what can and cannot be *true.* Children distinguish from an early age that certain experiences are considered unreal by their superiors, since eliciting either no adult responsive-verification or a negative adult response. This is mere arbitrariness to a child, however, not an absolute. A child's world is "quasi-hallucinatory," as Smythies calls it, though nonetheless real for that. Only little by little does a child adopt criteria for true-false in keeping with the relationship of parents and society. He does this as the rewards from and demands by that relationship grow. Piaget considers early adolescence the breakpoint for a new psychological stage and the full development of logic. It is not just fortuitous that this coincides with a growing peer group demand for other-directedness, culminating in that absolutely-other demand, sexuality.

Autistic thinking is self-contained. It operates beyond the restrictions and modifications of a world. That is why this kind of thinking can make an unlimited synthesis of experience. Anything is "true" in A-thinking; any of its constructions are "universals," or cosmic truths. It is just this capacity, still operating in the adult mind, even though only peripherally and unconsciously, that creates the postulate arriving full-blown in the brain.

The *Eureka!* illumination is unavailable to the constructions of logical thought, but *dependent* on the machinations *of* logical thought with its selective screening. Logical thought operates by limitation, selecting from potential some specific isolated desire. The autistic is a continuum, an "everything," and so nothing. A conscious desire held to passionately, or ultimately, until it excludes other ideas that would inhibit it, thus takes on the characteristics of autistic non-ambiguity, and furnishes a point of focus for this autistic capacity. The autistic can synthesize this desire into a unified postulate or answer relating far beyond the limited materials of the triggering passion. The given postulate can, in turn, change world views, and worlds-to-view.

The free-synthesis capacity of A-thinking, able to draw on the continuum of reality experience and potential as it does, is what gives all really new ideas their "initial element of foolishness," as Whitehead wrote of all genuinely new notions. Consider, for instance, David Bohm and all those billions of tons of energy from a cubic centimeter of nothing at all, or Jesus moving those mountains with the faith of a grain of mustard seed.

Piaget felt that autistic thinking corresponded with "primitive psychological causality, implying magic." Belief that any desire whatsoever can influence objects, the belief in the "obedience of external things," sets up a confusion "between self and world," Piaget claimed, which destroys both "logical truth and objective existence."

Piaget here expresses that intriguing fear the rational mind feels toward autistic processes. This is the cosmic egg's fear of being cracked. Piaget is here the voice of our eternal culture-priest, intoning the dangers of moving outside the common consensus of what constitutes our current egg-dimensions. Don Juan the sorcerer would be contemptuous of Piaget's timidity and narrowness, even as Piaget could rightfully dismiss don Juan.

Surely we must be selective. Surely we do not casually choose what makes up our current criteria for our "irreducible and stubborn facts" so longed for by the realists. These facts are our given world view and to question them is to threaten our ideation with collapse into chaos. Yet, "Logical truth" and "objective existence" are variables, formed by cultural agreement. These "Facts" change, much as fashions change—though to each generation they represent reality as it must then be.

We represent change as our own emerging from the dark and foolish superstitions of the past and the coming into the light of a final, true, and really *modern* understanding. Each age proclaims itself the *Ars Nova* and scorns the *Ars Antiqua*. Each man believes, as did Erasmus, that the world is just coming awake from a long sleep. Generation by generation we proclaim ourselves the enlightenment. Each age delights in singing a new requiem to its fathers. As we change our inherited representation of the world, the world we deal with changes accordingly.

In our struggle for an agreeable representation of reality, various systems rise as meteors, pronouncing, in their brief fling, absolutes concerning what we are. The mind is *only this, only that*. Each system is quietly bypassed as the mind and its reality prove always to be *more* than this, and *more* than that. A survey of this parade of self-asserting notions would be a history of the human race. A fairly recent episode lends itself well to the problem of autistic thinking, however, as well as to the nature of our shifting attitudes.

In the early 1960's there was a meeting of psychiatrists in San Francisco. One important dignitary mounted the rostrum and intoned that the problem of mental disease had been *solved*. Mental disease was just a chemical imbalance in that electrochemical machine called the brain. Now, chemistry had come to the rescue. Within about three years this certainty was quietly buried, quietly lest anyone be embarrassed. The issue will never prove so simple. The cause of this particular flurry was the growing experimentation with psychedelics, the mind-manifesting drugs, or hallucinogens, as they are variously called. Queen of the chemicals was LSD, and great were the wonders thereof. Apparently psychedelics enabled the mind to bypass the patterns of our ordinary, illusory world view and experience phenomena that had little relation to the everyday world. The experiences may have powerful subjective meaning, occasionally plunging the subject into "universals" and absolutes.

Psychedelics induce a kind of autistic experience and so are valuable to the present discussion. As stated before, there is no "value judgement" in the autistic mode of thinking. In the autistic mode anything conceivable is "true." The nature of the autistically perceived experience can thus become an exciting area for speculation since ordinary categories no longer apply.

Hoffer and Osmond, of the Saskatchewan group, in their early (1959) defense of a "chemical psychiatry," recognized that our beliefs influenced the way we perceived the world, and that the "mould for world-making," once formed, resisted change stubbornly. Psychedelics, they mused, allowed the mind to divest itself of the "protective yet dulling layers" of acquired assumptions and rationalizations with which all men are "encumbered." For a little while, it seemed, psychedelics allowed the mind to "see the universe again with an innocent, unshielded eye."

These early enthusiasms did not bear up well under experience. For one thing, a person's given conceptual frame of reference proved formative, even in the remote regions of psychedelic phenomena. When the patterns of the common world are fractured, our underlying attitudes still influence the nature of the experienced data. Cohen, of USC, pointed out that the "divergent expectations and intent" of the investigators made the difference between heaven and hell from the same hallucinogen. Cohen quoted Thomas Aquinas in one saying that can be considered a universal: "Whatever is received is received according to the nature of the recipient."

Hoffer and Osmond's notion of an "innocent, unshielded view of the universe" proved no more fruitful. So long as a thinking egocenter exists, its fundamental assumptions are a determinant in the experienced universe itself. Stripping off the acquired interests of our world view does not lead to a *true universe.* Our "acquisitions," as Hoffer and Osmond call them, are the very concepts directing the percepts that *constitute* the world in which we move, and there is no other world for us. We cannot free ourselves of our clearing in the forest and plunge out into the dark and find truth. If our acquired interests are a cloak that can be shed, we would immediately have to weave another, equally arbitrary garb. There is, in this sense, no going naked in the world.

Bruner of Harvard tells of studies in perception that have identified over seven million different shades of color between which we can differentiate. We categorize this spectrum into about a dozen groups, or families. This makes a practical, limited representation which we can respond to easily, talk about handily, and think about coherently.

The spectrum of light "as itself" might be analagous to the continuum of autistic thinking, lying free and untrammeled outside all categories. A handful of primary colors represent the defining disciplines of social thinking, our logic and objective reason. We impose our categories on what we see in order to see. We see through the prism of our categories.

The world view we inherit has been built up by putting things into objective pigeonholes like this, categories that can be *shared*. The psychedelic may fracture these structures. Under LSD, for instance, the categories of color, by which we help organize our field of visual possibility, may be dissolved. Then colors may merge, flow together, and not stay put. Faces may suddenly "drip" and run across the floor. Shapes may become fluid and mixing.

However, to shatter our working models of the universe does not lead to *truth,* any kind of new data, or, above all, a "true picture" of the universe. The universe, like nature, is a conceptual framework that changes from culture to culture and age to age. Our concepts are to some extent arbitrary constructs but to disrupt or dissolve them with drugs does not free us into some universal knowledge "out there" in the great beyond. There is, instead, the loss of meaningful structures of agreement needed for communion with others. This can lead to the loss of personality definition itself, that which don Juan meant by "loss of soul," or Jesus meant by the "outer darkness."

This "freedom from false concepts" notion is but a recurrence of the old Garden of Eden myth, the "noble savage," return-to-nature nonsense of the romantics. Any world view is a creative tension between possibility and choice. This is the tension that holds community and "real" world together. This is the cohesive force of our own center of awareness, the thin line between loss of self to autistic dissolution on the one hand, or slavery to the broad statistics of the world on the other. Perceptions relieved of this natural tension, through drugs or the various occult religious techniques, may well be profound or frightfully chaotic.

Price, in his preface to Carington's book *(Matter, Mind and Meaning),* discusses the physiological phenomenon of "ideomotor action." It has been found that an idea or response tends to fulfill itself or execute itself automatically through the muscular apparatus of the body, and will do so unless other ideas are present to inhibit it. Price suggests that this is indicative of a wider operation in life, namely that all ideas have a tendency to realize themselves in the material world in any way they can, unless inhibited by other ideas. This Price-Carington notion will be borne out, I believe, in the exploration taking place here in my book.

Solley and Murphy spoke of us as immersed in a "sea of stimuli," all "striving for dominance" within us. We are not so easily impinged upon by *things,* however, and the system of reality growing from our given stimuli is far more dynamic. The "striving" tensions are those of ideas, or ways for *grouping* this sea of stimuli. Surely a basic stimulus is given us, but each culture, discipline, or ideology, strives for dominance as the prism through which this stimulus will be ordered into a coherent, shared world. This fragmented striving is the charismatic curse of reason that drives us from innocence to experience, from circle to circle. The more thoroughly we search out our past, the more embracing and sweeping we find this "cosmic-egg structuring" to have always been, even in the most archaic of cultures.

Aldous Huxley considered our consciousness but a segment of a larger one. Normal consciousness is that which has been funneled through the "reducing valve" of brain, nervous system and sense organs. This protects us, Huxley believed, from being "overwhelmed on the surface of the planet." Through drugs, or the various mental cult systems, this valve-reduced reality can be bypassed and "mind at large" partially admitted by the personal psyche. The schizophrenic has lost the way back, and can no longer take refuge in the homemade universe of common sense, the strictly human world of useful notions, shared symbols and socially acceptable conventions. (Ronald Laing might say the schizophrenic may be hiding, not lost, or even on a private adventure from which he simply does not care to come back.)

"Mind at large" gives to a continuum of events an anthropomorphic shape that the situation may not warrant. Our "reducing valve" may be designed not so much to protect us from being overwhelmed (by those seven million shades of color, for instance?) as designed to simplify and realize, literally select, focus and make real a specific event out of a continuum of possible events. The only reality available in this universe may well be a homemade one.

Sherwood wrote of an apparent universality of perception in the psychedelic experience. He attributed this "universal central perception" to a single reality. Cohen takes a more nihilistic view, arguing that once the mind is unhinged from normal categories, regardless of the means used, it can only go in a limited number of directions. He called such departures "unsanity" to distinguish them from *in*sanity. He considered "unsanity" the common pathway of the stressed mind. Variations of the unhinged experience contain a common core of necessity, according to Cohen.

In another context, however, Cohen points out that the underlying motivation impelling the drug taker or systems-follower to *break* with the norm is the nucleus for what is *then* experienced. A combination of these two observations by Cohen gives insight into the reality function. The "common core of mind" may be the autistic mode of thinking, itself a kind of mirror for some ultimate notion or desire coming from consciousness.

Carington considered consciousness an intensified point on a spectrum of unconsciousness. He rejected the metaphors of a "layered consciousness," as found in depth psychology. He favored a "field of consciousness," the mind belonging to this field rather than the field belonging to the mind. Even material objects are only "logical constructions" from different appearances or possibilities for sense data. The limitations of the human mind are thus only matters of fact, not matters of some universal law.

Carington's working model is related to Whitehead's theory of *organism,* where the event is the core of reality. No simple location, or set of simple assumptions, can in themselves grasp the "unity of the event." For Whitehead, nature is a structure of evolving processes, and the reality is the *process.*

Bruner, in his *Study of Thinking,* discusses experiments in sensory deprivation. These experiments were designed to find out what happens when a person is shut off from all intake of perceptual data. A subject is isolated in a sound- and light-proofed room. He lies on foam rubber, wears velvet gloves, and everything is done to block out any possibility for sensory intake. Microphones, electrographic apparatus picking up brain waves which are amplified and recorded, and related devices keep tab on the subject's reactions.

After a period of this womb-like condition, the subject begins to hallucinate. Voices, images, movements, sensations, entire episodes begin to take place. Deprived of ordinary sensory data from which to select according to the needs of his world view, his mind structures a reality, drawing on past data. This structuring *happens* to the personality, too. He is not necessarily aware that he is hallucinating. He feels himself very much a part of the resulting event. The event takes place around him as an ordinary occasion. His sensory system is in full play, sending appropriate sights, smells, tastes, touches, and so on, as *needed* by the mind for its reality.

There is a rough similarity here with the Tibetan *tulpa* and other psychic creations such as Carlos Castenada's experiences with don Juan (as I will relate later.) Bruner's subjects, however, have no prestructured set of expectancies around which to orient their synthetic creations, and without such, and without the social world as definition and criteria, the experiences tend to become chaotic and nightmarish.

In 1963, two miners, Fellin and Throne, were isolated for nineteen days in a Pennsylvania mine collapse. After a while they began to be able to "see" and were able to maneuver and improve their conditions. They shared hallucinations, seeing the same imaginary things at the same time. At one time both men saw a great doorway rimmed in blue light, and a flight of marble steps beyond. At another time they saw two men walking along with miner's lanterns and called to them, at which the apparitions faded. The miners were, of course, in a tiny pocket nearly a mile underground, without lights of any sort. One wonders what would have happened had they gone up the blue-lit doorway and steps, as they debated trying. The experiences of *folie à deux,* or shared hallucinations, had a numinous quality deeply impressing the two rough miners, and the blue light described sounds quite similar to the light of the sacred mushroom experiences of the Mexicans.

Stephen McKellar argues that all mental experiences, no matter how bizarre and novel, are related to and originate in learned or subliminal information gained from experience. *Secondary* percepts, those gained vicariously from reading, listening to others, movies, and so on, must be taken into account. We can have perfectly real memories of other people's imaginings, just as we dream on former dream content or have specific childhood memories that originated in dreams or fantasies.

McKellar claims that no subject matter for thought is possible except from an external source. Our most unrestrained imaginings, works of art and science, all derive from "recent and/or remote perceptions." McKellar seems on strong grounds. Even so esoteric a production as the Yogic *tulpa* proves to have its inception in commonly-shared perceptions, and, as will be noted with Carlos Castenada's extremely strange experiences, the initial point of departure was some tangible perception from the mundane world.

Freud's analysis of dreams is one of McKellar's points of reference, however, and there is tacit acceptance of

Freud's interpretation of the unconscious as limited to the repressed, peripheral, forgotten episodes of an individual's experience. Yet there are experiences that suggest a mental structure more flexible than the Freudian. There are experiences that point to a collective level of consciousness, and unconscious exchanges. Suspending one's reality adjustment can open one to experiences neither available to, nor amenable to, examination by logical thinking.

For instance, one rainy afternoon when I was young, friends and I were pleasantly listening to Mahler and chatting of inanities when, crossing the room, I suddenly passed out. It was a bone-dry gathering, inside at least, and I had never done such an asinine thing before. Instantly I was "looking" at the hand of my girl, then some 250 miles away, writing me a letter. (She was "shooting me down" as we used to say, a point of no small emotional impact for me.) Immediately I regained consciousness, having been out only momentarily, just long enough to upset my roommate and friends. I told my friend of the letter, later that day. A couple of days later he brought in the mail, amused at the coincidence as he handed me the letter from the girl, postmarked the fateful afternoon. I made my roommate open the actual letter, however, and check as I recited the contents, burned into my brain as they were. This paled my friend and unhinged his day.

Unconscious exchanges and shared hallucinations between two or three gathered together in a common cause or belief express themselves in many ways. The experiences of Castenada and don Juan will prove to incorporate this phenomenon. Spiritualists, for instance, in their desire for information from "the other side" suspend all criteria of ordinary, social thinking. As a group they enter into a subset of experience, a kind of shared autistic hypnagogic state. Gathering together strengthens their faith in the validity of their system. Their *desire* for conviction suspends the criteria used in ordinary reality, criteria standing in the way of the esoterica desired.

The believers accept avidly everything produced, since doubt would split the fabric of their state. Eternal knaves feed on eternal fools, of course, and charlatanism runs rife, but so do genuine mind-picking, telepathy, clairvoyance, a kind of yogic-tulpa creation, and a variety of phenomena not available to the ordinary processes.

Having spent some time at a spritualist "camp," I attempted comment to a true-believing friend. He stated, however, that a *wise* person would spend twenty years or so in the brotherhood, in careful, devoted study, before attempting to draw any conclusion at all. Twenty years, indeed far less, of devoted study would only be sustained, of course, by one who had *already decided* that the framework offered sufficient reward to justify the life investment. That very decision would have set into motion *the kind of restructuring* of mind the new procedure would require. Further, the mind would *make* the adjustment, the restructuring of concept, sooner or later, in order to justify the investment of self. The mind would eventually reorganize to get the kind of percepts the new world view would need. It would be a self-verifying maneuver.

We easily dismiss as illusory and occult such esoteric plays of mind. Two things should be borne in mind, however. First, the productions of these "two or three gathered together" asking for certain things, and agreeing on the means of getting them, are quite genuine. The system produces as it aims to produce. Secondly, and more difficult to recognize, is that the same mirroring function underlies a science, a respectable discipline, a religion, or what have you. This assertion will equally offend the spiritualist, the scientist, and the theologian, since each apparently *must* represent his system as an absolute "out there" distinct from and objectively existing apart from himself, *in order to have* the nonambiguous faith to sustain the very fabric of his system.

Extrasensory experience may be a misnomer, but such occurrences are compatible with Carington's field of consciousness theory, as well as Whitehead's theory. "In a sense," Whitehead once said, "all things are in all places at the same time." Extrasensory influence of a sleeping person's dreams has been investigated at Brooklyn's

Maimonides Hospital. Dr. Montague Ullman and psychologist Stanley Krippner used the classic dream investigation technique devised by Nathaniel Kleitman at the University of Chicago. By using special equipment, much the same as in the sensory deprivation experiments, records can be made during sleep of eye movements, breathing, sub-vocal activity, brain wave patterns, and so on. From these it can be determined when a person is dreaming.

A sleeping subject is in one room, all the apparatus attached; a reseacher observing the equipment is in the next room; Dr. Ullman, in a third room, studies a "target picture" and tries to influence the dreams of the sleeping person. The equipment shows when the subject starts dreaming, after which he is awakened and asked to relate the dream. Sealed envelopes, containing pictures, one of which is the "target" picture, are then given the subject, who correctly chooses the one he "saw" in his dreams.

In one example, Ullman concentrated on a Gauguin painting, "Still Life with Three Puppies," which had blue goblets in it. The subject dreamed of "a couple of dogs making a noise, and dark blue bottles." In another trial, Ullman concentrated on a painting called "Zapatistas," showing followers of the Mexican revolutionary Zapata. The followers march along a road with a range of mountains in the background. The dreamer, when awakened, explained that his dream was about New Mexico. A file of Indians were going to Santa Fe for fiesta time, with great mountains in the background.

Now the subject had once lived in New Mexico and had seen Indians going to Santa Fe for fiesta. Simple fortuituousness could be presumed, but note that it is only *similar* data, found already in the subject's background, that is triggered up. Nothing *new* is given the subject, precisely as McKellar would claim. There is, instead, this calling-up and regrouping of previous perceptual contents in keeping with the stimulus of the nonsensory source. This justifies both Jung and McKellar, making them complementary rather than opposing.

The blueprint comes from the non-personal source, but it must be filled in with a content individual and unique.

Paul Tillich claims that divine answers are given the form of existential questions-rather the reverse of the above.

The Russian parapsychologist, Vasiliev, writes of subjecting hypnotized persons to fake mustard plasters. Peasants who had never heard of a mustard plaster had no reaction whatsoever to the fake application. Patients who had experienced a *real* one suffered the usual red-rashy, heat-irritated skin and sweated profusely. The inexperienced peasants were then given, in their normal state, a real mustard plaster treatment. After that, they produced all the appropriate symptoms in the hypnotic experiments.

Carl Jung found cases in madmen of experiences beyond the personal background. He told of a schizophrenic patient in his thirties, hospitalized since his early twenties with delusions of grandeur, visions, demonic seizures, and so on. One day the patient, blinking up at the sun, stopped Dr. Jung and showed him how by scrooching up his eyes, he could see the sun's phallus, swinging below the rim of the sun. When one moved one's head from side to side, the phallus could also seen to swing from side to side, and that was the "origin of the winds." This was such a strange hallucination that Jung carefully noted it, along with the patient's history.

In the course of his studies of mythology, Jung was sent a new book of translations by Dieterich, including the "Paris Magical Papyrus," thought to be a liturgy of the Mithraic cult. Here Jung found, stated in the same terms, but in cultic poetry, the identical sun-phallus-wind vision described by his patient. Cryptomnesia, or hidden memory, was ruled out. Jung later came across other references to the vision from Greek and medieval sources.

Jung used such cases to establish his three-tiered cosmology: consciousness, personal unconscious, and collective unconscious. Adopting his system, things can be seen in just this way, though others might use the material as grist for other mills. Anticipating my fourth chapter, on questions and answers, I would mention that the patient's history suggested just the kind of vision he experienced. It was the kind of esoteric, cultic "information" and secret insight for which he had longed in his mundane, uneventful and uneducated adolescence, the very drift which had eventually brought on his reality suspension and produced his retreat from the world.

Fulfillment of desire was surely one of the elements in the experience. The patient called up from the continuum of past experience the sort of thing he desired. The sun was the trigger for the ancient imagery, and the imagery was as valid to the patient as anything else, since all criteria of ordinary reality adjustment had long since been suspended.

None of this validates Jung against McKellar. Rather, it shows McKellar's "recent or remote" perceptions to be active on a wider scale than at first evident. The roots of our garden clearing in the forest are not shallow, and the common core of the unhinged mind may run deeper than Cohen suspects. This does not give to this background of ours a character of its own, however. If this continuum of experience is Huxley's "mind at large," such a mind has no criteria or value, and as such, "mind" as we know it is hardly the right term. A phallus swinging from the rim of the sun and causing winds is just as "true" within this continuum as the most sophisticated recent scientific jargon for the origin of solar winds.

In his book on mysticism, Princeton's elderly philosopher, Walter Stace, included an experience by the writer, Arthur Koestler. Koestler was in solitary confinement for several months during the Spanish Civil War. He was supposedly awaiting execution, and to while away the time he revived his esthetic interest in analytical geometry, scratching theorems on the wall. Euclid's proof that the number of primes is infinite led to a classical example of the spontaneous mystical experience.

Koestler became enchanted with the idea that a meaningful and comprehensive statement about the infinite could be arrived at by precise and finite means, without "treacly ambiguities." One day the significance of this swept over him "like a wave," leaving him in a "wordless essence, a fragrance of eternity, a quiver of the arrow in the blue." This led to a "river of peace, under bridges of silence," that came from nowhere and flowed nowhere.

Finally there was no river and no I. Koestler's *I* had ceased to exist-he had become one with that infinite.

Koestler apologized for such an embarrassing confession, stating that he had read the *Meaning of Meaning* and nibbled at logical positivism, and considered himself as tough-minded as anyone. He nevertheless recognized from his experience an "interlocking of all events," an interdependence in all things. He spoke of a "universal pool," and a unity of all things. He had many recurrences of the experience in prison, though they faded and disappeared after his return to normal life.

Consider now that Koestler's world at that time consisted of four grey stone walls. The only window was a tiny opening high in the wall, from which only a patch of sky could be seen. Week after week passed with no voices, no communications, no modifications to another. It was a kind of "sensory deprivation." All remaining was his growing fascination with geometry.

Consider, too, that he had been subject to an unannounced firing squad for months. Daily he had heard neighboring cell-mates being led into the courtyard onto which his tiny window opened. Daily he had heard the volley of shots. As with Feinberg's frustration at Einstein's speed limit, did the idea of *infinite* have real meaning to Koestler as a crack in his *finite* egg? As the full meaning of "finite" bore in on him inescapably, did his own synthesis of "infinite" begin? Was his finally-occurring experience not a *Eureka!* illumination in keeping with the nature of the trigger? Did his deep strata of desire not use as vehicle the only outlet available to his tough-minded world view, namely, geometry, free of those treacly ambiguities he had found in systems of belief? Was his experience, then, not only in keeping both with the nature of the trigger and the materials available for synthesis, yet satisfying the underlying ultimate desire? This is the case with all other mental experiences, regardless of the nature of the experience, as I will try to show with the scientific "breakthrough."

Was Koestler's experience not similar to my friend's Mozart-sonata, or my apple tree illumination? In Chapter Four I will outline other experiences in science, religion, philosophy, and so on, some of them radical ideas that have played a formative role in our modern world, and will show that they all follow this same general pattern. So we cannot disparage this type of experience as subjective illusion. Rather, it is the way by which the crack in the egg literally materializes.

The spiritually-minded may be upset that this greatest of human experiences, the religious illumination, is described as the synthetic production of a stressed mind, and not an opening to Huxley's mind at large, James's Over-Soul, the Stoic-Christian moral governor of the universe, or what have you. If the surface nihilism can be penetrated, however, a possibility more profound than either spiritualism or realism can be found. The same function of mind that gives Koestler "intimations of immortality" produces the scientific postulate that changes a reality structure, or allows the Ceylonese Hindu to walk through beds of fire. That the experience is a synthetic construct made by an ultimately committed mind does not lessen its realness, or the implications of the maneuver. *Every* aspect of our reality has this undercurrent of synthesis.

For now, I hope to have given some idea of what I mean by "autistic thinking," and the peculiar way in which it is unambiguous. I hope I have given some of its ramifications and suggested some of the ways it mirrors or responds to passionate commitments, tacit beliefs, unambiguous notions. I hope I have suggested how such notions tend to "realize" themselves. Understanding this mirroring capacity of thought we can avoid the spiritualist trap of granting an authentic or stable character of its own to this nebulous, indefinable, and haphazard play of mind, while yet recognizing the fathomless potential available there, a potential that goes beyond all naive-realist, biogenetic acceptances.

Jung, Carington, Teilhard, and others suggest a continuum of experience underlying our surface realities. To imply that this continuum is "thought" as we know it can cancel the open end it *holds,* and we must dismiss universal pools of metaphysical knowledge, a fixed scheme of *a priori* facts awaiting discovery "out there," or cosmic helping-hands available to clear-thinking minds or pure-minded souls. Attributing characteristics of personality to the function is a projection device which turns the open end into a mirror of ourselves, trapping us in our own logical devices.

The "universal pool" is as much "in here" as anywhere. Being autistic by nature, anything desired can be gotten from it, *if* one is willing to pay the price and has an ultimate commitment around which the process can orient. Hard discipline of mind and passionate adherence to a belief in spite of all obstacles and all evidence to the contrary, can overcome all obstacles and bring about the necessary evidence. The mirrors of reality play are brought into alignment by a non-ambiguous commitment from a conscious mind. The "other mirror" is automatically unambiguous.

The close relation between our commitments of life and what we perceive was explored by Livingston in the *Bulletin of Atomic Science,* February, 1963. Livingston discussed the idea, inherited from the Greeks, of a common logic of thinking. Recent studies have questioned this Greek notion. Culture and language affect one's world view, the very process by which we think, and the "logic assumed for the operation of the whole universal process."

We inherited from Descartes the notion that there is a close correspondence between what we perceive and the "real nature of our environment." Descartes believed that a world of objects existed in a stable form and that reasonable men could "divest themselves of their passions" and by methods of reasoning arrive at an objective comprehension of physical things, social events, and forces.

Descartes granted us a relatively one-to-one correspondence between our subjective experience and the world "out there." He also gave us the notion that each of us has access to a relatively uncontaminated screen of perceptual experience upon which our judgements and actions can be based.

Livingston points out that our logical processes of thinking are relative to the language learned. He questions the correspondence between what we perceive and the "real nature of our environment." I would extend his question to ask: Is there such a *thing* as a "real nature of our environment"? Cohen assumes that if there is, man can never know it. All we can know, as Bruner says, is our own representation of the world; a representation, Jung might add, carried as a blueprint within our culture, filled with an endless variety of diverse content-from Solley-Murphy's sea of stimuli, shaped by Sapir-Whorf's concept-percept in this semantic universe of Lévi-Strauss's, and so on.

There is nothing orderly or logical to the function I am trying to outline. I find no evidence that great cosmic powers keep the process on an upward trend, keeping an eye on us to assure our eventual success. There is no hierarchy of criteria or value for what is or is not "realized," made real, by the function. It is a contest of inhibitions and strengths, choices and allegiances. We are the source of value and choice, the source of ideas around which the procedure of our reality orients.

On the one hand it is argued that there is no world "out there" available to dispassionate observation. Objectivity in relation to reality is a naive delusion on our part. On the other hand, a universal common knowledge is denied. There appears to be no world-mind from which we may get cues, no secret wavelengths for our perceptors.

There is, nevertheless, an open-ended aspect for us, a creative one, and glimpsed through autistic thinking. There is a bridge between clearing and forest, between logical man and his non-logical potential. William Blake claimed that "anything capable of being imagined is an image of truth." We openly shape reality when we diligently apply every ounce of our logical process to a given desire. We are subject to the same effect on less conscious levels. Our confused, conflicting, and inchoate assumptions also enter as shaping forces in reality, and happen to us as a random, confused fate.

It takes an ultimate commitment to damp out and exclude other possibilities so that one possibility might formulate and be realized. Autistic thought can synthesize and break into consciousness with anything desired, if the conscious desire is strong enough to win the struggle for dominance. Non-ambiguity is the shaping force of reality. This capacity of mind is remote, elusive, whimsical, but it can catalyze and synthesize ideas, notions, desires, and quests drawn from or suggested by a realized world of events. From this catalytic synthesis we have presented back an enhanced mirror of our concepts that can enlarge our reality itself. This is the way in which "eternity is in love with time."

Next I will explore the shaping of a world view, our set of concepts built from infancy and childhood, its structure determining the kind of world then available to the mind so shaped.

3

blueprints and viewpoints

A social world view, one shared with other people, is structured from our infant minds by the impingements on us from, and the verifying responses to us by, other people. A mind finds its definition of itself not by confrontation with *things* so much as other minds. We are shaped by each other. We adjust not to the reality of a *world* but to the reality of other thinkers. When we have finally persuaded and/or badgered our children into "looking objectively" at their situation, taking into consideration those things other to themselves, we relax since they are being *realistic*. What we mean is that they have finally begun to mirror our commitments, verify our life investments, and strengthen and preserve the cosmic egg of our culture.

Occasionally we hear of people found chained in attics and such places from infancy. Their world view is either scanty or different for they are always feeble minded at best. In 1951 a child was found in an Irish chicken-house, having somehow survived there with the chickens, since infancy. The ten-year old's long hair was matted with filth; he ate at the chicken trough; roosted with the flock; his fingernails had grown, fittingly, to semicircular claws; he made chicken-like noises, not surprisingly; he had no speech and showed no promise of learning any in the time he survived his rescue.

Forty years ago there was interest in two feral children found in India. They had apparently been raised by wolves. They were taken from an actual wolf den along with some cubs, the older wolves scattering or being killed. One of the children, Kamala they called her, survived for nine years. Only with difficulty was she taught table manners and such niceties as walking on the hind legs. Nevertheless she exhibited a growing awareness of the reward system of her new group, and displayed a strong drive toward such orientation. As with the chicken-child, however, she had missed the formative period of human infant development, and there was no easy or complete going back to retrace the steps. Kamala had formed according to the pattern eliciting response around her during her mirroring period. For her first two years of captivity—or rescue—she howled faithfully at ten, twelve, and three at night, as all Indian wolves do. She would also, in spite of precautions, manage to get at the chickens, rip them apart alive and eat them raw. Only when the new social reward system grew strong enough to outweigh the earlier rewards did she abandon her early training.*

What kind of minds did these feral children have? Jung claimed that no one is born a *tabula rasa,* a blank slate. As the body carries features specifically human yet individually varied, so does the psychic organism. The psyche preserves an unconscious stratum of elements going back to the invertebrates and ultimately the protozoa. Jung speaks of a hypothetical peeling of the collective unconscious, layer by layer, down to the psychology of the ameoba. We can trace a rough parallel in the development of the foetus.

As the body must be fed to realize the potential built into the genes as a blueprint waiting development, so must the mind. Jung used the term *archetype* to describe "recurrent impressions made by subjective reactions." We inherit such ideas as part of our potential mind pattern. *Archetypes,* however, are only a kind of *readiness* to produce over and again the same mythical ideas. If the

---

* There has been an accepted disparaging of the reports by Kellog, Gesell, Singh, and others concerning these children, until one now hears this case blithely dismissed as a fraud. No one reading the original publications, studying the photographs, the diaries, and the overall picture will dismiss the case, however.

readiness is not triggered by a response or a demand, that particular possibility remains dormant and even steadily diminishes.

Linguists are intrigued by the readiness with which the infant seizes a language, *if* given the referents. The "readiness" of language can miscarry, as Susanne Langer put it, because of lack of the trigger-response interplay. If this happens, the world view shaped by that language miscarries too and never forms. Then participation in that kind of world is permanently blocked. Leonard Hall writes that our culture and our reality are not separate phenomena. People of different cultures not only speak different languages, but inherit different sensory worlds.

Lévi-Strauss uses the term "semantic-universe" to describe our intellectual-scientific-technological fabric of reality. Jerome Bruner suggested that language is our most powerful means for performing "transformations" on the world. We transmute the world's shape by metaphoric mutations. We recombine our verbal structures in the interest of new possibilities.

Susanne Langer considered language to be conception and concept the frame of perception. Thus, for Langer, we live in a "primary world" of reality that is verbal. The *word* for a thing helps to arrest an infant's visual process and focus it on a specific thing. It is the combination of sensory possibilities, parental focus, and innate drives for ordering, that organizes the child's visual field. Then the word-thing growth becomes exponential, growing like a tree at every tip. Grouping, identifying, correlating, with a constant check with his exemplars, gives the young child an exciting participation and communion, a defining of self and world. Langer calls even nature a "language-made affair," made for understanding, and "prone to collapse into chaos if ideation fails." Fear of this collapse may be the most potent fear in civilized man.

It is our ideation that shapes our children. We provide an enriched environment, visual, aural, tactile stimuli to furnish the best supply of raw materials, but our own background determines what we decide makes up a "rich environment." And then, quite naturally, we expect our children to shape this material into a pattern verifying our commitments. We look for agreement.

A "semantic universe" can be built only on a background of language, but a considerable input of raw materials of every kind is necessary to build a language. The mind has to have a world to draw on in order to organize a world-to-view. In my opening broadside I have emphasized thinking as the director of percepts, and surely our developed concepts shape our world. But an initial impingement on perception by a world "out there," of things and people, enters as the other mirror in the two-way interaction of development of mind. Infant thinking is probably autistic, gradually structuring into reality-thinking, but even autistic thinking cannot arise from a vacuum. The mill of the mind is the chief element in reality, but before it can grind, at least for our table, it must have some of our kind of grist. Missing this, a mind might still grind marvelous stuff, but we could never know it.

In the last chapter I presented evidence against a universal pool of knowledge or a common logic of thinking. Evidence points toward the infant mind being prestructured along clearly marked drives toward communion with others, toward speech, response and so on, but the *content* for the drives is acquired. Bruner points out that *intent* precedes both acquisition of knowledge and ability to do. Acquisition of language and the ability to *do* in an infant are brought about by nurturing and fostering the inborn intent. Raw material must be given the mind; the blueprint must be filled in by responsive and guiding actions and reactions from other minds. The infant mind then makes syntheses of these acquisitions of possibilities.

The kind of syntheses that can occur, once material is available to mind, is varied, however. Smythies, as mentioned before, assumes that *hallucinations* are a part of the normal child's psychic experience. As the child grows older, he selectively represses the hallucinatory fabric according to the "current negative social value." Syntheses accepted *as* the "current social value," and given "positive reward" are considered real.

Bracken pointed out that the distinction between autistic and reality-adjusted thinking corresponds with the German theory that new and more complex neurological structures, as the mid-brain and cortex, grow as superimpositions upon older and more primitive brain structures, such as the "old brain," or brain-stem. These older thinking devices (there is no being but in a *mode* of being,) continue to function, however, even after the higher ones are developed. McKeller presumes that A-thinking takes place in these lower centers, and Smythies' *hallucinatory* psychic experiences of childhood would fall into the same classification. Jung's notion of a collective response would fit in with this kind of representation. The mid-brain, old brain and stem being structures shared by all animals, one can see how the psyche might be peeled layer by layer down to the psychology of lower creatures. Polanyi's "primary process" thinking of animals and children could be understood in this sense.

Perhaps, then, the education of a child is unlearning as well as learning, and perhaps many possibilities are *lost* through lack of triggering response, possibilities that may have been of worth. James Old, in his experiments on rats (giving electrode stimulus to various parts of the brain), presumed a kind of ecstacy-response was created by stimulus of a certain area of the mid-brain. In the human, stimulus of this area makes "all the bells of heaven ring," as one subject expressed it. Hallucinogens must occasionally stimulate this area, as well as dissolving the ordinary categories of reality.

This kind of ecstatic experience is negated by logical thinking. Old found that the rapture *faded* as the stimulus was moved away from the mid-brain and toward the rat's thin layer of cortex. And life has moved toward an abundance of cortex, this thinking material giving us our superior discontinuity over the animals. Our logical process has been bought at too stiff a price, though, and life moves toward the further possibility of getting around the price paid. That is, life moves toward correcting the imbalance of mind that the development of logic has brought on. If balanced, a logical process could then selectively direct an infinite potential.

At any rate, while we can say the chicken-child was

not really human, we cannot say his experience was that of a vegetable. A low level of cortical activity might allow free development of mid-brain experience. We tend to deny consciousness to other things (or other people), but, as Blake put it:

How do you know but every bird
That wings the airy way
Is an immense world of delight,
Closed to your senses five?

Bruner's *Center for Cognitive Studies* proposes a "programmed infant mind," a mind only awaiting the proper stimulus to flower. Bruner argues that if language were the result of a learning process alone, man's grasp would be forever limited by what he has already learned to reach. The infant is a bud, ready to bloom. The intention, the will to do, precedes the skill, the ability to do.

William Blake, in his outrage against the dead world of a John Locke, cried: "Man's mind is like a garden ready planted. This world is too poor to produce one seed." We find, nevertheless, that the specifics of the plantings are given shape by the kind of weeding, thinning, and fertilizing done by other minds. Arnold Gesell noted with wonder that the wolf-child, Kamala, eventually *did* respond to her human environment in a "slow and orderly recovery of obstructed mental growth." The recovery was only partial, certainly. It took some five years of care before she had reached an approximate age development of an eighteen-month-old; at her death at seventeen, after nine years of human environment, she had reached something approximating a three-year-old level. Scant progress as it seems, this was from a child who had spent her first eight years in a wolf-den, and whose learning and unlearning problems must have been considerable.

Gesell considered the capacity of an individual to acquire and create culture to be inborn, but he pointed out that the culture which surrounds an individual operates as a "large-scale molding matrix, a gigantic conditioning apparatus." He warned against oversimplifying the complex and interwoven riddle of "nature versus nurture."

And surely if only a wolf-culture is offered as the mirroring pattern, this is nevertheless seized upon by the programmed patterns of response and responded to, giving a structured world in which to move.

An error causing grief in our time is the idea that culture and civilization are recent acquisitions, and that all previous cultures were but crude gestures laying the groundwork for our own enlightened emergence into truth. Erickson denies that primitive societies are "infantile stages of mankind," or arrested deviations from the "proud progressive norms which we represent." They are, he states, a "complete form of mature human living." Levy-Bruhl spoke of prehistoric man not as a *protoscientist* who arrived at false conclusions, but another type of man entirely, whose mental life differed from ours in kind. I would qualify this by observing that primitive man is not so much a different type as of a different esthetic bent. Lévi-Strauss finds archaic cultures a unified, coherent, intellectual scheme, based on different logical premises from our own. Jensen deplores the theory that early man arrived at totally erroneous conclusions regarding cause and effect.

Culture is not an autonomous venture; autistic thinking remains autistic until modified by another mind which is also modified by the relation. But the capacity and drive to create a culture *is* innate. It is an enormous formative potential that realizes itself against the most extreme odds.

Oversold on the splendors of "realistic," tough-minded thinking, we are led to believe that current methods represent discovery of universal truths and are thus sacred, rather than particular esthetic choices. Notions of what we are, and of what our capabilities are, change with a marvelous disregard for consistency. Yet these world views tend to bring about the very state of mind they hold to be the case. We become what we behold.

The danger of accepting a programmed infant mind is that we might decide the mind was really programmed for *our* particular show, and that all the dark ages preceded this final light. We must, rather, realize the program capacity to be the universal, the current programs the particular, and that particulars are variable, flexible, even expendable, and never sacrosanct.

The child's mind is autistic, a rich texture of free synthesis, hallucinatory and unlimited. His mind can skip over syllogisms with ease, in a non-logical, dream-sequence kind of "knight's-move" continuum. He nevertheless shows a strong desire to participate in a world of others. Eventually his willingness for self-modification, necessary to win rapport with his world, is stronger than his desire for autonomy. Were it not, civilization would not be possible. That we succeed in moulding him to respond to our criteria shows the innate drive for communion and the flexibility of a young mind. It doesn't prove an essential and sanctified rightness of our own constructs.

Maturity, or becoming reality adjusted, restricts and diminishes this "knight's-move" thinking, and tends to make pawns of us in the process. The kind of adult logic that results is dependent on the kinds of demands made on the young mind by parents and society. If we believe our social view sacred and made in heaven, we tend to shut off a deep potential in which many of the terrors and shortcomings of our logic and reason might be averted. Exclusion of possibility is necessary to narrow and hold the mind to a world of others. The price of excluded possibility buys a prism that opens on specialized worlds. We lose and gain. But the autistic mode of mind offers a way around severe loss.

Benjamin Lee Whorf recognized cultural *agreement* as implicit and unstated, but absolutely obligatory. Agreement determines the way we organize nature into concepts giving nature significance. Agreement underlies our codified patterns of language. We cannot talk at all, Whorf claimed, except by "subscribing to the organization and classification of data which the agreement decrees." Whatever this agreement decrees is what then makes up reality. Cultural agreements are automatic and unconscious, built-in and unquestioned, furnishing the "obvious facts" of experience. These are the other factors moving into and synthesizing our "visual world" from the visual field.

We force our children, consciously and unconsciously, to selectively ignore certain phenomena and look for and nourish other phenomena. The child's capacity for imagination may put up a struggle. All of us "attend the world" only from necessity or specific reward. The mind wanders into byways every second it can. Its moments of attention are fragmented. Concrete things do not impinge on this flux of mind very much. Defensively tending to the world can be handled mechanically, but other people cannot. Jean-Paul Sartre spoke of hell as "other people," and his hell was well placed. Without others I could reign supreme, except that I must have others to reign at all.

All parties in a reality event are modified by each other. All create the common denominator through which they relate. To take part in society we must accept the social definitions and agreements that make up the society's reality picture. Our definitions outline the socially acceptable framework for what shall be considered real. This network of definition changes from culture to culture and period to period. It is arbitrary to an indeterminable degree, but is always the form for the only reality available.

Langer was one of the first to question the old concept of speech as a survival technique of evolution. Thirty years ago she wrote of the beginnings of speech as purposeless lalling-instincts, "primitive aesthetic reactions, and dreamlike association of ideas," all of which sound autistic. Langer denies that speech was a "natural adjustment." (Recent studies of the cultures and esthetics of the higher apes by C. E. Carpenter and others lend an interesting overtone to Langer's proposal.) Our dreamlike autistic quality is structured into a world of categories and logical shapes through language. The stage of this development lasts throughout infancy and early childhood. The word and the concept become fused in that early period of development and grow up together.

If language is not built in during this formative period, it cannot be built at all. Bruner refers to the child as father to the man in an irreversible way. Piaget's stages of learning make clear that it is not just a lack of phonetic material (Langer's *lalling*) that blocks language learning later on. More important than this is the fact that the emerging mind will have mirrored *whatever model it had* during that formative period. The pattern formed in this plastic stage becomes firm. It hardens into the functional system of representation-response we call a world view. Once done, there is no undoing of the system except by *metanoia* resyntheses, that capacity for mutation which will occupy the next portion of this book. Even this mutation is dependent on the materials available *for* mutation—conversion is a creative process, but not magical.

This pattern formed by the mirroring of child mind and social pressure is not only the means then available for *coping* with a world and other people, it largely determines what shall be coped *with.* This world view is then the screen allowing only related data in, as well as the synthetic process determining the final cognitive shape *of* that admitted material. The pattern shapes the kind of world to respond to, and the world response that must then be made.

The infant's dream-like association of ideas is slowly won over to an agreement of *what* should constitute reality. By the time our reasoning has developed enough to reflect on the process by which our reasoning has formed, we are part and parcel of the whole process, caught up in and sustaining it. By the time the young rebel reaches the age of rebellion he is inevitably that against which he would rebel, his linear thrust ending as a pale reflection of the circle from which he would break.

Edward Hall writes that it is impossible for us to divest ourselves of culture, for it has penetrated to the roots of our nervous system and determines how we perceive the world. We cannot act or interact except through the medium of culture. Thus Whitehead could write of "fundamental assumptions" unconsciously presupposed by all the variant systems within an epoch. People do not know that they are tacitly assuming, for no other way of putting things has ever occurred to them; they are always merely responding to "obvious facts."

Whately Carington spoke of the limitations of the individual mind as matters of fact, not of law. We are limited by our agreements on possibility. Agreement is a common exclusion of alternate possibilities. Agreement is the cement of social structure. Two or three gathered together, agreeing on what they are after, may create a subset in which their goals can be achieved, even though folly in the eyes of the world. The world in this case means a set of expectancies agreed upon, a set excluding other possibilities.

Cornell's Gibson referred to a "visual field" as a constantly-shifting light pattern, bringing to mind Bruner's seven million shades of color. Gibson refers to the "visual world" as distinct from this "field." In the formation of a visual *world,* sensory data from *other sources* are used to correct the visual field. These "other sources" are the conceptual framework, the world view formation, built in the formative years. Seeing is a synthetic process incorporating our conceptual assumptions and esthetic conditionings.

Edward Hall points out that we are less actively aware of seeing than we are of talking. It is difficult to grasp that talking and understanding are synthetic processes, overlapping and incorporating an intricate network of varied responses. Much more difficult is the idea that *seeing* is subject to the same qualification. The variables that enter into seeing prove enormous, nevertheless, and people from different cultures not only use a different language, but inhabit a different sensory world, as Hall puts it.

So, when Cohen wrote that the world we see is far from an exact image of the physical world, I wondered how one could ever tell. He added that this was the case since perception is hightly variable and often erroneous, and that we can only perceive what we can conceive. Cohen observed that we tend to see only what can be incorporated into our established frame of reference, and tend to reject anything not fitting. Cohen then presumed, however, that our notions of what is "out there" are based on an "indistinct uncertainty," and I thought of Blake's comment: "If the sun and moon should doubt, they'd immediately go out." Failure of nerve is the major sin. Cohen went on to conclude that for all we know, the "thing called reality may exist, but we shall never see it," and at this point I protested.

Is there an "exact image" of a physical world? Consider even photography. The same subject can be hideous or lovely according to the skill of the photographer. Photography is an *art* because it can catch aspects of reality that escape us, precisely as painting can do. I can traverse the same tired street year in and year out, familiar with every twig and stone—but a photographer can suddenly present me with a photograph of it that makes me catch my breath much as from a poem or a piece of music. I refuse to believe the "police lineup" photograph on my driver's license is my real image; as with all aspects of the police mentality it somehow has sought out the worst possible aspects of me.

Is the strange abstraction of the physicist an "exact image" of a world? The physicist is the last to claim this. But his at times absurd abstractions become contingencies *in* the processes of a physical world. Does the word *real* mean at all what the naive realists and the tough-minded have claimed? What could the "atomically-verifiable statement" conceivably mean? Our error is in considering our concept-percept function to be separate and distinct *from* reality, rather than a dominant force in the *shaping* of it.

The condition called reality exists as an ever-current sum total of our representations and responses. Whatever we *see* is what reality *is* for us, and there will never be, from here to eternity, any other kind of reality for us. And this reality will always be in a process of mutation and change. Huxley's "homemade world" is a necessity in any context. There is no magic, there is only The Creation. There is no supernatural, but there are an infinite number of possible natures. A point of centered thinking organizes and survives by relationship with similar points of thinking. It is a matter of agreement, a structuring of similar patterns of shared response.

We know now, according to Jerome Bruner, that our nervous system is *not* the "one-way street" it was long considered to be. All minds have a program of their own. The mind sends out monitoring orders to the sense organs and the "relay stations." The orders specify priorities for different kinds of environmental message. Selectivity is the rule. We used to think of the nervous system as a simple telephone switchboard, bringing in messages from outside. We know now, Bruner claims, that the system is every bit as much an "editorial hierarchy"—a policy-making device determining what is perceived.

Edward Hall, with his "proxemic research," speaks of *vision* as a "transaction between man and his environment in which both participate." Hall explores how we unconsciously structure our *visual world*. Perhaps we can consciously seize the process. William Blake antedated all this by two centuries. He said he used his eyes to see *with,* in active *vision*—a process in which creative imagination played a principal role. He did not look *from* his eyes as through a window, in passive sight, as Descartes or Locke would claim.

How can firm statements be made about a world to itself? The very statement enters as a contingency *in* that world. What is real is a variable. Though a regressing contingency stretches back to a hypothetical First Day, the visual world is what we *practice* day by day, and our capacity for practice is infinitely varied. Our "editorial policies" are more flexible than we dare imagine. Our range of selectivity is boundless. All things are possible to him who believes—that is, to him who believes in the possibility.

We feel that surely, to a man of good will and honesty, an honest look should inform of an honest reality—and we mean, of course, our reality. This common assumption has been questioned in our day—and this is a crack in the cosmic egg of the realisms of the past few centuries. Our survival may well depend on this crack splitting the blind world of politician and pentagonian. The crack should lead us to find an open-ended possibility, provided we can open to other world views, those of Oriental and archaic cultures for instance, as valid, rather than as objects for destruction that our own might reign supreme.

The open end of human potential is built into the blueprint of mind, and is contained in that mode I have called *autistic*. This is blocked, however, by blindness of *viewpoint,* and yet the autistic can be structured and realized only by assuming viewpoints. The openness nevertheless happens to us in peripheral and unsuspected ways. One of the most intriguing of these ways is the procedure of ultimately asked and passionately adhered to *questions*. The ways in which questions form in the mind and are answered is the next part, and the central part, of my exploration.

4

questions and answers

The English scientist, Edward de Bono, writes of "lateral and vertical thinking." Since Aristotle, he points out, vertical thinking, which I have called reality-adjusted thinking, or logic, has been given the place of supremacy. In actuality, de Bono writes, all truly new ideas, by which new eras of reality have come into play, have been products of lateral thinking. Following on one great lateral opening of mind, the vertical thinkers can busy themselves for generations. De Bono likens the activity of vertical thinking to digging post holes deeper and deeper, along the lines established by lateral breakthroughs of thinking.

In this chapter I will elaborate on how the postulate, the *Eureka!* discovery, the illumination, of lateral thinking, come about. A few examples were given in Chapter Two, when I claimed that these "autistic eruptions" into logical thinking suggested a clue to the way reality shapes, the way the potential of the "dark forest" is given shape by ideas arising from our cultural clearings.

The relation of questions and answers is an example of the mirroring function between the modes of mind. Answers are shaped by the questions demanding them, just as the question is finally shaped by the nature of the answer desired. In this way our experience shapes and moves as desire reaching for the unknown.

A question is a seed of suggestion which we plant into that continuum of synthesis I have called autistic thinking. The question's germination takes place in ways unavailable to conscious thought, but only in a ground prepared and nourished *by* conscious thought. The synthesis flowers as the *Eureka!* illumination, that dramatic breakthrough wherein we are convinced of having received a universal truth.

There are no limits to the kinds of *Eureka!* we may experience. Verification of any prejudice, fulfillment of any desire, can be obtained. Polanyi pointed out that the procedure of mind involved here follows St. Paul's formula of faith, works, and grace. Faith is a neutral function, however, and any kind of belief can stimulate passionate work. Grace, unfortunately, is given according to the nature of the faith, the content of the work, the triggers around which the synthesis can organize.

The scientist, the idiot-fringe philosopher, the cult prophet, the devout Christian, the withdrawn Hindu, may each find their respective pearls in this same sea of thought. The function of question-answer is the same in all cases. The triggering desires, the metaphors of allegiance, the dictates of training, the techniques of attainment, may all differ radically, and give correspondingly different products, but underneath is the single function of representation-response, undergoing analysis throughout this book.

Back in 1935, Bertrand Russell, in his book *Religion and Science,* pointed out that Catholics, but not Protestants, could have visions in which the Virgin Mary appeared. Christians and Mohammedans, but not Buddhists, may have great truths revealed to them by the Archangel Gabriel. The list could go on, of course, and Russell was obviously right—but he was right for the wrong reasons. His conclusion was a product of nineteenth century naive realism, and a defense of vertical thinking as the only true indicator of "real things." In this chapter I hope to show the sterility and narrowness of Russell's viewpoint, and to suggest that his attack on religion was a case of pot calling kettle black.

Sir William Rowan Hamilton was professor of mathematics and astronomy at the University of Dublin. His *Quaternion Theory* has played a vital role in modern mechanics. The theory "happened to him" as a *Eureka!* discovery, an illumination, while walking to Dublin one morning with Lady Hamilton. As they started across Grougham Bridge, which his boys afterward called Quaternion Bridge, right there, in such an unlikely spot, the "galvanic circuit of thought closed," as Hamilton put it in metaphor fitting to the interests current to his time, and the "sparks which fell" from the closing of this circuitry were the fundamental equations making up his famous theory—a theory which generations of vertical thinkers have happily explored.

At the very moment of illumination there washed over Hamilton the understanding that an additional ten to fifteen years of his life would be required to translate fully the enormity of the insight given in that second. Marghanita Laski, investigating the nature of the mental maneuver involved, notes that the experience itself filled an *intellectual want* of long standing. In a letter written shortly before the discovery, Hamilton spoke of his long-cherished notion having "haunted" him for some fifteen years. A recent renewal of his old passion had given him a "certain strength and earnestness for years dormant." This renewed diligence and application to the mathematics involved furthered the long collection of material for the synthesis of the desired answer.

The historian, Arnold Toynbee, had a mental illumination of *history,* fittingly enough, and in the incongruously prosaic setting of Buckingham Palace Road. There he suddenly found himself in "communion" not with just some particular episode of history, but with "all that had been, and was, and was to come," an apt description of a mystical-autistic seizure. In that experience Toynbee was directly aware of the "Passage of History" gently flowing through him in a mighty current, his own life "welling like a wave in the flow of this vast tide." His communion both verified his life investment, and furthered it as stimulus.

Albert Einstein spoke in reverent tones of his illumination giving rise to his famous theory. He never doubted that he had been privileged to glimpse into the very mathematical mind and physical heart of all things. James R. Newman spoke of Einstein's 30-page paper "On the Electrodynamics of Moving Bodies," as embodying a "vision." He observed that poets and prophets are not the only ones to have visions, but that scientists do so as well. They glimpse a peak perhaps never again seen, but the landscape is "forever changed." Their life is then spent describing what was seen, elaborating on the vision that others might follow.

Nikos Kazantzakis was a Greek novelist and poet. He was an adherent to the Bergsonian concept of the *élan vital,* a spirit transcending matter and transforming it into spirit; an "onrushing force throughout all creation which strives for purer and more rarified freedom."

In a final assault on the meaning of existence, Kazantzakis retreated to Mount Athos, that near-legendary Greek mountain where no woman has ever set foot, but ascetics and monastics abound. For two years Kazantzakis devoted himself to contemplation. He spent months teaching his body to endure cold, hunger, thirst, sleeplessness and every privation. Then he turned to his spirit, where, in painful concentration he sought to conquer within himself the "minor passions, the easy virtues, the cheap spiritual joys, the convenient hopes."

Kazantzakis finally experienced a tremendous vision, in keeping with his desire for verification of his ultimate concern. In his numinous experience his life-work, the belief he had hammered out all his years, was both clarified and verified. His illumination happened one night and he "started up in great joy," seeing the "red ribbon" left behind in the ascent, within us and in all the universe, by his "certain Combatant." Kazantzakis clearly saw those "bloody footprints ascending from inorganic matter into life and from life into spirit." It was this, the transmutation of matter into spirit that was the great secret. Here was the meaning of his own life, to transmute, even in his own small capacity, matter into Spirit, the highest endeavor, and by which he might reach a harmony with the universe.

Jean-Paul Sartre had a diabolical mystical experience, an "extraverted," or conscious one, in which he "saw" the whole world to be a single, unified, grey, jelly-like protoplasm of pain, horror, and meaninglessness. This is completely opposite to the mystical experience of Jacob

Boehme, also a conscious one. Walter Kaufman, with his "Faith of a Heretic," claimed a negative experience that verified, that is gave a numinous, "universal" kind of rightness to, his agnostic position.

St. Augustine was driven by his desire for religious conviction, but felt blocked by a myraid of minor allegiances inhibiting the single devotion demanded by Christian belief. Little by little he damped down and inhibited the various drives of ego and flesh that prevented his opening to transformation. Augustine knew what his goals were, however. He longed for a certain experience of total seizure because he had heard others speak of such an experience, and he had seen the evident results. His longing finally reoriented his own "hierarchy of mind," making his own "new-seeing" possible. (That what he finally "saw" was a synthesis of his own desires—not some absolute or universal "out there" knowledge—is clearly evident from the Stoic nature of the Christianity *resulting* from Augustine, a point to which I will briefly return in the last part of this book.)

Laski contrasts Augustine's complex personality and search with John Wesley's simpler one. Wesley was, though a sincere, practicing Christian, not one of the twice-born. He had simply never doubted God or felt removed from a divine presence. All around him his fellow workers were experiencing dramatic conversions, however, and Wesley wanted the same stamp of authenticity for his own formulations. He investigated in detail the moment he sought; he knew what it must feel like. He was moved by "appropriate influences at significant moments," according to Laski's study. He knew the question he was asking, and the answer desired. He finally achieved his conversion and it was just as dramatic as that hoped for, just as real as could be desired, precisely toward which he had long aimed.

The asking of a question with passionate concern for its answer, a concern which demands life investment, suggests a door which will sooner or later be found. Whether it is successfully opened to the public is another matter, but if a current world view can *accommodate* a new synthesis, the new idea may prove to be the case. A new idea fails if it involves too great a sacrifice of invested belief. If the new idea triggers a passionate enough pursuit to make suspension or abandonment of previous beliefs, or current criteria worth the risk, however, the new idea can *change* the reality structure.

Price spoke of an idea's propensity for achieving reality unless inhibited by other ideas. A new idea can be killed by the pressure of inhibiting investments. On the other hand, and happening a bit more as fate, a new idea can breed the very ecology necessary to its own translation, testability, and realization. In the next chapter I will explore this function as seen in the posing of the "empty category" in science, and how this can bring about the content needed to fill the category.

A person with passionate concern for the successful translation of his *Eureka!* (itself produced by passionate pursuit of an idea) can transform the very common domain with which adjustment of his new idea is sought. Whether the energy equivalent of ten billion tons of uranium fission will ever be obtained from a single cubic centimeter of empty space, as proposed by Bohm, depends on how passionately such an idea might be sustained and followed by enough people long enough for sufficient realignment of a vast network of assumptions.

If the current reality cannot contain a new idea, if the current allegiances inhibit the idea and prevent its completing its circuitry and fulfilling itself, never mind. Those current allegiances can be replaced, if slowly, until the new idea achieves its goal and is "real-ized," made real. Einstein's equations helped bring about the current scientific fabric that in turn verified Einstein's equations. New ideas must agree with this fabric or be discarded. On the other hand, for a new world view to develop, Einstein's ideas must be subtly changed or selectively abandoned. Such metaphoric mutations or discards require, however, a certain good taste, an esthetic protocol acceptable to the brotherhood of believers.

Passionate conviction can change the very adjusted reality with which testable correspondence is needed. The true believer can bring about the very changes and adjustments within his reality that can fit his new idea into the then altered background.

The double-helix formation for the chromosome gene was proposed as an "empty category" sixteen or so years before it was finally "photographed" and verified. Even then the photography was not direct, but only possible after suitable preparation allowed the photographing of an otherwise unphotographable entity.

How does the mind arrive at such remote and difficult theories when there is no tangible sign or even rudimentary hint, and when no way exists for verifying even the first part of the newly-forming fabric?

The Platonic retreat is an accepted evasion: Plato's God built into the mind the hidden idea of how he, God, created the mechanism to begin with. In a kind of Jungian extension of this, perhaps the mind itself, built up from the simplest combinations of a thinking phylum, contains within its labyrinthine corridors a kind of memory of its own structure. Or, of course, we can always attribute these *Eureka!s* to good, solid, scientific detective work and dismiss the problem.

Père Teilhard said that whatever was put together could be taken apart. But our method of taking apart plays an indeterminately formative role in what is then taken apart. The nature of question-answer, filling the "empty categories," indicates that a kind of thinking encompasses the most remote regions of energy organization, much as Teilhard proposed. And the function of question-answer is an expression of the ontological, reality-shaping process itself.

Common sense tells us that certain ideas are true because they prove to be backed by actual events; they were obviously triggered by real things. The "light of day" is the final arbiter. The cold facts of real things dispel the illusions of mind, and leave only the hard kernels of clear thinking. Piaget observed that we are continually hatching an enormous number of false ideas, conceits, Utopias, mystical explanations, superstitions, and megalomanic fantasies. All of these disappear when brought into contact with other people.

They do not all disappear, however; some remain to

change the very framework and criteria of what makes real and what makes fantasy. There is more than a fortuitous connection between science fiction and scientific fact, though a one-for-one correspondence would be magic. That which is superstition and fantasy to Piaget was obvious fact to a previous age, and many of Piaget's cherished notions will themselves someday prove amusing and quaint.

There is a strong possibility that there is no *a priori* status for any one idea as against another idea. Teilhard observed that nature operates by profusion. According to Nietzche, we hear only the question to which we are capable of finding an answer. A question to which we can respond with a full investment of life and energy will influence our "editorial hierarchy" of mind. Then the kind of data we *accept* as *evidential* will be different. We will screen out and let in, interpret and synthesize, on a different basis.

The success of the atomic postulate influences the way we look on the birth and history of that hypothesis. Our current reality is not just represented as atomic, it *is* atomic. The atomic hypothesis, therefore, must have been a correct "hunch" about a pre-existing state of mechanical affairs. Any other attitude is surely madness.

Consider, however, that the final fruits of the atomic notion were born from an ecology greatly different from the original grounds wherein the early and tentative questions first appeared. And pursuit of the notion was one of the formative processes in changing the ecology itself. The translations and testings of all the myriad pieces of the puzzle expanded the original basis for possible thoughts about atoms. The expansion of the ecology was the result of both a peripheral and direct play of passionate believers, all those people working out the contingencies and correspondences with reality that would prove necessary for the answer's fruition. We tend to forget that a century and a half separated Dalton's early overtures from the final fruits at Alamogordo, and that Dalton himself was a late-comer to the atomic fantasy. Each of the many people involved could hardly have been aware that they were laying the groundwork for

Oak Ridge or Hiroshima. The overall drift of possibility toward such a thing as atomic energy may be seen as a kind of self-sustaining idea seeking its own expression over many centuries.

Passionate belief is the chief ingredient in any question-answer function. William James referred to "overbelief" as the subjective gloss given by people to an experience or an idea that they felt revealed a universal truth. Laski considers *overbelief* the most desired answer to an urgently-asked question. Once we have been seized by a question, that is, once we have accepted a question as ultimately meaningful to us, we set about gathering the kinds of material the question needs to build its answer.

Poincaré was fascinated by the way ideas coalesce in the mind to produce original thinking. He thought of all the related ideas as "hooked atoms," which, in the unconscious work of mind, collide and give rise to new combinations. The process is hardly one of chance, he noted, since the separate ideas involved have been selected according to the definite purpose in mind, and are the ones from which the desired solution may reasonably be expected.

Wallas distinguished four stages in the process of postulate building: preparation, incubation, illumination, and verification. The preparation period is the seizure by the notion; Laski would call this the asking of the question. This dedicates the mind, rules out conflicting drives, and organizes the energy to the task. Laski's search for materials for answer is the gathering of Poincaré's "hooked atoms," feeding them into the hopper with selective care. This part of the process may take many years, as with Hamilton's quaternions, or may be comparatively rapid, as with Einstein's idea.

The incubation period is the "unconscious work," wherein the collisions of hooked atoms occur. Laski speaks of the fusion of materials, which is an unconscious process. This is the stage I have called autistic, since it grinds along its way without conscious control. The illumination is the *Eureka!* experience itself, the final fusion of all materials, the breakthrough when the barriers of ordinary logical screening are relaxed.

Verification involves the translation of the experience, as found in Hamilton's ten to fifteen years needed to work out all the ramifications. This is the point separating wheat from chaff. Laski speaks of the crucial "testing of the answer" to see if it can be fitted into the common domain. This is no simple jigsaw puzzle placement, however, but is rather a subtle play of many contingencies.

Bruner points out that our ordinary experience is a categorizing, a placing in a syntax of concepts. We can explore connections heretofore unsuspected by metaphoric combinations that leap beyond regular systematic placements. In his *Essays for the Left Hand,* Bruner explores the creative process and ends with a pattern similar to that of Laski and Wallas. First in Bruner's outline, there must be a *detachment* from the commonplace. (You could not be a follower of Jesus until you hated the ordinary world, rejected it, gave it up as your "systematic placement.") One detaches from the world in order to commit oneself to the *replacing* of the conventional with a new construct.

After this commitment of self to the task, the work itself becomes a balance between the *passion,* which gives a "superior degree of attention," (the capacity for selective blindness), and a *decorum* that counters the enthusiasms with a "love of form," an *etiquette* toward the object of passionate effort, and a respect for the materials involved.

The creative movement, according to Bruner, is rounded out by the "freedom to be dominated by the object." Blake noted that only by a long and intensive training and discipline, getting beyond the mechanics of technique, could the mind truly utilize its imagination. Yet this utilization meant a final breaking with all the forms and boundaries of the very discipline necessary for the ability to develop. The Divine Imagination moves the mind as it pleases, the wind bloweth where it listeth, but only when the way has been prepared by a discipline of mind. In every recorded case of *Eureka!* illumination, the final breakthrough of the postulate occurs at a moment when the logical processes have been momentarily suspended, a moment of relaxation from serious work.

If one is dominated by the object of desire, the work of creation takes over, Bruner says, and "assumes the role of dominance." Then the artist or scientist serves the new work. I would add saint to Bruner's listing. In turn, the life, then committed to that line of action, is justified only if the work succeeds. Thus the initial commitment breeds an ever more stringent allegiance and striving for successful completion. The new work is served since the new work serves the life and justifies it.

Mircea Eliade spent several years in the Orient, studying the Yoga discipline. He was quite struck by it, and his exhaustive book on the subject was sympathetic. He found it an arduous discipline, requiring years of development. The real technique hinges on a mental "blankness" that bypasses the world of "false and illusory notions." Stilling the flux of mental activity is in itself no small achievement. Having done this, the Yoga is convinced that a truth *happens* to him. What happens is so totally at variance with the "world" that no prestructuring on his part seems possible as a determinant.

On examination, however, the Yoga system proves to be a clear example of the question-answer function as outlined by Laski, Bruner, and Wallas. Eliade writes that *this* world is rejected, *this* life depreciated, because it is *known* that something else exists. And that something else is beyond temporality, beyond suffering. The Indian rejects the profane world because he believes without question in the reality of a sacred mode of being, and so we find from the very outset what Bruner calls the *detachment* from the commonplace.

The *commitment* to the new construct is adhered to passionately. All around him the Yogin sees his superiors able to do things that cannot be done so long as one remains in the ordinary world. Nothing less than concrete production is ever the motivation or the expectation. By their fruits they are known. Each particular discipline had its particular short-term rewards in addition to the long-range goal of Nirvana. The initiate absorbed an expectancy of the goals as he was incorporated into the system, just as a physics student does. Should the novitiate fail to produce tangible results, his life had failed. His long associative learning provided strong stimulus to overbelief formation in keeping with his traditions. His passion was carefully balanced with his decorum and respect for the tradition. His mind was finally transformed, just as Kazantzakis', Hamilton's, or Einstein's, in respect to each of their disciplines and goals. Where the faith is simple the test of the faith is simple. The Yogin had to produce: walk on fire, produce extraordinary body heat, reverse any of the bodily functions, and in general overcome the ordinary fated necessities of life. Nothing less than actuality was expected, or accepted as proof of "arrival."

The Yogin's environment was one of *expectation* of esoteric phenomena, and acceptance of such esoterica is commonplace within that environment. This is no small part of the entire fabric and possibility therein. It took several centuries to build up the kind of scientific environment we have today, the ecology in which the particular esoterica *we* produce can be thought of, accepted by mind, and brought about. Countless centuries have gone into the production of the sets of expectancies shaping the Yoga's sensory world. And, of course, the realists from *our* system smugly dismiss as nonsense reports of the non-ordinary reality produced by Yoga.

Answers arrive through novel media. It is a matter of esthetics what label is given, but the mind's predisposition toward one metaphor and against another has a damping effect on the kinds of possibilities open to it. The English occultist, Douglas Hunt, for instance, relates a story from Benker's *Gepenster und Spuk* in which a Munich engineer came home one day to find, to his alarm, none other than himself, "seated at the drawing board," busily sketching. This "mirror-image," or "Doppelgänger," which has caused some terror through the ages, had worked out the solution to a problem which had worried the engineer for days. The twin-image had supposedly penned out the entire problem, and there it lay before the startled engineer's eyes. The example is given by Hunt as proof of astral projection, exteriorization, or out-of-the-body experience, as it is variously called.

No scientist could tolerate such occultist terminology or definitions. *Hypnagogic imagery,* however, is quite respectable. No less than the great Friedrich August Kekule von Stradonitz, otherwise just Kekule, professor of organic chemistry at Bonn from 1865 till his death in 1896, conceived the theory of the benzene ring, one of the most important theories in all modern chemistry, and one of the most original ideas of modern times, in a *hypnagogic state.* He actually "saw" the ring in visual image clearly and distinctly right before him, as occurs in all hypnagogic imagery. Surely it took no little doing to translate the strange imagery into terms compatible with his brotherhood, but the nature of the whole experience is typical of most discoveries. In the same way, Descartes appears to have encountered the basic notions of his analytical geometry—in this quasi-dream state.

Laski wondered about all those scientific breakthroughs that fail to "pass the appropriate tests" of translation. Obviously they, too, arrive with initial certitude and conviction. We seldom hear of the ones that fail, she noted, though evidence strongly suggests they are in a majority. The question arises *why* wrong *Eureka!s* arrive at all.

Bruner supposes it to be an heuristic device of the mind, leading us on until we finally arrive at proper conclusions. This attributes to the mind a subconscious foreknowledge of the proper answer, which automatically places the proper answer in an *a priori* state of permanence. Why, with the foreknowledge already there (wherever *there* could be), would the mind keep stopping at so many false or premature places—playing tricks on itself, as it were, and hardly just for fun since lives invest in answers and are ruined when the answers prove unacceptable. This further attributes to unconscious processes a value-judging capacity quite counter to evidence.

Rather, autistic thinking acts on *all* possibility, without judgment, since value is a capacity of logical reasoning only. The choices for possibility are suggested by the conscious mind's own value selections, and the material with which the autistic synthesis must work are those drawn from the experienced world. Nature operates by profusion as Teilhard said. All answers created are "true" to this nature, but not all will fit the tight limitations of the logical framework of the recipients triggering the very procedure. We might say that an infinite potential casually produces a thousand answers, one of which fits the carefully-defined jigsaw puzzle of the rational mind. A new puzzle could be organized around any of the pieces randomly produced, provided the rational mind were willing or able—which it is not—to change its total orientation so casually. All postulates are thus "true" in some context.

The sum total of the experienced world does not necessarily afford the new knowledge attained by the *Eureka!* hypothesis. The illumination "given" is generally of a character and nature larger than life, greater than the sum total of all data leading up to it. For instance, you can add the total thought from John Dalton, through Avogardo, Mendelejeff, Arrhenius, Planck, Bohr and all the others of that rich century and a half preceding and contemporaneous with Einstein, and never come up with a final sum that is Einstein.

There is a catalystic quality in autistic thinking, and this catalyst hinges on its very "non-judging" aspects. The *Eureka!* is traceable to its parts for genesis, yet is larger than their sum, or else attainment of radically new viewpoints, producing dramatically new results, could become a commonplace formula. The unconscious autistic continuum is a sort of total wealth where all things, or any thing, are true, where the energy of thought and the energy of adhered-to forms of matter appear to merge. There are no polarities in this "ultimate reconciliation of opposites," as those people falling into the mystic states have reported. In autistic thinking nothing is either true or false, it simply *is*.

The rationale of consciousness is what gives a particular value; that makes meaningful by limitation; that gives the form of a necessarily limited fact to the unlimited formlessness of fantasy. Thus a revolutionary idea that has no possibilities within the context that triggers it, and is thus stillborn or a failure, is still as valid within the synthesis function of mind as is anything else. On the other hand, ideas that are highly irrational, such as the atomic notion with its vast interplay of particle physics, can, if adhered to by true believers long enough, build up an ecology giving them the necessary possibilities for expression and realization.

Jung talks about unconscious processes being in a continual state of synthesis, which brings to mind Poincaré's hooked-atom collision process. David Bohm, seeing the world from the eyes of a convert to the physicist's brotherhood, contends that all processes of nature are in a constant state of change. If we ourselves could shake off a Cartesian dualism, we might see the full shape of the procedure. Descartes believed that God was the mediator between a mechanistic world and the non-involved thinking mind. Since God was presumably honest, he would not deceive the mind with perceptions that were illusions—provided, of course, that the mind under question were equally honest and open to the mediator. Jesus, on the other hand, said God judged not at *all,* and that we reaped as we sowed—a notion that does not fit the Greek orientation, but does fit quite well the question-answer function under consideration.

Carl Jung observed that a psychology reflected the background of the psychologist propounding it. Jung did not see how a Chinese psychologist and a Swiss one would reach the same conclusions. Cohen mused on the curious way the Jungian analyst's patient confirmed the fondest Jungian theories when under LSD, while the drugged Freudian patient gave back the proper Freudian symbol—verifying the therapist's own most basic assumptions. The patient "senses the frame of reference to be employed," suggests Cohen, and his associations and dreams are molded to it.

Kline of New York University, for several years head of the Society for Clinical and Experimental Hypnosis, observed the same interaction between a hypnotist and his subject. Kline found that the unconscious mind of the subject made every effort to comply with the demands of the hypnotist. The hypnotist serves as the logical value-selector in the resulting relation. Material ordinarily inaccessible to consciousness, forgotten or subliminal impressions, synthetic combinations of childhood fantasies, dreams, secondary percepts and so on, all become available as valid events and "real" contents under hypnosis. The association between hypnotist and subject takes on a marked affinity over a period of time. Material can be exchanged unconsciously between the two. The unexpressed desires of the hypnotist may affect the subject, who begins to fabricate from the unconscious of both parties, finally giving valid responses to the hypnotist's hidden desires. (In amateurs such desires are most often esoteric and cultic.)

The experience of Fellin and Throne, the two miners mentioned before, shows the extent to which unconscious exchanges can occur. Cases of *folie à deux*, or shared hallucination, bear a relation to hypnosis, where fantasies from the unconscious may be built into logical and airtight structures creating non-ordinary states. This is particularly evident in cults (though of course a *cult* is a discipline not in the current acceptancies). For instance, insistence on the part of the hypnotist that the subject "rediscover a past life" can plant a seed of suggestion in the unconscious around which related materials, that is, materials that *can* be used for such a synthesis, gather into a coherent pattern and finally present themselves as a valid memory of an actual occurrence.

In variations of this, a person's own desires, particularly cultic, can produce the same kind of unconscious synthesis which then breaks in automatically as verification. (Someone might make a study of the personality backgrounds of subjects seeing flying-saucers.) The conscious mind of the subject, since his desire has to some extent suspended his ordinary system of judgment *in favor of* the experience, suspends the ability to distinguish the "remembered" synthetic event from a "real" one.

William Butler Yeats's biographer, Ellman, wrote that had Yeats died in 1917 at the age of 52, instead of marrying as he did, he would be remembered as a remarkable minor poet who "achieved a diction more powerful than that of his contemporaries," but who did not have much to say with it, except in a handful of poems. The difference between his being a minor poet or a major one rested, strangely enough, on the talent for automatic writing which Yeats, an enthusiast of the occult, found in his new bride. With great excitement Yeats drove her to hours of automatic writing daily, to her general weariness. Out of the results Yeats found emerging the crystalized metaphors with which he had struggled, with only partial success, all his life. Mrs. Yeats uncovered his thought in a synthesized and clarified imagery beyond his own abilities, and it was this esoteric venture that produced those last fruitful decades on which Yeats's greatness lies.

Under the spellbinding situations hypnotic interplay often creates, the questions asked will tend to be in keeping with desire for esoteric or cultic knowledge. Conscious value judgment is precisely what is set aside by the subject in order to enter the hypnotic state—a point to which I will return later. Value judgment is often willingly suspended by the hypnotist himself, if half-unconsciously, in his desire for conviction. Thus there is set up a possibility for *folie à deux,* and a ready granting of authenticity to the revelatory content.

Laski dwelt at some length on P. W. Martin's *Experiment in Depth.* The major premise and purpose of Martin's book is to bring to those who treat life responsibly and with devotion, an experience of the *deep center* of mind that has in the past been available only to the "highly percipient man or woman, the mystic, the saint, or seer."

Some idea of the goals of the experiment is made known immediately. The focus has narrowed. The reader who continues with Martin's book will have acknowledged tacitly that the prospect of such a goal is intriguing enough to warrant further investigation. Perseverance along the actual path outlined in the book would further the expectations and the desirability of the end product.

Laski notes that the entire venture is cast in Jungian terms, and that it will be Jungian terms in which the final overbelief is expressed. Martin's process for arriving at the deep center entails working with a small group (two or three gathered together). It is far better to have one member of the group be someone who has already gone "some way along the search." This means, of necessity, someone of the Jungian bent. According to Martin the group would need to read and discuss appropriate literature, such as William James's *Varieties of Religious Experience,* Jung's *Two Essays on Analytical Psychology,* the *Journals of George Fox,* or such related materials. (Bertrand Russell, for instance, would hardly be in keeping with the desired end.)

Needless to say, no one will involve themselves in such reading and discussion without implanting the necessary material needed for synthesis of the desired goal. The time and energy would only be expended for a desirable reward. Some suspension of ordinary criteria will have unconsciously been made. Some expectation for renewal or reshaping will have been nursed from the outset.

As a part of the preliminary training, members will find it helpful to work out their psychological compass bearing according to Jung's "four functions." Threading their way through this elaborate, complex, and intellectual system would of itself necessitate considerable understanding and adoption of Jungian ideas.

Other ventures for opening to the unconscious are "active imagination," a kind of conscious entry into autistic realms, automatic drawing, painting, writing, the inward conversation, and so on. Watch for the appearance of the *Friend,* the symbol of the helpful figure of the unconscious. (The Spritualists have "Indian Guides" as mediators between the two worlds, and their use of pidgin English was probably the esthetic offense that kept my own hardness of heart quite intact.) If the helpful figure appears, the seeker must establish contact with it and not let go. Finally, if the deep center itself appears in any of its forms, *by then readily known,* hold on to it.

Thus will the shadow of the unconscious appear, and

then the anima-animus, and finally, the active archetypes. This is the great possibility and the perilous encounter. Perilous, because the unconscious content can engulf, seize, and dissolve the ego-centered person. Jung speaks of the psyche being flooded or inflated by the contents of the collective unconscious.

However, the man centered in depth (knowing what he is doing), the man who has properly prepared himself and has the right attitude toward the venture, can *hold.* (Rather as the fire-walker, whose attitude of mind *holds,* is not burned.) Since experience from the "other side" of consciousness goes by like the wind, a journal should be kept of one's subjective impressions. Thus the psyche will be vastly enriched.

Laski asks: "Who can doubt but that the technique will work?" After all that effort, no small investment, something recognizable as the desired experience will be achieved. Laski feels that preliminary training has ensured that those who persist with the experiment know explicitly both the question and the answer. The steps taken are those necessary both to clarify the question and bring about the answer. They further ensure that the answer will be lasting and felt to deepen progressively in significance. Laski observes that these very steps have been tried and true procedures from time immemorial. All the older disciplines have used the same procedure. (Education is but a confused, fragmented form of it.) Future catechumens, she feels, will have their own sectarian "confession" and journals to get the initial group discussion going along the right lines.

Were you to undergo an *Experiment in Depth* along some other line than Jungian, without those indications of what to expect, it is hard to see how the Jungian pattern would develop. (Should the "Friend" appear to a non-Jungian, he might not seem so friendly.) The stylized archetypes might not occur, but *something* would. The energy of all the effort could only be generated for a reason and the reason would have given the nucleus determining the end result. There is no possibility of opening to some unconscious level except through a technique of opening, and the technique determines the nature of what is found. Such an experience would shape around the individual's background and the trigger of the search device itself.

The illumination resulting would have been synthesized by a catalyst giving something larger than the sum total of the background, however, and would move the subject beyond himself. That the end result is arbitrary does not affect its realness. Approximately the same procedure gave atoms and atom splitting which are real enough.

Consider again Russell's observation that mystic revelations prove to be pretty much shaped by our culture and training, not by great cosmic powers "out there." Mr. Russell's purpose, of course, was to disparage religion. I think some basis has now been given for saying he was right for the wrong reasons.

Mozart was born to an Austrian family and "ecology" of rich artistic bent. No Mozarts have been found in Bedouin tribes. Bach was a fifth-generation musician, not an Eskimo. And my truisms are no more fatuous than Russell's. Sartre's truth and Kazantzakis' truth are mutually exclusive, but equally valid within their respective frameworks. Adopt either viewpoint, invest your life in the sets and expectancies involved, and your life will bend to make good the investment. Then you may live with your gains. We seek and we find. What we find is up to us. We knock and the door opens to us. There are an unlimited number of doors. We choose some, even as we are born with others ajar and absorbing us into their interiors, whether we like it or not, or *know* it or not.

So I would say to Russell: "Were God to speak to *me* from the burning bush, He had better use English, not some heathenish Semitic tongue." I should be even more perturbed than Clarence Day* to find God speaking *French* or something, like a *foreigner.*

In my next chapter I hope to show how this question-

* In *Life with Father,* by Clarence Day (Alfred Knopf, N.Y., 1935, p. 132). Day writes of finding a Bible which ". . . was in French and it sometimes shocked me deeply to read it. . . . Imagine the Lord talking French."

answer function shapes not only those subjective things so much beneath Russell's contempt, but also that very scientific structure that seized him, and which he, in turn, has made into the same kind of idol he disparages in other casts.

5

mirror to mirror

Singer closed his *History of Science* (1941) with the observation that in the future the frontiers of scientific abstractions may be rendered more fluid. The philosophical method might have a share in determining the nature of change. The idea that mind is separated from mind, and mind from matter, might need modification, he felt. He suggested that the tendencies of science since the later nineteenth century may well have been working in just this direction.

The late English physicist, Eddington, who was instrumental in helping translate and bring into being Einstein's relative universe, was deeply impressed by the way a short, tidy little equation, the product of a *Eureka!* image arriving full blown in the mind, could open our experience to a whole new aspect of concrete reality. He felt that man's mind must be a "mirror of the universe."

Singer wrote that the processes of mind seemed to reflect the processes of nature. He felt that our minds were as much the product of evolution as were our bodies, an idea both Jung and Teilhard developed. We have developed through the ages as "mirrors of the world in which we dwell," wrote Singer, and spoke of us as "attuned to nature."

Newton saw science as a voyage of discovery, coming across islands of truth in that great ocean. Jerome Bruner questions this discovery aspect of Newton's genius. Science and common-sense inquiry do not *discover* the ways in which events are grouped in the world, claims

Bruner, they *invent* ways of grouping. Newton was a creative inventor, if unknowingly.

Warren Weaver calls science a very human enterprise, exhibiting the same "lively and useful diversity" which is to be found in philosophy, art, or music. Bronowski claimed original scientific thought to be the same act of mind found in original artistic thinking. Sir Cyril Hinshelwood also spoke of scence as a creative art, "joining hands with all human endeavors, learning by its mistakes."

"By their fruits you shall know them" is the criterion that underlies scientific success. As with a piece of music the final question has been: how well does it perform, and how well does it listen? Performers will not consistently play, neither will an audience long support, a poor work. Time screens out the charlatans.

Teilhard, reflecting a Bergsonian evolutionary theology, claimed that intellectual discovery and synthesis are no longer merely speculation, but *creation*. From our time on in history, some "physical consummation of things" is bound up with the "explicit perception" we make of them. What a thing *is* is to an unknowable extent determined by or influenced by what we *think* it is. This may be as much a growing conscious awareness of the basic ontology as it is an evolutionary development.

Singer sees our minds reflecting nature, and we must go a step further and see this as a dynamic, an interrelation that will always deny clear categorization or a one-for-one correspondence. We must push Eddington's and Singer's reflecting mind one step further and recognize that man's mind is a mirror of a universe that mirrors man's mind, though the mirroring is subtle, random and unfathomable.

Michael Polanyi has championed the subjective aspects of the scientific faith, an irritant to many in his field. Jerome Bruner is an articulate spokesman for this "contemporary nominalism" that senses science to be a process of inventive synthesis rather than discovery.

A "contemporary nominalism" is possible, however, only because of a security and certainty in the scientific position. Hostility to such ideas of the creative power of thought may be the last lingering aspect of the very *position of mind* necessary to bring about the current confidence itself. As Jung pointed out, only the most secure of psyches can open to and face up to their own capacity for and tendency toward automatic projection. Current resistance to recognizing science projected as a synthetic creativity may be the last stand of science projected as sacred "out there," a stand necessary to establish the entire structure.

Descartes' notion of a fixed "out there," and a separate "in here," with God the honest mediator between the two, may have been naive realism, but it is possible that science could only have developed through such a faith projection—a faith which produces, as all faiths do, according to the nature of its postulates.

Apropos of this, in the early 1950's kidney transplants were a fascinating possibility. A Chicago doctor finally made an apparently successful transplant of one kidney, in a patient with a good one left. The doctor and his staff kept extremely accurate and detailed reports, covering every conceivable bit of data on the entire affair. After a few months the doctor cautiously published his reports on the apparent success, that others might benefit and follow suit with further lifesaving attempts. Immediately the performance was known to be workable, similar operations were tried all over the world, and the margin of success soared beyond all previous expectations.

To his alarm, however, the doctor later found that he had erred in his interpretations. The transplant had failed, probably from the beginning; the other kidney had carried a double load plus the added strains of rejection and so on. The data so cautiously published had been erroneous. In what was admirable honesty, the doctor published a retraction and apology, but by then, of course, his error was incidental. Who cared? Success was at every hand, and has been growing ever since. All that may have been needed was sureness, belief, a concrete hope.

Science is full, in fact, of cases where perfectly workable, fruitful productions have been organized on grounds later found fallacious. Gone, Popper says, is the old scientific ideal of *episteme,* the absolutely certain, demonstrable knowledge. Every scientific statement, he claimed, must remain tentative forever.

Warren Weaver likens the foundations of science to piles driven into soft and swampy terrain. We simply stop driving the piles down, he said, when we are satisfied that they are firm enough to carry the kind of structure we want, at least for the time being. Euclid called "axiomatic" the step on which he stood to build his system. Weaver says this bottom step is not axiomatic but simply a postulate, assumed to be true in order to obtain what we *hope* to find by following it to its conclusions. He speaks of an "ultimate mysticism" at the bottom of this type of scientific explanation.

Such attitudes are new in the history of thought. They might well be luxuries of mind that only a very rich discipline can afford. We are on the way, at least, to opening to both mirrors of reality—mind and its source of possibilities—and perhaps this could not have been done earlier.

Whitehead traced the rise of science from its religious conviction that God being rational, His Creation must also be rational and, therefore, available to the process of reasoning. The early scientist saw subjectivity as the illusion. Since Augustine the neoplatonic view had held full sway, and one got outside such quicksands by concentrating on the "natural world." An interest in natural objects of the most mundane sort for their own sake grew. The seventeenth and eighteenth centuries displayed a mania for labeling and cataloging every commonplace item on the globe.

This encyclopedic name-passion was another chapter in the building of a semantic universe. These obvious and self-evident events made up those "irreducible and stubborn facts" so loved by the earlier scientists. Whitehead felt that several centuries of contemplation of this basic stuff was needed. What grew from all this was a method of *agreement*—agreement on the kinds of phenomena that could be "objectively" considered, and the way by which such speculation could be verified. The method of agreement was strengthened by its own careful restriction to those events amenable to the same "common objectivity." This kept intact the particular fabric of belief in process of being woven. Thus the growing frame of reference centered on a desire for an *order of nature* that would reflect the medieval faith in the rational order of God. The transition was slow, orderly, and smooth. The name displacement, the change of metaphor that would allow mutations of a more direct sort, followed a certain protocol of decorum.

Faith in the rational order of God, and thus of His Nature, was perfectly genuine. This faith gave the prism through which those events examined were seen. Events not fitting the prism were simply ignored. Order was imposed upon basically random disorder through this prism of prejudice. The prism dictated the kinds of events which were given the energy of attention. Whitehead pointed out that the narrow efficiency of the scheme was the very cause of its "supreme methodological success." The scheme directed attention to the groupings and correlations that lent themselves to that *kind* of investigation, and that in turn verified the system.

The efficiency, while narrow and selective, gave success within its confines. The success gave ever-growing boldness for speculations. This enlarged the selectivity itself. Whitehead observed that the early scientists confined themselves to certain types of facts, abstracted from the complete circumstances in which those facts occurred. This gave rise to the materialistic assumption of "simple locations in time and space," an assumption which fit to perfection the facts so abstracted. The given confines were expanded by this very activity, and the store of "facts" grew apace. Postulating empty categories, for instance, gave the passionate focus of attention to find the particular facts that would fill the categories. Trial and error determined the general nature of empty categories likely to be filled by the accepted kinds of facts.

Eventually these self-verifying successes built a system of hypotheses that became self-sustaining. Science became a *reality-shaping* structure, creating its own unique ecology, much as the Pentagonian mind tends to produce the very events which make necessary an ever-expanding Pentagon structure, and justify such things as Pentagons.

The original "stubborn and irreducible facts" of science faded into the background as they were no longer needed. An equally stubborn fact, that of science as an event-producing activity, rooted itself into the growing reality structure that science itself had fostered and brought about. Scientific growth became a process of metaphoric combinations and mutations of existing scientific metaphor, a continual expansion of an inherited web of ideas.

Though nothing in this web remains static, each generation's "facts" produce the reality which that generation finds itself in, facts with which it must deal. Feinberg feels confident that we have found the basic substructure of matter. Yet a short two generations or so ago an eminent scientist could write, rather with a sigh, that at *least* one sure fact could finally be counted on by science, and that was that *ether* filled all space.

A certain egotism marks all men of science simply because nothing less than sureness can sustain any system, much less give the confidence to blithely contradict their elders and "discover" anew the *real* way things work. McKellar speaks disparagingly of the "certainty systems," religions and cults, and lauds the reality-adjusted methods of the humble scientists who only *serve* truth. The reality adjustments of science are made to the continual metaphoric mutations occurring in the scramble for success and fame within the brotherhood. The only humility ever exhibited is when their systems fail or are in process of being outmoded by their very techniques.

Edwin G. Boring writes that examination of new facts, new truths, new theories, immerses one in the history of *controversy*. Men get their egos tied up with their theories and their facts and "fight one another for intellectual self-preservation." Boring speaks of science as a policy, not a picture of truth, but a policy that has to *work* to be retained.

McKellar says the biggest error that underlies much thinking today is the belief that scientific concepts refer to things which actually exist, that science cleverly isolates existing things and measures or uses them. The idea that scientific principles are parts of nature can seriously impede the progress of our knowledge, McKellar wrote. In the same sense, Bruner referred to scientific discovery not as "engineered tinkering," as commonly conceived, but as an enterprise of thinking.

It is doubtful, however, that science could have built its constructs and sustained its passion without the sure confidence of those earlier scientists that they were only discovering God's preordained secrets and laws. Policies are put into effect by people who believe in them. It is doubtful that even today scientists will concede that they are involved in synthetic creativity rather than discovery of *a priori* truth. As doubtful, in fact, as that theologians and preachers could open to the same possibility for their own systems.

Michael Polanyi wrote of the *metanoia* changing a student into the true physicist. A brilliant array of facts, proofs, laws, theories, and an impressive body of empirical evidence, will not in themselves create a science, Polanyi claimed. Only as all this is given meaning and purpose through the intellectual passion of a true believer does the real science emerge. A belief in the basic tenets determines the criteria by which an investigator works. Science, states Polanyi, can provide no procedure for deciding issues by systematic and dispassionate empirical investigation.

The scientific audience is won over to a new system by intellectual sympathy. A hostile audience may deliberately refuse to entertain novel conceptions for fear of being led to conclusions they abhor, rightly or wrongly. Sympathetic listening allows one to discover what cannot be understood in any other way. This kind of openness, which alone can lead us into true agreement and "hearing," Polanyi notes, is a self-modifying act. To elaborate on Polanyi a bit, I would explain this self-modifying by saying each of us has an autistic openness for unlimited synthesis, but agreement on *another's* synthesis then limits *our* openness. It defines a specific area that can then no longer be open for us.

Hardness of heart, the refusal to listen sympathetically and open-mindedly, with its corollary, unbelief, is the stumbling block which no theoretical system can overcome.

Polanyi claims that "intellectual passions" affirm the scientific interest and value of certain facts as against lack of such interest and value in others. Without this selective function science could not be defined at all. A "vision of reality" serves as the scientific guide to enquiry. Passion and vision are the "mainsprings of originality." A new idea may impel a scientist to abandon an accepted framework of interpretation and commit himself, by the leaping of a logical gap, to the use of a new framework.

Note how Polanyi's picture fills Bruner's outline for creativity: the scientist detaches himself from the common-place assumptions of his discipline; commits himself to a new construct; his passion gives him his selective blindness to ignore the contradictions and negatives, and, by his superior degree of attention, he sees what he needs to see; his decorum assures the love of form, the etiquette toward the object of desire, that keeps him in the brotherhood. Having placed his intellectual and professional life on the line (losing his life that he may find it), he has the freedom and willingness to be dominated by the object until the work of creation takes over. Then his life both serves the new work and is justified by it.

A scientific education does more than develop the skill to handle scientific ideas. It brings about that change in thinking that determines the ideas which will be accepted to begin with, the new ideas most likely to occur to mind, and the phenomena accepted as factual. "Unscientific" ideas tend to be dismissed, should they even occur, and "unscientific" facts tend not to be recognized as phenomena.

Claude Bernard admits that "facts" are necessary materials, but points out that it is their manipulation by experimental reasoning, or theory, that establishes and builds science. "Ideas given form by facts," was his expression. The idea is the *prime movens* of all scientific reasoning.

We point to a "realized fact" that was not a part of

former realizations, and insist that the fact must have always existed. Existed as *what* may well be asked. The atom did not "exist" for Democritus, or even Dalton, as it exists for us today. A rich network of explorers had to develop correspondences to the point where inclusion of the atomic fact would be, if not observable, at least possible and maybe even *necessary* to the resulting framework—a framework which itself may prove to have resulted from the acceptance of the idea of atoms. The long-nourished idea may well have brought about the facts to support the idea. This does not imply that we can pull a rabbit out of the hat whether or not there is first a rabbit in the hat. It means that we must question the nature of rabbits and hats. Perhaps we can breed any number of varieties of rabbits in the hat, given time, effort, passion, and all the rest of the triggers for catalytic synthesis.

Bruner wrote of how science postulates empty categories on purely logical grounds, and then, when appropriate measures have been found, "discovers" the content needed to fill the category. When the neutron was disintegrated, its products, the electron and proton, did not behave according to the law of the conservation of momentum. Something had to yield; surely it was not going to be the law, on which too much else depended, so the Italian physicist, Enrico Fermi, postulated a third particle of zero charge and zero mass, which he called the "neutrino" or little neutron. The mysterious third particle, without mass, charge, or much of anything, was finally considered to have a spiral orbit; several years after its hypothetical beginnings, evidence for it took on more and more reality aspects until finally it was "discovered."

Discovery of the planet Neptune followed the same pattern. Twenty-three years separated Bessel's logical conclusions that a trans-Uranian planet should exist, and the computing by Adams and LeVerrier of the possible orbits for the undiscovered planet, which finally led to its "discovery." The elements in the sun were identified through spectroscopic research. During an eclipse in 1869, the solar spectrum was found to include an unknown gas which was named helium. Twenty-seven years later the gas was discovered or at least identified on earth.

Bode's Law of 1772 offers a fascinating example. Bode found that if you took the simple sequence; 0, 3, 6, 12, 24, 48, 96, and so on (each number doubling the previous one), and added to each member the number 4, then producing: 4, 7, 10, 16, 28, 52, 100, and so on, you obtained approximately the proportionate distances from the sun of Mercury, Venus, Earth, Mars, Jupiter, Saturn—but, disturbingly enough, with a blank for the number 28. The numbers game gave rise to a great search for the missing planet (so great our faith in numbers). In 1801 Guiseppe Piazze of Palermo found at the required distance a very small planet, only a fourth as big as our moon, which he named Ceres. The attention of all astronomers then focussed on this orbit and in time over a thousand of these "asteroids" or pieces of planet were found. The lapse between postulate and discovery was twenty-nine years.

David Bohm notes that the evolution of scientific concept has been due more to scientific experience than to observations of everyday experience. Imaginative analysis of the experimental and theoretical results of the science of mechanics has given rise to our concepts of the motions of bodies. Observing and measuring actual bodies in motion has not played much part. Mathematics in general, (justifying Roger Bacon's thirteenth-century observation), and differential calculus in particular, Bohm says, have played the key role in guiding the development of a clear concept of accelerating motion, just as our concept of wave motion comes from theoretical and experimental studies of the interference and propagation of waves in the various sciences such as optics and acoustics, not from watching water waves themselves.

The physicist Pauli wrote that intuition and the direction of attention far transcend mere experience in the erection of a system of natural law.

Polanyi went to great length to show that true discovery, in its scientific sense, is irreversible. That is, the procedure cannot be traced back stepwise to its beginnings and repeated *ad lib.* any number of times. True discovery is not logical in its performance. Polanyi describes the obstacle to be overcome by any new idea as a "logical gap." *Illumination* was his term for the leap by which the logical gap is crossed. The scientist stakes his life on his leaps, and science grows and changes thereby.

Gerald Feinberg spoke of James Clerk Maxwell's desire for a mechanical model of the electromagnetic field, and Albert Einstein's desire for a deterministic substratum of quantum phenomena. The world, Feinberg sighs, is not so simple. The proper understanding of matter requires, he says, the imagination to *invent* entities not apparent in everyday phenomena. It is the enduring miracle of creative thought, he wrote, that the mind is equal to the task.

William Blake considered our capacity for imagination to be our "divine genius." Jesus was Blake's most truly imaginative man, since he could bridge the logical gaps. In his marginalia to Reynolds, Blake claimed that our truest self was in our innate ideas with which we are born. He did not mean this in the Platonic sense, but as the capacity for creative and original thinking, independent of mechanical information from a world. Biological and economic necessities as formative devices were denied by Blake. "The eternal body of man is the Imagination, that is, God himself . . . It manifests itself in his works of art (in Eternity all is Vision). Man is all Imagination; God is Man and exists in us and we in Him."

What Blake's vision releases on earth is released in heaven. If an imaginative seed, the gist of an idea, can be planted, even though contrary to existent evidence, the seed can still grow and sooner or later produce confirmation. Data can be found to bolster the conviction. The desire for conviction can produce its own data, its own metaphoric mutation, even to its visual demonstration.

A system is outlandish only to opposing systems. How great must be the pressure before a new idea succumbs depends on the "correspondence gap" and the tenacity of the believers. Even if the gap is great, even if there is no evidence at all, even if the bulk of current belief would have to be sacrificed to give the new idea grounds for growth, a tenacious adherence in spite of all the contrary evidence will nevertheless slowly build up the possibility for the needs of the new idea to be met. It may take more than one lifetime for the new evidence to accumulate, establish correspondences, and bring about a new seeing.

Jean Ladrier wondered about the mysterious connection between our own potentials, the power for action we bear within us, and the potentials of the world. In the same vein, the physicist Pauli asks about the nature of the bridge between sense perceptions and concepts. Logic, Pauli notes, has been incapable of constructing the link. Pauli feels it satisfactory, however, and to him necessary, to postulate a "cosmic order" independent of our choice, and "distinct from the world of phenomena." The relation of sense perception and idea remains predicated, he claims, on the fact that perceiver and perceived are subject to an order thought to be objective.

Pauli's notion is a commonly held one, but questionable. We are prone to resort to a *deus ex machina* when forced into a corner. We are always plagued with the idea that "out there" is a great, eternal, and *a priori* state of truth. That the "realness" of our lives might hinge on *our* choice is disquieting. All postulates, systems, and accepted facts tend to be superseded by future systems, however, as even today the inevitable margin of error grows in the Einsteinian system. Desire frets always at the boundaries.

David Bohm rejects "eternal forms" as well as randomness or strict causal laws. He holds that all things are interconnected and influenced by contingencies with all other things, traceable to so remote an interrelation that they may be considered chance for all practical purposes. To associative causes and contingencies Bohm adds the element of satisfying *necessary relationships*. Opposing and contradictory motions are the rule throughout the universe, he believes, an essential aspect of the very mode of things. The existence of anything is made possible by a balancing of contingent and opposing processes. These very processes will tend to change a thing in various directions, and eventually always will change it.

In Bohm's "Natural Law" there is no limit to the new kinds of things that can come into being, to the number of transformations, both qualitative and quantitative that can occur. This echoes Whitehead's "structure of evolving processes," and brings to mind Carington's theory that an idea tends to realize itself in any way it can unless inhibited by opposing ideas.

Teilhard spoke of a "biological change of state" terminating in thought, a comparatively recent development in evolution, and affecting life itself in its "organic totality" on the entire planet. I think, too, of Jung whose "unconscious contents" were always in a process of new combinations and syntheses.

Bohm's "natural law" is of a "nature" shot through and through with the mind of man. Thinking is the most important of all the "necessary relations" that must be satisfied. Singer mused that the philosophical method might have a share in determining the nature of change. An energetic focus of thought weighs heavily as a determinant among the contingencies in any context. To focus is to narrow to a specific, to agree on a single aspect in an infinitely contingent possibility. The wider the agreement, the wider the context influenced. In oder to achieve focused agreement there must be a nucleus of ideas around which the participants—and possibilities—can organize. The ideas come first. The mythos leads the logos.

Bohm writes that scientific history is full of examples in which it was fruitful to assume that certain objects or elements might be real long before any procedures were known that would permit them to be observed directly. The atomic theory, a subject very near to our lives, is the best example.

According to tradition Leucippus and Democritus first proposed an atomic theory, some two thousand years ago, though Singer says *they* got the idea from the Pythagoreans. Though abandoned in that great "failure of nerve" suffered in those waning years of antiquity, the notion never completely died. Atomic views were coming to the fore again in Galileo's day, stimulated by discoveries of the microscope. A considerable philosophical literature on the subject grew, now largely forgotten since it led to nothing dramatic, but the curiosity it aroused had a decided influence in "directing the biological observation" of the generations that followed.

Newton incorporated atoms in Question 31 of his *Optiks.* The whole subject was very much in the common domain before Dalton moved the idea directly to the fore of tangibles by postulating the existence of individual atoms to explain the various large-scale regularities, such as the laws of chemical combination, the gas laws, and so on. Dalton gave the old idea new life by drawing up a hypothetical table of atomic weights, treating the imaginary things as actualities and giving them a real place in the sun. Putting things on paper, backing them with mathematical correlations, relating them to the basic stuff of the world, proves to be a strong catalytic tonic.

It was possible to treat these large-scale regularities of gasses directly in terms of macroscopic concepts alone, without the introduction of new notions. Certain nineteenth century positivists, notably Mach, insisted on purely philosophical grounds that the concept of atoms was meaningless and nonsensical because it was not then possible to observe them as such—and, indeed, by their very nature they could never be observed. Nevertheless, Bohm points out, evidence for the existence of individual atoms was eventually discovered by people who took the atomic hypothesis *seriously* enough to suppose that atoms might exist, even though no one had actually observed them.

James B. Conant claims that a theory is only overthrown by a better theory, never merely by contradictory facts. Certainly the contradictory facts for atoms were many and severe. But the "questions" had been asked, and a long series of believers set about directly and indirectly contributing to the gathering of material for the answer. The unfolding history covered many generations and gives a fine example of the question-answer function in cultural form, moving over many lives, a cultural drift taking on power and characteristics. That people took the idea *seriously* enough was the key.

Only a sustained passionate belief could have leaped the logical gap between that "imagined," created within the mind's eye, imaged from possibility in spite of the lack of sensory evidence, and the final answer, translated into reality through enormous expenditures of time, effort, group belief, money, and with even the passionate urgency of war to hasten its final birth.

Interestingly enough, Newton's laws of motion could not cover the new atoms, and the emerging postulates of Einstein and Planck shook the early twentieth-century physicists who had felt satisfied with the world system long since discovered and formulated. Weaver mentions how the new ideas recharged all the scientific fields. Journals and learned magazines which were thin and anemic burgeoned into fat and exciting adventures in every issue.

Today atomicity is the energy basis of all things, commonplace, taken for granted. Newton's cosmic egg has been expanded enormously, but resealed with splendid logic. Now we see the current egg as an *a priori* structure. This always *was,* this is the way the sun works, billions of years of development were involved, this is the very underpinning of all things.

Was this a breakthrough of Pauli's "cosmic order"? Was it a truth glimpsed through some temporary freeing of the cave-encompassed mind and brought back as light into our sphere? In fact, can we claim something really different and not speak madness? Yes. If we *cannot* see beyond this apparent chasm, we will miss something vital.

Exploring Bohm's "qualitative infinity of nature" a bit further I found Bohm postulating that the universe may have existed, and in his system must either *once* have existed or necessarily will *someday* exist on a basis totally unrelated to atoms, molecules, and such aggregates of energy. (Gerald Feinberg cannot rule out such a possibility on purely logical grounds, but is content to wait, skeptically, for such a development. He feels we have arrived at a final understanding of the basic stuff of which our world is made.) Thus Bohm postulates his *sub-quantum* theory of an "infinite substructure of matter." No matter how fine a breakdown of particles we ever achieve, there will be that many more—and there is always the possibility of their eventual reorganization in non-molecular atomic form.

Where, then, would be the cosmic order? Or is it not also a *process,* a process of change and possibility? Are both men, Bohm and Pauli, correct in their own ways? Is the true cosmic order some law like Bohm's that might thus, as an abstraction, always be independent of the products of its function? Wherever we are, whatever we may be, that which we *are* is the true and objective reality. Is that process itself a cosmic order?

Several years before Bohm's work, Teilhard spoke of man's dream being mastery of the ultimate energy, *beyond all atomic or molecular affinities.* And I think of William Blake's great romantic affirmation: "More! More! is the cry of a mistaken soul. Less than *all* will never satisfy man."

In these poetic, quasi-religious, and scientific expressions there is a *question* tentatively and ever more strongly asserting itself. A seed of possibility is being planted into the continuum of potential.

Bohm talked about *new* sources of energy from this "infinite process of becoming." New energy might be available even now when atoms, molecules and so on continue to exist. Bohm points out that in the last century only mechanical, chemical, thermal, electrical, luminous, and gravitational energies were known. Today we have at our disposal *nuclear* energy, a far larger reservoir of energy.

Bohm then follows with a statement that creates, in effect, a kind of rudimentary shaping of the question into tighter form. For he muses that the infinite substructure of matter very probably contains energies that are as far beyond nuclear energy as that great force is beyond chemical energies.

What follows this is both the rough formulation of a possible direction for the question to move in which will help determine the nature of the question and the basis for the first tentative steps in the gathering of materials for an answer. For Bohm next shows how, by computing the "zero point" energy due to quantum-mechanical fluctuations, something on the order of 10^{38} ergs is attained in "even one cubic centimetre of space." As I wrote when citing this assertion in my first chapter, this comes out to the explosive energy of roughly ten billion *tons* of uranium fission.

Bohm qualifies by saying this kind of energy provides a constant background not available under *present* conditions, but he dreams that, as conditions change, a part of it might be made available at our level.

Does Bohm believe that man will *wait* for conditions to change in order to have new energy? Did conditions in the universe change for man's atomic age to come about? Or for the discovery and development of the laser? No. Man's conceptual level changed, and the kind of universe with which he dealt proved to be different from that of previous dealings. No amount of waiting would have ever brought about man's atomic age *naturally*. There is no such nature.

The evolving processes of an "infinite substructure of matter," or whatever it may be called, evolve around suggestions, ideas, and notions passionately adhered to, triggers for what might be. Eventually Bohm's postulate, or one by another Bohm or Feinberg or whoever, *will* formulate an equation that *will* break into some future mind as a *Eureka!* revelation. Scoffed at for lack of evidence, perhaps, it will find its passionate believers, those who simply like the notion and see it a way to their own expression, their own ambition's fulfillment. They will start driving piles into shaky ground, working out the correspondences, trying to develop a mathematics to cover all the contingencies. Some day they will make the translations, they will achieve the testings, and the results in reasonable facsimile will be produced. Then the technicians, the mechanics, the brass-tack realists who deal with the obvious and evident, will start exploiting and exhausting the possibilities—filling in the new circles of reason.

Max Planck once wrote that when an experimental result contradicts an existing theory in some way, progress is in sight, for the theory is even then in process of being changed and improved. Consider then, the discovery of that tiny *quasar* (*i.e.* seemingly a stellar object) 3C-273. Pouring through it, or from it, or something, is energy enough to power up to 1000 times the usual sized galaxy like our Milky Way. At least, that was the estimate in 1965, when Dr. Herbert Friedman, head of the Atmosphere and Astrophysics Division of the U.S. Navy Research Laboratory, reported on it, saying that the release of such energy fits nothing in modern physics at all, and that we may be witnessing an entirely new source of energy.

Since then *pulsars* have been discovered, which apparently incorporate an energy far exceeding the speed-of-light limit demanded by the Einsteinian universe in which we live at present. These new phenomena have triggered off an immense excitement of speculation. Probably no single topic in decades has stimulated such an outpouring of theorizing among astronomers, physicists, and men of all the sciences. Each month the new offerings come forward in large quantity.

Consider now that ideas of radical energies were assumed as a matter of course by Teilhard, back in the 1940's before development of the hydrogen bomb. Bohm's proposal was published in 1957, about four years before the great quasar show began. Indeed, Bohm's notion and quasar 3C-273 seem made for each other. At any rate, it is not simple fortuitousness that these ideas were in the domain *before* people began to "see" quasars and pulsars.

Teilhard saw thought "artificially perfecting" the thinking instrument itself. We rebound forward under the collective effect of our reflection. And, he prophesied, we foster the dream of that "energy of which all other energies are merely servants." Teilhard saw mankind "grasping the very mainspring of evolution, seizing the tiller of the world."

Do you not see that our Catholic paleontologist and our Jewish physicist, each in his own sphere, explore the same capacity for potential, funneled through their prism of prejudice, their molds for world-making, and their heart's desire? Can we do other than acknowledge

Blake's dictum from *The Marriage of Heaven and Hell* that "The Worship of God is: Honouring his gifts in other men, each according to his genius, and loving the greatest men best: those who envy or calumniate great men hate God; for there is no other God."

Bohm searches beneath the *quantum;* Jung talks of the psyche speaking about the psyche; Teilhard said the Great Stability is not at the bottom, in the infra-elementary sphere of quantums and their sub-levels, but at the top, in the ultra-synthetic sphere of thought. They are all really talking about the same process, for at some point along the way the categories dissolve and things merge.

Teilhard claimed that what is "spontaneously psychical" is no longer merely an "aura around the soma," but a part, even a principal part, of the phenomenon. Intellectual synthesis is no longer speculation, he speculated, but is creation.

Now the passion, the belief, the imagination, the intuitive analysis, and the insight that brought about the logical gap that could then be leapt to bring into being man's atomic age were all psychic phenomena. Imagination and idea preceded, and in fact created, this new age which is, in turn, transforming and reshaping the whole of our reality. We are the determinant, the prism that shapes inner and outer into a meaningful pattern that is the only reality we shall ever know.

David Bohm's idea, or a compatible equivalent, as H-bombs or atomic generating stations are at best rather strained equivalents of Democritus' idea, may eventually produce its own structure. Infinite changes are taking place as consciousness enters into contingencies, altering courses, searching for a way to interpret, to broaden, to explore.

At our present rate who dares suggest how far this interference might extend in, say, another century. That attractive seizing of the tiller is there—perhaps cloaked as 10^{38} ergs. Surely it does not *exist;* there is no such animal except as a dream-figure in some physicist's creative mind.

Yet from there it will be translated, sooner or later,

into reality. And the reality into which it will be translated will be a reality that has, itself, been translated, or transformed, into terms compatible with the new desire. The "ecological" satisfactions demanded by the new idea and its radiating contingencies will somehow be met. The vast network of our reality will make adjustments for inclusion and support of the new concept. The infinite process of change will have its logical, normal, and reasonable working out. The action of psyche and *physis* will have gone full circle.

Then, at that point, the new will become obvious. We will say: "Why, of course. This is the way the *universe* works. This is the real secret of the sun, and the stars. This was obviously *a priori,* for its processes involve billions of years. We simply never had the proper tools, the proper insight, we did not understand the Laws."

Laws there will be, and the only breaking of them will be through that crack-forming procedure. What we will have loosed on earth will have been loosed in heaven. Theologians will grudgingly admit, in a kind of sour-grapes way: that the scientists have discovered more of God's eternal secrets by which He built the universe. And the laws *will be* "true" ones, of the only truth there can *be.* They will be universal. They will reflect the cosmic order. They will be the underpinnings of the very ground on which we stand. The level between our idea and the resultant fact will be difficult to assess, for the very ground from which the assessment must be attempted will be, then as now, itself a product of the function of mirroring in question.

6

fire-burn

In the *Atlantic Monthly* of May, 1959, appeared an article by Leonard Feinberg, Ph.D., University of Illinois, on fire-walking in Ceylon. Feinberg had observed several fire-walkings while serving as an officer in the South Pacific during World War II. As a Fulbright Professor to the University of Ceylon in 1956-1957, he had the opportunity to follow the full development of the chief ceremony held on that island.

Preparations for this annual affair, held in honor of the god Kataragama, lasted three months. The applicants lived that entire time under the constant surveillance of the priests of the god, and in the main temple. It was a time of abstinence, vegetarianism, drinking only water, daily baptisms in the holy river, constant sprinklings with holy water, continual religious instruction, prayer, meditation, and communion with the god.

It was a serious undertaking, a 24-hour a day investment of self. If the believer did all these things, he would finally achieve the proper state of mind, an absolute and unquestioning belief in Kataragama, a seizure by the god himself. Then he could walk the fire unafraid and unharmed.

Numerous benefits could be gained from a successful walking: success in business, love, health, forgiveness of sins for oneself or for another, and oneness with the living god. Death, disfigurement, or crippling awaited the failures, and there were enough of these to attest the seriousness of the venture.

When the end of the long period of asceticism approached, Hindus from all over the island began to arrive. Fire-walking was far more than just a spectacle to these people, Feinberg noted, although he detected a "note of malevolent sadism" in the air. The affair was a concrete symbol of intimate identification with Kataragama, who, within his domain—a fourteen-mile radius from his temple—was in absolute, if whimsical and good-natured, control.

The families nearest the fire-pit held their places for days. Among the ordinarily fastidious islanders, sanitation became a bit slack. At the very last, the usual European dignitaries and bumptious tourists arrived and tried to push their way to the ringside, but were resisted firmly by the otherwise courteous Hindus.

Sensational preliminaries began in the afternoon when native women tried to attract the attention of the priests, and probably everyone, by parading up and down in front of the temple gates carrying in their bare hands iron pots filled with burning coconut husks. After dark the pots could be seen glowing quite red. One woman, carrying her redhot pot on her head in the conventional Ceylonese fashion, removed it for Feinberg's inspection, and "neither her hair nor her hands showed any signs of scorching."

The crowd was feverishly tense when the great hardwood logs were ignited, well before midnight. The logs filled a pit twenty feet long and six feet wide. The spectators did not know exactly when the walkers would appear, neither did the priests nor walkers—for that could only be when they were "ready," seized and changed by the god. The fire burned to a bed of deep charcoal, raked smooth by attendants with long branches. At four o'clock in the morning, when the final moment came, Feinberg found it difficult to breathe within ten feet of the incandescent pit, neither could he stand that close for any time.

The drums had built up to a great crescendo when the huge temple doors swung open and the priests and initiates came streaming out, straight into the pit of fire without pause. Eighty people, including ten women, most of whom held hands, walked the fire that night. One small, slim man in a white sarong strolled slowly and serenely through the fire, stepping gently onto the earth at the far end. Another danced gaily into the center of the pit, turned, did a wild jig for a few minutes, then danced madly on across the coals and out.

Of the eighty people walking that night twelve failed. Some required lengthy hospitalization and one man was burned to death. The devout dismiss these accidents. Those people, Feinberg was told, simply lacked faith or proper preparation. Feinberg then related the fate of a young English missionary who was quite upset by the ceremony and vowed to walk the fire next time, to show Christian faith to be as firm as Hindu. He did walk the fire, somehow, and spent the next six months in the hospital where doctors barely managed to save his life.

These failures stand as a kind of macabre control group that make credible the entire incredible business. Recently in our own country the annual spring beach frolics of the college set have been turning up cases of severe burns suffered by LSD addicts who think they can walk fire. Apparently there are no shortcuts to union with the gods.

Another splendid account of fire-walking appeared in the *National Geographic Magazine* for April, 1966. It was written by the Senior Assistant Editor, Gilbert Grosvenor and his wife, Donna. Color photographs made the story quite vivid. The Grosvenors were visiting Ceylon and heard by chance of a fire-walking ceremony in a nearby village.

This ceremony was held in the private courtyard of one Mohotty, who, as a young boy, had vowed to Katar-agama to walk the fire yearly if his father could be cleared of a murder charge. Sensational preliminaries again led up to the annual walking. The dancers all knelt to have their cheeks, arms, and chests rubbed with sacred ash. As they stared with glazed, half-closed eyes, Mohotty forced steel skewers through each man's cheeks. Not a drop of blood appeared, there were no indications of pain or feeling, and when the skewers were later removed, no sign of a wound could be detected.

Then Mohotty's own cheeks were pierced by attendants who next drove needles into his arms from shoulder to wrist, sank little arrowheads into his chest and stomach, lashed spiked wooden clogs securely to his bare feet, and finally, with real effort, drove fearsome hooks into Mohotty's lower back. The hooks had ropes attached and by this strange method Mohotty pulled an enormous sledge, a kind of sedan chair, about the courtyard, the several hooks pulling the flesh quite taut. Removing the hooks left no signs of blood or wounds of any sort.

When Mr. Grosvenor asked Mohotty his "secret," the Hindu answered, "Faith total faith in my gods."

The fire in the pit, which was of the standard twenty by six dimensions, though shallow, smoldered until long after midnight while the chanting dancers, gleaming with perspiration, circled the red-hot embers. One man fainted, and was dragged away. At 4 A.M. Ed Lark, a member of the *Geographic* team, measured the coals with an optical pyrometer from the Ceylon Institute of Scientific and Industrial research. The pyrometer registered 1328° Fahrenheit. The photographs show the onlookers quite close to the coals, however, and there were no fatalities or even minor failures; it appears that most of the dancers were yearly repeats, old hands at the game, and that the fire was not the intense deep pit such as that prepared by the priests of the temple itself.

The crowds grew still as the first young man danced across the carpet of coals, twisting his body, shuffling his feet, digging into the fire. Another followed, scooping up handfuls of embers and throwing them over his shoulders. Nearly twenty people, men, women, boys, and girls, walked the fire. Some walked it several times. Mohotty crossed four times—twice with his own young son on his *shoulders.*

Mohotty quite willingly allowed his feet to be examined and photographed afterward. They showed no signs of any blisters or burns. The Grosvenors got back to their room long after dawn, exhausted but unable to sleep. They said they just could not digest the incredible sights they had witnessed. "What we saw was real," they wrote, "as real as the faith upon which these believers base their immunity from pain of steel or flame."

Dr. Arnold Krechmal, Fulbright Professor teaching in Greece, wrote an article on Greek fire-walking, published in *Travel* Magazine. *The New York Times* also gave an account from Ayia Heleni, where fire-walking activities have been happily seized upon by the Greek National Tourist Organization. Frowned upon by the church as a carry-over from pagan times, the ceremonies are only practiced in the remote mountain villages where the priests are sympathetic.

The ceremonies are held in honor of Saint Constantine and his mother, Helen; and these two, in return, protect the dancers from all hurt. Intensive preparations last for several days. Prayers, meditations, constant sprinkling of holy water, drums, and so on, prepare the dancers for seizure. They, too, must wait until "ready," which according to accounts is a bit more dramatic—even if their bonfires are less extreme—than their Asian counterparts. Seized, they shout, gesticulate, roll their eyes, and sigh heavily as they move onto the coals. No drink or drug is used, and doctors' examinations detect no signs of either protection or injury.

A gentleman in California traveled the world studying fire-walking, convinced that great cosmic secrets were hidden there. He set up his own publishing house for the numerous books and tracts concerning these mysteries, but I found my heart hard against his cult. I *was* interested to read that in Indonesia stones are heated for days for a walking and that wads of paper thrown into the pit will burst into flame before touching. As with all the firewalkers, the long togas they wear are not even scorched, unless the walker's faith snaps, whereupon the toga bursts into flame. Admission to the priesthood hinged on a successful walking over the stones, and attendants stood by with long wooden hooks to try to rake failures off before cooked.

Enough for examples. By now the brass-tack realist may have abandoned me in disgust. I recall being so pleased with the *Geographic* article since I knew Grosvenor to be quite reputable, the recipient of many scientific honors and so on, that I showed the article to a colleague who was particularly scathing in his attitudes to superstitious nonsense. Indeed, he dismissed the *Geographic* article as either a cheap trick to bolster circulation, or indicative of how the best of us could be duped and led astray. I was reminded of the farmer who, taken for his first zoo visit, saw a giraffe, spat, and snorted that there was no such animal.

One of the tenets of science is of a basic uniform causality operating as a unifying force throughout all the universe. Dr. Weaver speaks of this as a kind of statistical necessity, but points out that this can never be proved to *have* to apply to any particular specific. No individual event *has* to follow the pattern, but among all events, the pattern is the case. Jesus differentiated between the *broad way,* which leads to destruction, and a *narrow way,* which few find, but which leads to life.

For centuries a certain locality in India chose a sacrificial victim for each spring's planting. The victim was properly initiated by the priests, anointed as a temporary god, enthroned in the temple with pomp, and then, on the fatal day, with all the tribes in attendance, amid great praying and commotion, two large eye-hooks, big enough to hang a side of beef on, were run through the victim's back. Ropes, run through the eyes of the big hooks, were tied to a tall pole carried as a boom on an ox-cart, and, as propitiation to the fertility gods, the victim was swung out in great arcs over the various fields being planted.

Some two thousand years ago a victim survived this ordeal, without pain or injury. Perhaps he was intensely religious, seeing himself in a Messianic light, rejoicing that the salvation of the crops rested with him. When he was anointed and made a temporary god, perhaps he was seized in ecstasy and became, in effect, that which was claimed. At any rate, from that point on—*once it was known to be possible*—the yearly victim went unscathed. The position grew highly exalted, the subject honored for the entire year, and *elected* by all the tribes. It is still practiced today, in spite of government disapproval. Photographs in the *Scientific American* show the elation of the subject, who sheds no blood and shows no signs of a wound, literally no puncture signs in the flesh itself, when the huge hooks are removed.

Life moves by historical accident, and random incident. Under Manasseh (697-643 B.C.), who followed Hezekiah as the ruler of the Hebrews, Assyrian religious forms were instituted from the cult of Moloch, an Ammonite deity closely associated with astral divination. Among these cult-forms was the practice of compelling one's firstborn child to pass through or into a furnace of fire. The practice had come from the orient, was widespread, and had many variations down through the centuries.

The ordeal of judgment was one such variation. The accused was thrown into a pit of fire. If he could survive, the gods were obviously with him, and his innocence was established. (The European practice of freeing a suspect if he could pick coins from the bottom of a pot of boiling oil had a roughly similar sadistic origin.) Somewhere back in the dim past someone believed, in that final gruesome moment, not only in his innocence, but that the gods *were* with him. Doubtless carried into ecstatic trance, he then walked the fire unscathed and elated. From that point on, *once the notion that it could really be done* was implanted in experience, it became a part of our reality-potential, and the practice grew.

Now here we get back to my first chapter's "clearing in the forest" metaphor. God did not build such a possibility into the universe and sit back waiting for man to have the fun of discovery. Neither in all the ramifications of "nature" is such a cause-effect bypass hidden. Man's discovery of the idea was the phenomenon's creation—this is the way, or a way, by which God *creates* things. The notion arises from experience. Painted into a corner, caught in a cul-de-sac, out on that final last-chance limb, life scrabbles around, searching for a way out. If there is no logical way out, reason is impaled and must be abandoned.

Fire burns; without this as a fact there could not be the kind of reality we have. Man sees fire not burning himself as a possibility through an alliance with God—that which is beyond one's control, an outer limit, as Bruner called fate. Fire-walking is an *autistic* venture.

It would seem that fire-walking could never prove

amenable to laboratory testing, but at Surrey, England, in 1935-36, the English Society for Psychical Research ran a series of tests on two Indian fakirs imported expressly for the purpose. The tests were graded by physicians, chemists, physicists, and psychologists of Oxford. The Indians walked the fire under control conditions, under the skeptical and probing eyes of science itself. The emotive-religious buildups reported by observers in Ceylon and Greece were not reported here. The Indians had their *metanoia* well in hand. No chemicals were used, no preparations made, they repeated the performances under a variety of conditions and over a period of several weeks, on demand. Surface temperatures were between 450–500° Centigrade, the interior temperatures 1400° C. There was no trickery or hallucination.

A high point was reached when one of the fakirs noticed a professor of psychology avidly intrigued and dumbfounded. The fakir, sensing the longing, told the good professor he, too, could walk the fire if he so desired—by *holding the fakir's hand.* The good man was seized with faith that he could, shed his shoes, and hand-in-hand they walked the fire ecstatic and unharmed.

These phenomena question our assumptions concerning biological necessities. They are the margins of error in our tightknit world view. In the scientific picture these margins of error prove to be passports to new areas of thought, as Max Planck said. But this never invalidates the functional reality of current postulates and systems. That the quasars may lead to concepts of speed and energy beyond those given by the Einsteinian universe does not lessen in any way the truth of Einstein's system or denigrate one of history's proudest times. New constructs are no more true than false, but matters of choice. The new, in fact, needs the old against which to move to gain meaning or value. The riddle of the quasars, and the inherent promise of them, is comprehensible only against the backdrop of our current viewpoints. The quasars will not fit *into* these current viewpoints—and *only by the misfitting itself* are the quasars in fact *noticeable*—or *nameable as quasars.*

And so—fire burns. The cause-effect of fire burn underlies the physical world. There could be no such phenomenon as fire did fire not *burn.* But fire does not have to burn a person in this particular case at this particular time. Neither does cancer have to kill this particular person at this particular time; nor do any of the other grim dragons of necessity *have* to apply to *this* person or *that* person—nor to *any* person who can believe in another way, or another construct.

Is there a pattern? Yes. There is the conscious *desire* for the experience, the asking of the question. There is the *detachment* from the commonplace; the *commitment* to replace the conventional with a new construct; the *passion and decorum*—the intensive preparation, the gathering of materials for the answer; the *freedom to be dominated* by the subject of desire—the sudden seizure, the breakthrough of mind that gives the inexplicable conviction that it can, after all, be done; and then the *serving* of the new construct, the instant application.

If a few lone people can reverse causality in isolated cases, what could truly-agreeing people in a mass do with broad statistics? (And in this new worldwide monoculture our technological push is so bent on achieving, what kind of agreement concerning reality is going to be the dominant shaping force?)

Erich Neumann, in an unrelated context, contended that the actual process of fire is experienced "with the aid of images" which derive from the interior of one's psychic world, and are "projected upon the external world." The subjective reaction, he claims, always takes precedence historically. Fire-walking seems to confirm this. Fire-walking is made possible by replacing "historical precedents" with non-ordinary images. The non-ordinary event takes place in the external world through the same reality function by which all events take place.

Fire-walking is found in "simpler" societies probably because these people have fewer investments in strict causal modes. We are so heavily committed to our constructs that any suggestion of their relativeness fills us with anxiety. It is for *reward* that the Hindu undergoes the discipline and risk. The followers of Jesus were those who "hated the world." One does not abandon an eminently satisfactory system. New life can only be created by metaphoric mutation—synthetic re-creation of the old, and the old must be surrendered for this synthesis to take place.

To give up one's belief concerning some structure of reality, there must be an image that stands for the new goal or framework, even if the specifics of that goal are unclear. The new goal must be ultimately desirable or ambiguity results, an ambiguity which prevents the new from forming and only fragments and weakens the old. It is an all-or-nothing process.

Voodoo, for instance, is a potent and real power in the Caribbean and other areas. If a man learns that he is destined to die, he tends to oblige. The same force is operative in our culture, but under sophisticated metaphors and more subtle sureties. If we are told that one of every four of us is destined to die of a certain disease, we fill the social requirements. The one on whom the lot randomly falls feels fated to oblige as surely as the black victim of voodoo.

If an arbitrary and premature death is announced as your statistical imperative, why not give up allegiance to that system and devote yourself to something less statistical? With death the alternative, surely you could generate the same intensity the Hindu does with Kataragama, and find a new structure of concept-percept. Granted, the statistical world is a broad and powerful way. You would need a strong image for the new goal to break completely with the bad-news system and risk your life in a new one. It is the equivalent of asking a passionate question. If you hold and serve the question, until all ambiguity is erased and you really believe in your question, it will be answered; the break-point will arrive when you will suddenly be "ready." Then you must put your hand to the plow and not look back; walk out onto the water unmindful of the waves.

Jung speaks of life's potential as governed by law and yet not governed by law, rational and irrational. Bruner refers to *fate* as that which is beyond one's control, a residuum left after one has run through the census of our possibilities.

"Running through the census" is an act of reason. Fire-walking shows that possibility opens to extremities beyond our census. I cannot reason out fire-walking. There are things to which our intellect gives assent, and vague things to which only our soul can give assent. I know that two plus two must make four or our house of cards comes tumbling down. I also know that three loaves and two fishes can equal five thousand hungry mouths fed.

Tillich speaks of God as the *ground* of our being. Our ultimate concerns are what this ground is for us. They shape God as He is for us. A faith in God as an ultimate beyond the perimeters of our reason and experience can give an ontological "warp." We may assume and by the assumption be open to new ground. Our images of belief are clothed in the flesh and blood of reality by action. The broad stream of semi-conscious belief cannot see any possibility but imitation of those actions already given form. This limits possibility to *a priori* modes of social acceptance, harmful or not. This is the broad road of automata leading to its own destruction. Blake wrote that the man who did not believe in miracles surely made it certain that he would never take part in one.

The Hindu's belief restructures the way in which he shapes his data. Something unusual happens to his "editorial hierarchy" and something unusual happens in the world in which he moves. It is the function of structuring that counts. No claim is made for mind over matter. The successful fire-walker or hook-swinger simply alters and reshapes an event by an ultimate allegiance or commitment. He is then in the world, but not quite of its ordinary makeup.

If for any reason, under any circumstances, hypnagogic, anagogic, hypnotic, spiritual, metaphysical, or what have you, fire does not burn a man, the cause-effect framework, considered a final arbiter all to itself and the means by which our current priesthood holds us in bondage, cannot be held as unalterable by the mind of even a single person. The hard-line realist, the biogenetic and determinist psychologist and their like are simply inadequate to cover life in its fullest, actual terms. We are sold short by our tough-minded dogmatists. The state of mind referred to as *faith,* bandied about though it is, is profound beyond all "objective truth and logical thinking."

7

behold and become

The word hypnotism alienates some people, creating a semantic barrier to hearing, even when the point to be made lies considerably beyond the ordinary impressions of what the word implies. Ernest Hilgard, of Stanford University, spent ten years in research on one question: why can only about twenty percent of the population undergo a deep trance experience? In his exploration, Dr. Hilgard threw light on the whole problem of mind, differences of world view and personality, as well as on the characteristics of the trance state. Hilgard's text makes for rather specialized reading, however, and the occultic, popular approach too often is accepted as the norm for hypnotism. Legitimate studies offer a far more sensational, radical, and novel picture, in their cautious and subdued tones, than those writers whose intent is generally toward sensationalism and whose uncritical extravagances prejudice many in the scientific field from "hearing" the significance of legitimate trance studies.

The trance state is another manifestation of the *autistic* mode of mind. Bloodless wounds can be inflicted on a hypnotized person, or undergone by a conscious person in a voluntary, self-induced trance. Enormous strength and ridiculous weakness can be induced. Earlier notions of the powers of suggestion, as a kind of super-adrenalin enhancing native capabilities, no longer will cover all cases of trance phenomena, though it surely enters as an element.

Carl Jung told of a young lady patient, disabled by

anemia, whose body weight had dropped to seventy pounds. Hypnotized, she was told of her enormous strength. Her head was then placed on one chair, her heels on another, her body easily spanning the gap in a straight line—a feat the best of athletes have difficulty doing. Jung must have been fond of this trick, for he recounted a similar case in which he and several other doctors then *sat* on the patient—and Jung was himself a very large man—without any detectable strain, discomfort, or after-effects on the patient.

In 1966 interesting experiments were performed on student volunteers who fasted for three days until blood samples showed their blood sugar to be extremely low. Hypnotized, they were given imaginary bowls of sugar to eat. Then samples were again taken, which showed a several hundred percent increase in blood sugar. Others fasted for three days; samples showed the basic food nutrients of the blood to be very low. Hypnotized, the students were given imaginary meals which they "ate" with gusto. Blood samples taken afterward showed a several hundred percent increase in the basic food nutrients.

This cannot imply pulling a rabbit out of the hat when there is no rabbit in the hat, neither does it suggest a quick, magical way out of the food problem. Perhaps the body reverses the blood-ingestion process, drawing on tissue *for* the nutrients. Even this would be no small thing. The body manages, somehow and at all costs, to respond to the *conceptual framework* induced by the hypnotist. Somehow the materials are found to make real, to realize, the mind's notion. A conceptual demand brings about a change in the ordinary mechanisms of life. The same process can be seen in the fire-walker, who reverses or nullifies or bypasses the most extreme cause-effect to be found in life.

The term *a-causal* used to appeal to me, tinged with a bit of magic perhaps, but something causes non-ordinary events even though the causality falls outside the criteria of the times. Perhaps the focus of attention has been misdirected heretofore. Perhaps the "cause" of non-ordinary effects and the "cause" of ordinary effects are simply different points of emphasis of a single causal function. Are we not dealing with the Price-Carington notion that any idea will realize itself in any way it can—unless inhibited by conflicting notions? In the trance state, the world of conflicting notions is temporarily set aside.

Carington would claim that there are phenomena that achieve only some aspects of a reality event, but not a sufficient number. Mirages, apparitions, many occultic experiences, hallucinations, and so on could be explored from this standpoint. Suppose a group of people were to experience a non-ordinary event that would not fit their conceptual frame of possibility—that agreement on which their normal world hangs together. They would call the event an hallucination, or *folie à deux,* and so keep their categories for the norm intact, lest their ideation collapse and they fall into chaos.

The situation is complicated by the fact that not every personality type will experience a non-ordinary event. Hilgard searched for the properties of mind that made one student capable of entering deep trance, another not. The backgrounds proved varied and general, but one feature came to light and proved to be the decisive element.

As children, all those capable of deep trance as adults had shared in fantasy play and imaginative ventures of some sort with their parents. Their parents had read to them a great deal, entering with them into the "inner space travel" that reading brings about. Or their parents told them tales, ghostly stories, saw giant-castles in the clouds with them, played "let's-pretend" with them, listened to the children's fantasies with respect. And, not incidentally at all, always brought them back to reality of the norm with "Enough of that now, back we come," back to the world of real people.

This background gives the temperament capable of deep religious experiences, empathy, compassion, ability to see from a different world view, willingness to agree quickly with the adversary, and other marks of a flexible tolerance that does not feel threatened by strangeness. Surely the problem of the "hawk" and "dove" sets of mind can be understood within this line of study, and some grasp gained of the fundamental gap between the two that logic alone cannot bridge.

Smythies, you recall, considered hallucination to be a normal part of every child's psychological life. These hallucinatory capacities are gradually repressed because of negative social values. It is said that Blake's father paddled him for seeing angels in the windows, so it must have been Blake's mother who helped keep his threshold of mind open. Carl Jung's father was a stiff and pedantic cleric, but according to Jung his mother was almost mystically inclined. Both Blake and Jung retained a marked degree of hallucinatory capacity and were capable of creative and imaginative thought.

Trance experience is a disengagement from ordinary reality orientation. It is a suspension of the ordinary criteria, or common consensus. Trance falls into the autistic mode of thinking. The kind of grown person who is able to suspend his reality orientation is the one who retains a pleasant recollection of former disengagements. His childhood fantasies were forms of play in which parental tolerance, approval, or participation played a specific part. The child could always come back to a warm security. The threshold between autistic and reality thinking became a well worn path, a door well hinged and oiled, through which access was easy and safe.

The parents were the ones who had structured the infant autistic responses into a communicable world of others in the first place. Fantasy play then repeated the essentials of the long development, each time for a new and novel kind of mental adventure. The child who feels secure and comfortable in "flexible role taking," as Hilgard called it, and in creating fantasy and adventure without intense self-criticism, can learn to become absorbed easily in new interests or esoteric points of view. A variety of such new experience will keep alive in adolescence and adulthood the ability to relinquish reality and enter non-ordinary states.

Having found that he can let go of reality adjustment in favor of other experiences, confident in his ability to return to the world, he has a favorable background for acceptance of novelty. On this background new experience can be grafted, constantly reinforcing the native autistic ability. Without this uncritical spirit of adventure, however, this faculty of mind is repressed until it atrophies, rather as speech in a child missing the formative elements in language development.

Jane Belo, in her study *Trance in Bali,* makes it clear that when trance seizure is socially acceptable, desirable, and a mark of esteem, as it is among the Balinese, it is found on a wider scale than in the west. Trance entrance was the high point of Balinese social life. It provided each participant with a unique expression and outlet, and was for onlookers an adventure otherwise lacking in the easy, static, island life.

The characteristics of the trance state, according to Hilgard, are directly related to childhood. There is the same blurring of fantasy and reality, the enjoyment of pretense and sensation, the excitement of omnipotence, and the implicit following of *adult* words.

These traits are easily seen in the Balinese child trance-dancers, who function as an integral part of the society. Chosen for their trance ability at age seven or so, the children demonstrated immediately on first seizure an uncanny ability to perform automatically and with finesse the highly ornate and difficult Balinese dances. This impressed Jane Belo, but I would point out that the children had watched such dancing all their short lives. A seven-year-old has pretty well absorbed his culture. And trance seizure gives complete confidence, a total recall, and perfect synthesis of material.

In this activity childhood autisms, with their excitements of pseudo-dangers, could merge with the adult world itself and win approval and acclaim. Small wonder the young eyes missed nothing, and that the unconscious synthesis was made so readily once the mind had developed to the point where such was possible. The little boys, meanwhile, played at Kris-dancing, mimicking with sticks the self-stabbing (ngoerek) postures of the adult males, laying all the groundwork needed for their own seizures when the time came that such would be in keeping with the social modes. This self-stabbing of the adult Kris-dancers, by the way, was designed to really stab and draw blood, unlike the Ceylonese whose purpose was a-causal by nature, designed to bypass the world of cause-effect. On the other hand, the little girl trance-dancers danced blithely over hot coals without fear or harm.

Back to the Western world, Hilgard points out that the hypnotist fills the same role in the trance state that the parent once filled for the child. The final phase of the hypnotic process parallels precisely that phase in the development of the infant's ego in which its boundaries *initially expanded,* that is, when his world view was inculcated by parental response and demand. This procedure, if you recall my second and third chapters, unconsciously patterns the image of the parents, an image shaping the autistic mind into a reality-adjusted, communicable member of the society. The adult who can freely *abandon* his common world view and retreat to the unformed *autistic* is the one who feels security with the hypnotist, as he once was secure with his parents in a similar function, crossing the same threshold passage between autisms and the world of others. What takes place is a reproduction of the natural developmental processes of early experience.

The ability to relinquish reality and enter trance states must wait until a fairly firm reality picture is itself built up. Trance abilities are lost, unless retained by the associations mentioned, somewhere in early adolescence. Somewhere between twelve and fourteen logical development, which means a final adjustment to the world-of-others, becomes the complete criterion of concept—the ruling hierarchy of mind. This hardening of world view generally represses the autistic modes, with their free synthesis, into fully unconscious, lost potentials.

The small percentage under discussion retain the autistic mode as a freely-possible subset. Trance entrance bypasses the ordinary criteria for data selection, and draws on the ordinary world as needed by the novel suggestions induced.

The most important aspect of autistic thinking, and one I may have emphasized *ad nauseam,* is that it has no value judgment. It has no criteria for what shall or shall not be synthesized. This same qualification and limitation holds in all trance states, a point of major importance, and one overlooked by cults. The person in trance, though he has an enormously rich background to draw on for synthesis, remains a blank slate—at least when his entrance is through a hypnotist. The person can draw on background not from his *own* value system, since that has been suspended to *create* the trance state, but draws on his background perceptually in response to the concepts of the hypnotist. The "over-all ego" retains its ordinary relationship with both hypnotist and world. It is the partially-regressed subsystem that is surrendered to the hypnotist's control. And it is this subsystem that is receptive to novel thought formations, novel restructuring of the perceptual world.

Immediately it should be asked, concerning the Balinese trance states: *Who,* then, is directing *their* conceptual systems? Who is determining the selection of concepts for response in self-induced trance? For the Balinese it is the cultural image, the socially-shared set of expectancies, built up over untold generations, that acts as the trigger for autistic synthesis. The trances are self-induced, but within the confines of the proper social setting. The cultural image functions as the directing selector; it functions as the hierarchy of mind—a factor that enters heavily into Jesus' Kingdom and don Juan's path, as will be explored later.

This cultural imagery was clearly evident in the Ceylonese experience, and was one of the many reasons the poor Protestant missionary nearly burned to death. As with the language trigger, the process seems to be the sowing of a small wind to reap a whirlwind. The cultural image, given the proper triggering for synthesis, seems to carry an enormous force of its own.

Hilgard likens the surrender of world view for restructuring by a hypnotist to the transference of patient to analyst attempted in psychiatry. A successful transfer is both subject to and limited only *by* the conceptual framework and capacity for belief of the hypnotist himself.

The function of world view development is a natural, imitative process, building on acquisition of given data. It is profoundly complex within this simple pattern, however, and there may be an untold number of innate capacities inborn and awaiting the proper triggers that would give unique and novel experiences. The partial restructuring of world view, by repeating the initial steps through trance induction, indicates some of the range of possibility, a range going beyond any *particular* world view or set of concepts.

An interesting account of a self-induced anesthesia appeared in a medical journal (1963), when the well-known doctor, Ainslie Meares, underwent a tooth extraction. The dental surgeon performing the operation described the details. First, an incision had to be made in the gums, laying bare the bone over the third molar. This bone was then removed with a chisel, exposing the roots of the tooth near the apices, after which the tooth was removed by forceps. No anesthetic was used. The dental surgeon asked Dr. Meares to write out his own subjective reactions.

Dr. Meares, the patient, had published widely on therapy, and had served as president of the International Society for Clinical and Experimental Hypnosis. Thus the integrity of the two doctors seems beyond question. Meares was capable of self-induced trance. Though normally sensitive to pain, he was well aware of the anesthetic possibilities of trance. He explained to the surgeon that he would signal "ready" when in the proper state of mind, and that he would also signal should it be necessary to halt the proceedings.

The idea of halting the operation never occurred to Meares. When he heard the chiseling of the bone he knew an instant's irrational anger that the surgeon might have injected anesthetic without his knowledge since he felt no pain. The doubt quickly vanished, however, since he realized that he felt every detail of the work being done, just without the pain of it. There was, further, almost no sign of blood during the operation, or any trace afterward. Dr. Meares suffered no after-effects, felt perfectly normal and took his family out to dinner that night.

Here then is the technique of the hook-swinger, the fire-walker, the cultist, adapted to specific beneficial needs by an intelligent medical man. He carried into a trance state his own ego awareness. He had predetermined the idea around which his subset would orient. He had filtered out those elements of his ordinary world that he did not want, and had set up his expectancies for those he needed to retain.

The trance part of his experience was a voluntary releasing of his ordinary logic, while logically controlling the autistic results. That portion of logic which cannot escape ambiguity, which cannot avoid the excluded possibilities, was bypassed. The secret involved is thus an inner agreement with one's self.

There is, then, this capacity of the adult to bypass the world selectively, while drawing on that world for a particular synthesis. This is only a peculiar and specialized form of the way all pursuits and disciplines work, as briefly outlined so far in my book.

Hilgard presumes that our trance experiments have so far been role-playing only, and wonders what trance possibilities there are for "inner experience" itself. If the autistic mode *were* an experience level in its own right, this might be another possibility. Evidence is so far against the notion. The necessity for some sort of guiding stimulus or triggering, some seed for synthesis, cannot be avoided. The kind of trigger, whether furnished by the conscious manipulations of a hypnotist or the cultural patterns of expectancy unconsciously assumed and synthesized, will determine the nature of the "inner experience."* That is the way it works, and no system or method, including religion and science, has yet gotten around it, because there is no place to get to—the function is the only thing there is. The light of the clearing still

* Please note the commentary in Reference section concerning Dr. Charles Tart's work in this field.

determines what is seen in the dark forest; eternity is still in love with the productions of time; and what we loose on earth is still loosed in heaven.

Carl Jung's structural analysis of the processes of mind involved various psychological "figures," as you recall from P. W. Martin's *Experiment in Depth.* These represented levels or depths of psychic experience: the friend, the shadow, the anima and animus, the old man, the final deep center. One had to have a fairly good grasp of these images beforehand, in order to comprehend them when they occurred. If they occurred to an unprepared mind, the person would not recognize the experience for what it was. It would be literally un-cognized and so lost. One must be primed beforehand for the introductions.

Now this is perfectly logical, and try as you may, you can find no way around it. Simultaneously, however, the mind has then been given the necessary materials and triggers the syntheses of the very figures under consideration. The seed will grow to fruition, as Martin pointed out, if the desire is sufficient. Do you not see the unavoidable symmetry of the problem? This in no way denigrates the profound personality healing this "integration experience" can bring about. It can surely open one to levels of experience beyond previous conception. The materials emerging seem vastly larger than the synthetic possibilities of one's own unconscious workings. The material always seems to have had an *a priori* existence. But the mirroring function is clearly evident.

Following my own absorption with Jung's works, the extent of my psychological awareness, the contents of my dreams, my hypnagogic capacities, underwent a profound enrichment and expansion. But not until my exposure to and fascination with Jung.

Somewhere around adolescence the Australian aborigine boy undergoes a rite of initiation that is probably the most extreme known to anthropology. The resulting hierarchy of mind is also the most markedly different of any known (except perhaps that world view of modern physicists.)

The young boy is taken from his mother, isolated in a wilderness spot from which he may not move on pain of death. He is starved for a prolonged number of days, kept awake at night by the terrifyng sounds of the bull-roarer (a device kept hidden until needed in the rites, and never seen by women). Finally, after this long solitude, starvation, and sleeplessness, he is suddenly surrounded by the elders in hideous body-paints and masks, and subjected to an ordeal of fear and pain against which ordinary circumcision is idle pleasantry. Through it all he must remain stock still, silent, and impassive. By this enormous shock, his psyche is very literally shattered and disintegrated. At that moment of disintegration, the inculcation of the totem world view begins. It is an elaborate and complex system, intellectual, logically cohesive, completely interrelated.

Many of the raw materials have been sensed and unconsciously assimilated, of course, throughout childhood. The sets and expectancies are all there. Nevertheless the rites initiate a logical, intellectual synthesis only available once the logical phase of normal maturation had set in.

After this, if the young man has survived, his acceptance and unquestioning, automatic response, according to his totem world, is complete. He takes his place with the two great mythical Brothers who eternally create the world. His every move is dictated by the strict traditions of what the Brothers did on that first great day of creation. These are the very movements by which creation is sustained. The stance he takes for his Dream-Time is rigorous and exact. Dream-Time is that mode of trance communication with the Brothers by which he attains that clairvoyant and telepathic rapport with his ecology—clan, animal, nature, world. The stance he takes for urination, the manner in which he runs, hurls his spear and boomerang (that most sophisticated of labor-saving implements), his mode of eating, copulation, addressing others, dancing, fire-building, painting his body, every facet of life is controlled by the taboos of his totem world.

In return, everything has meaning, a definite place in a specific hierarchy of events. His clairvoyancy and telepathy are natural results of his total rapport. He knows when his own totem food animal is in his vicinity, though a hill intervenes. At the closest point of interception, he breaks his stance, and, in the least number of moves, intercepts his game.

His discipline is complete. He is seldom bothered by choice, since his totemism decides most issues. Spontaneity is at a minimum, and, as a result, so is ambiguity. The mesh of threatening, excluded possibilities of western man plays no part in his world at all. He stands on one leg, immobile for hours, in that Dream-Time state that is apparently a cross between a nature rapport and a mystical trance. Flies crawl unmolested across his open eyes; no movement such as blinking is wasted.

Lévi-Strauss champions the aborigine totem-cosmology as an intellectual refinement as well knit and coherent as any culture's in history. Jung aped the graces of the naive realism of his day to state that primitive thinking and feeling were "exclusively concretistic," always related to "sensation." Primitive thought has no "detached independence," he wrote, but "clings to material phenomena." The primitive could not, for instance, experience the idea of the divinity as a subjective content, but the "sacred tree is the habitat," if not the deity himself. Behind such "primitive" projections, however, lay a rich intellectual scheme—as found today in our own activities. Will history recognize only *our* projection symbols, and not our intellectual schemes behind them, and so view us as we now view the "primitive"?

One aborigine explained that he knew others would come along and paint over his own cave-painting. But, he mused, "they" would see his art there, and know that, though dead, he too had once lived and painted, and they would be sad for him, and remember him. Now this is individualization—this is the keenest expression of being human. We deny soul or psyche of "real feelings" to those we are in process of removing or dominating. Just as the Germans with the Jews, we find it hard to accept that the dry statistics of dead Vietcong, for instance, could also be those who lived, felt dawn, saw sunset glow.

Lévi-Strauss was the most articulate, though not the

first, to insist that the aborigine long ago *rejected* the more common world views, by *choice,* and isolated himself to develop, undisturbed, his highly-refined and abstract intellectual cosmology. Adaptive techniques, so loved by the nineteenth century evolutionists, play almost no part in totemism. Necessity could have been met on far less rigorous terms.

George Peter Murdock, writing in 1934, summed up the destructive and limited view we have long held of man, when he wrote (apparently from second-hand information): "The idea of using skins as clothing seems never to have dawned upon the Aranda," (a central tribe of Australia). What seems never to have dawned on Murdock was to research his information before echoing the mistaken views of E. B. Tylor.

Murdock went on to say: "The Aranda cannot conceive of death from natural causes." Neither, might I add, can we. Our own medicine men, to whom word-magic and cabbalistic signs have only assumed more arrogance, give elaborate, preferably alien, awesome-to-laymen, Latin or synthetic cult-names to excuse or write off their failures.

The aborigine Dream-Time is a highly-specialized form of trance, unique as the other growths of that strange land. The aborigine has been on that continent, isolated from the rest of mankind, for at least 16,000 years, and probably much longer. His cultural expectations are not dismissible. Refinements of the system were long in building, and his Dream-Time totemism probably represents the longest unbroken intellectual scheme in man's history.

My interest here is Dream-Time itself. The aborigine may be in a state of permanent trance, or rather, trance may be the normal state of the mature aborigine. It was his socially-shared state of mind—not just "approved" as with the Balinese—and certainly not necessary for survival. Through this state, and only through it, he knew communion and relation with his gods, his world, his society, his family, and himself.

In his state of permanent trance—at least his threshold was so low as to be nonexistent—it was the Two Brothers who served as his conscious selector system, his value system directing his perceptual screening of a world. In this respect the Two Brothers could be said to serve as the hypnotist does a subject. The totem structure was developed over thousands of years. The subset was created by careful trial and error, achieving a perfect balance between mind and nature. Before dismissing the potentials of this long period, consider what science has done in only a few, short, half-dozen centuries. (And the two systems differ only quantitatively according to the kinds of choice made.)

The aboriginal subset screened out everything not needed for the intellectual refinement, precisely as the scientific world so rigorously denies and screens out the aboriginal world view. The aborigine could *use* the world of others, however, but only as needed within his own. He drew on others from strict choice, not fate. Adoption to necessity played a negligible part in his abstractions. He was the only predator on the continent except for the dingo dog which he half domesticated, after his own fashion. He had no real competition, and life supported him without trouble. None of the survival-adaptation ideology of the nineteenth century can account for the elaborate ritual of aboriginal life. His primary necessity was an intellectual craving for a system encompassing all things of his life and relating them to a single center.

Berndt was impressed and puzzled by those "miles of cave-paintings," those enormous quantities of carvings, and above all, by the series of great festivals and religious rites, lasting for weeks, that filled the aboriginal calendar. Life was one long pageant, a colorful ritual, a cosmic play. For a people considered animal-like, grazing all the time to sustain themselves, how did they possibly have the time for such frills?

Berndt speaks of the way the aborigine overcame his limited tools to produce his art as "nothing less than genius." I would point out that he always produced the kinds of tools necessary to or desired by his interests. And his interests were solely in his symbols, totems, rites, and that joyous union with the Two Brothers.

Archeology has discovered that, at one stage of his

development, the aborigine developed a splendid pottery industry, so fine it was sought by cultures from that entire area on the Pacific. The aborigine assiduously avoided use of the pottery *himself,* however, using it only for trade purposes, and probably for hallucinogens to enhance his religious ceremonies and Dream-Time experiences.

The naive viewpoint of western man, as exemplified in Murdock for instance, points to the nudity and houselessness of the aborigine as evidence of a remarkably low level of mind. Even wolves make dens, after all. But this fatuous assumption did not hold. The aborigine eschewed houses, clothing, articles and things—other than a few sacred articles, bull-roarer, spear, boomerang, a few beads and feathers as ornaments, and even his own skillfully-designed and esthetic pottery—because these things *interfered* with Dream-Time. Allegiance had to be solely to the Two Brothers, and not to acquisitions. And—know them by their fruits—the rewards of Dream-Time were greater for the aborigine than all other visible rewards from the world of the "unreal men."

The aborigine considered "sufficient unto the day were the evils thereof," and very literally took no thought of the morrow. He sought always only his own particular kingdom of heaven, and all other things were "added unto it." Jesus insisted it would be harder for a camel to get through the eye of a needle than for the rich man to get into heaven. Riches were not the point, as they were not with the aborigine; allegiance of mind was the thing. Ambiguity does not find the narrow gate. Morality or ethics is not the issue, but rather a simple, mechanical, ontological fact.

Surely the aborigine's system gave no basis for spontaneous creativity, and here the analogy with Jesus breaks down. The stringency of their system allowed neither flexibility nor adaptiveness to other systems. Aborigines were courteous as all primitives, but were seriously disoriented when intruded upon by the spontaneous and disorganized aggressions of western man. The centuries of selective isolation broke down under the white man's invasion. Outsiders were called "unreal" for logical reasons. Outsiders responded to none of the modes for a coherent and meaningful reality.

Scholars found the aborigine's powers of mind exceptional, if narrowed to specific limits. On a bright, clear day a tribe would suddenly move off in a slow, loping, loose-limbed run, twenty miles straight over a high ridge, to intercept a rainfall, rare and sacred, and also undetectable by any ordinary means from their point of departure. To test their proverbial tracking skill, a single man traveled on foot for many miles over widely-different terrain, sandy desert, marsh, rocky country, following no trail, leaving no detectable trail. The route was nevertheless followed unhesitatingly a year later by a cooperative aborigine. Their ability for "ground reading" is famous, but here the contemporaneousness with the Two Brothers was called on. The aborigine had to have an article of clothing from the man leaving the original trail. This he held while going into Dream-Time. The Two Brothers, of course, were contemporaneous with the original event itself. Having made his connections with the Two Brothers, the tracker connected with the event which was then contemporaneous with himself as well. He followed the trail rapidly, unerringly, and without pause, never giving any indication of looking for signs, should any have conceivably remained.

It might be wondered why the aborigine boy had to undergo a terrible initiation in order to enter Dream-Time and its totem world. According to my third chapter, he should have mirrored his adult world. The reason is that the adult world of Dream-Time was an abstract, intellectual construct. It was not just raw material from an informational "out there." Its logical complexity could only be grasped by a mind that had developed to the logical level, which, as Piaget points out, is in early adolescence. Then the world view developed to that point was disintegrated as a rational structure, while its acquired information was retained. The totem and dream state then acted as screens channeling percepts and determining the autistic synthesis. The system produced according to its premises, as any cohesive, logical structure should.

The aborigine, the Balinese, the Ceylonese, the doctor having a tooth extraction, all show the wide scope and variety of the trance state, and suggest its potential, and its limitation. Trance states repeat the basic process by which world views originally form in the mind, by first bypassing that world view and opening the autistic or unconscious to restructuring. The triggers for the new syntheses are given either by a conscious directive or by assumed cultural expectancies. These serve as concepts for the directing of percepts in new ways. Trance is a dramatic, if temporary and limited, kind of *metanoia.*

In my second chapter I mentioned some ways of dissolving the categories that make up our shared world, and spoke disparagingly of any great truths to be gained thereby. An extraordinary and beautiful little volume has recently (1968) been published that at first glance calls my assumption to question. On close examination, however, the volume, entitled *The Teachings of don Juan,* verifies my contention. The author, a young anthropologist named Carlos Castaneda, is probably one of the bravest and most intelligent persons I have ever read about, and I plainly loved don Juan, the Yaqui Indian Sorcerer, of whom Carlos wrote with rightful respect, reverence, and awe. I envied Castaneda his experience, frightful and hazardous as it was, with that vigorous and powerful old magician who, at seventy, still saw life as a great adventure opening ever before him.

For the first year of his growing friendship with don Juan, Carlos tried unsuccessfully to get information about "mescalito," the peyote cactus that is hallucinogenic. He knew that an elaborate ritual and tradition surround the Indian practice, and that the plant itself was of small value. Finally don Juan agreed, not just to tell Carlos about "mescalito," but, surprisingly, to initiate him into the actual "path of knowledge itself," the entire practice of Yaqui magic. Don Juan had seen in Carlos a possible heir of the ancient way itself.

First, though, Carlos must be sure of his own heart. Unbending intent was the prime requisite. Clarity of mind, singleness of devotion, and other qualities must be carefully built up if one were to survive the deadly dangers of the path, perils that could so easily kill a man or rob him of his soul.

Hallucinogens were the gateway, but hardly the path. Ingested by the uneducated and unguided, the plants destroy or produce only horror. A long, detailed instruction and a hard, self-disciplined life were necessary preliminaries and constant requisites. Fear was a major stumbling block and had to be faced, acknowledged, accepted, and gone beyond. Power when it came, and it would come, was a temptation to be spurned if further progress was to be realized. The practice would lead into the right way to live, though there was no goal other than the *way* itself. Death was the final victor and one's impermanence had to be accepted.

The hallucinogens themselves were used sparingly, and then only after the proper instruction and elaborate, intricate preparations. A full year of acquaintance passed before even the first, introductory hallucinogen was tried. This initiatory move was hardly made by an unprepared mind, although no specific talks about it had taken place. Associative learning is no small force, even if unconscious, and Carlos' background of inquiry into the Southwest Indians, his scientific detachment coupled with an adventurous, inquiring mind, his growing respect for don Juan, his avid desire to learn of the Indian world view, all entered as factors making this a deeply-serious undertaking. Carlos was aware of the dangers of his undertaking, and his whole set of mind made him susceptible to many cues that an untrained or uncommitted observer, looking only for personal titillation, would never have brought into the relationship. Thus there was an indeterminable amount of serious, unconscious exchange between the two men.

Two full years of instruction passed before don Juan thought Carlos ready for the really serious business of "introduction to an *ally.*" This ally was a "spirit" that would give assistance in moving in non-ordinary reality, if they were successful in *taming* the ally, which apparently meant successfully bringing about the necessary state for introduction, *surviving* the rigors of the hallucinogen used, and coming to grips with the peculiarities of the resulting state. Through the ally the apprentice could gain that unlimited power which could transport a man beyond the "boundaries of himself," and open to the really great fields beyond, traveling freely through different reality states. Each specific drug experience was followed by long periods of evaluation and digestion of the events that had transpired during the experience. Don Juan's techniques of evaluation skilfully guided the course of future *expectancies.* Certain occurrences were dismissed as unimportant by don Juan, though Carlos could not distinguish the reason for the value of others which were seized upon and heavily emphasized and approved by don Juan. This, note, was the equivalent of those childhood experiences that are dismissed and those that are complimented and rewarded by superiors though the child sees no difference in value himself. Negative and positive reward-reactions are strong, suggestive triggers toward future acceptances and rejections, and we see the way in which Carlos made a transference to don Juan, and underwent a reshaping of conceptual framework.

The actual state of non-ordinary reality, or the state of "special consensus," varied. Often the materials of Carlos' surroundings became the basis of the new state, but increasingly the non-ordinary materials of his previous experiences became the materials for further synthesis in new experiences, as shaped by don Juan's evaluation techniques. At times Carlos' perceptions themselves underwent change in relation to his ordinary reality. Objects glowed with their own light and Carlos could see quite clearly in the darkest night, across the hills, close up, and so on. At times solid objects lost their solidity and Carlos passed through them—one of his most frightful ordeals.

Each of the hallucinogen families had its special techniques for approach, its particular purpose, and its unique non-ordinary reality reward. Each hallucinogen group was consistent in the kinds of state created, though, of course, each required its own unique period of instruction, preparation, and sets of mind.

The states of special consensus had three common

characteristics. They were *stable*. Carlos could not distinguish any difference between the non-ordinary reality components, the things, materials, physical objects, of his special states. The materials of those states remained stationary for minute and repeated examination. They could be returned to as ordinary reality objects. They did not shift and flow as in a dream sequence, Secondly, they possessed *singularity*. Every detail of the components was a single, individual item, existing of itself, isolated from other details. The non-ordinary reality was composed of solid, stable objects, as in ordinary reality. The experiences contained an inner coherency, the overall reality was cohesive and indistinguishable from any ordinary state. There was no flux of detail, no blurring of the guidelines, as in LSD or mescalin experiences, for instance. Carlos was aware of being *in* a special state; the occurrences followed unusual sequences and cause-effect patterns, but there was no dream quality to distinguish the special reality from the ordinary. Except, that is, the third characteristic: lack of ordinary consensus. The perceptions of the non-ordinary states were in complete solitude.

Consider, now, that the guide in this long procedure was an intelligent, pragmatic Mexican Indian with many centuries of tradition behind him. He taught Carlos "exactly as his own benefactor had taught him." The complex system had been handed down by just such relationships since time immemorial.

The capacity for unconscious exchange between hypnotist and subject has been mentioned before. Cohen spoke, you recall, of a Freudian analyst's patient immediately reflecting Freudian symbolism when under LSD, verifying the assumptions of the analyst, (the same holding, of course, for Jungians). The effects of unconscious exchange can be safely assumed for the Australian aboriginal initiation rites. P. W. Martin mentioned in his *Experiment in Depth* that one's unconscious immediately reflected and responded to all the attention given it, greatly increasing the flow of unconscious material. (I found this to be very much the case.)

Anthropologists keep finding more and more evidence

of great civilizations in the early Americas. Those civilizations are now seen to extend many thousands of years further into the past than previously suspected. Evidence indicates that the Indians of our continent were remnants of very advanced and complex civilizations. The achievements of the mound-builders in our own Mid-west put to shame our original notions of our innate superiority, and the "concept of the primitive" is undergoing profound, if belated, change.

Not to be discounted, then, is the full extent of the "archetypal" heritage don Juan possessed. And Carlos, a true anthropologist (that is, free of that obnoxious chauvinism that destroys), opened to and entered into don Juan's frame of reference to *learn*. He was susceptible, by cast of personality and profession, to the drama, rich historical atmosphere, and emotional investments of a once-powerful race.

All this entered into those long months of instructions from don Juan, as he and Carlos would sit on the dirt porch, in their particular "places of strength," where one did not tire but was renewed from the earth. Twilight, don Juan told Carlos, was the crack between the two worlds. Little by little don Juan prepared Carlos to find that crack. When the crack appeared, Carlos did not enter ignorant or empty-handed.

So we find that what Carlos experienced under "mescalito," the peyote cactus, the sacred mushroom, or the Jimson weed, was vastly different from that which the marginally-adjusted sensation-seeker could possibly discover. Recall Jesus' admonition to the man gathering grain on the Sabbath: "If you know *what* you are doing, you are blest. If you know *not* what you are doing, you are accurst and a transgressor of the Law."

Don Juan left very little to chance, or not-knowing. The system was thorough; centuries had gone into its perfection, and it produced exactly according to its precepts and intent.

Ingesting or smoking the hallucinatory plants dissolved the ordinary categories of reality for Carlos, just as the initiation shocks of the aborigine dissolved the natural world view of the young man, and just as the person under hypnosis voluntarily leaves his structured world to play at fantasy. Dr. Meares carried over into his actual operation a certain set of assumptions which altered the reality of that procedure so that blood, pain and after-effects did not enter as parts of that reality. The Ceylonese Hindu fire-walker also comes to mind.

In the same way, Carlos carried into his non-ordinary states the long instruction period's products. Don Juan had so thoroughly traversed the paths for certain portions of the system he himself no longer needed the threshold-lowering hallucinogens. He stepped from one world to the other at will, and led his protégé carefully and well. It was, in fact, the onslaught of this phenomenon of spontaneous threshold dissolution that horrified Carlos and terminated his apprenticeship after six years.

Critics have complained that Castaneda's dry analyses in the back of his book were in effect a "sellout" to the mechanistic gods of the time. This is unfair and misses the point. Had don Juan been completely successful, no one would ever have known. That Carlos *did* sustain his sharp, trained intellect throughout these traumatic, often dreadful experiences, and retain his analytical perspective, is in itself a remarkable display of strength of mind. His analysis is not only logical, it is far more awesome than some cultic enthusiasm might have produced.

Surely Castaneda in no way disbelieved that other world. Perhaps it was its all-too-frightful reality from which he had to retreat finally in order to hope to stay in this one. In no way does Carlos denigrate or diminish the authenticity of the states of mind so created. In no way does he call into question the possibility that those states might exist, somehow, within their own right, as self-sufficient possibilities of organization within the discipline. The creative element was clearly recognizable to him as was the archetypal potential. He recognized the two-way interaction between the drugs, the relation with don Juan which shaped the expectancies, and the necessity of unquestioned following of instructions. In spite of his remarkable objectivity and his final analysis, Carlos never retreated to scientific dodge or psychological cliché. He accepted his experiences for what they were: non-ordinary reality states created by a complex interplay of carefully-controlled events, a definition which might fit ordinary reality except for the element of control itself.

In his Foreword to *don Juan*, Walter Goldschmidt clearly points up the real importance of anthropology to "this entering into other worlds than our own." This leads us, he writes, to realize that our own world is "also a cultural construct." This has been the whole thrust of this first part of my own book, to claim that no other world could ever *be* for us except through the very creative technique found underlying these dramatically differing pursuits; that this process has happened to us, but can be consciously controlled.

Goldschmidt realizes the intriguing riddle to lie in don Juan's *twilight*—that crack between the worlds. Goldschmidt concludes, however, that through this crack we can then see, fleetingly, what the *"real world,* the one between our own cultural constructs and those other worlds, must in fact be like." Here, I do believe, we have an example of the perpetual error at one remove. The "crack between the worlds" is neither a "real world" nor an opening into such—for there is no such thing as a "real world" other than that one from which one makes such a statement. The crack is only a capacity, an ontological function, a possibility for processing an infinite number of worlds—none of which is absolute. To leave one you can only structure another one or face dissolution.

I was particularly struck with the frustrations Carlos and don Juan faced in trying to reach a consensus of what was actually achieved during the non-ordinary states. Carlos tried to elicit from don Juan a description of what he, Carlos, looked like to don Juan when he, Carlos, was to himself a crow, flying in beautiful skies with other beautiful crows. Don Juan insisted he *had* been a crow. Carlos asked, though, about his *body:* it had not changed had it?; surely it was the same body as it ordinarily was? Don Juan said of course it was not the same body at all. Carlos countered that surely only his *mind* had been a crow; surely his *body* had not flown? Of *course* your body flew, was don Juan's retort, that's what the devil's weed is *for*. So Carlos asked whether, if friends of his had been there to see him, they would have seen him as a crow. That, don Juan answered, depended on his friends. If they understood about the *devil's weed* they would certainly have done so. Finally, Carlos asked don Juan what would happen, say, if he tied himself to a large rock by a heavy chain before flying? Don Juan looked at him incredulously and replied that he would certainly have to fly holding the rock with its heavy chain.

Reading this brought back memories of my equally frustrated evenings with my mathematical neighbor and those topological eggs he could remove from the shell without damage to the shell, through his mathematical four-spaces, and my trying so desperately to link it up with a tangible concreteness that I could grasp. The situation between don Juan and Carlos was surely analogous to that of the nonbeliever who asked Jesus for a sign, a miracle, that he might then believe in him. And of course the dilemma was that the sign could only be given through belief—the two in agreement—suspending the ordinary for the non-ordinary.

Mathematical magic has built magical machines now quite in the ascendancy. Don Juan's magic created magical places to go, but they are almost extinct. I sensed some of don Juan's sadness that his great adventure was fading from this earth as a meaningful mark of a "warrior"—the reward for bravery and skill. His enormous powers were of no use anymore. Surely he could clip the tops of the tallest trees in his great leaps—but it only scared his own Indians, who no longer understood, while the white man only saw something blurry and dismissible in the treetops.

The path of knowledge was no longer important maybe, but to *have* a path of knowledge, a path with a *heart,* made for a joyful journey, and was the only conceivable way to live. Don Juan had spent his life traversing his path, and intended going to its fullest and final length "looking, looking, breathlessly."

Don Juan advised us to think carefully about our paths before we set out on them. For by the time a man discovers that his path "has no heart," the path is ready to kill him. At that point, he cautions, very few men can stop to deliberate, and *leave that path.* Surely the nuclear Pentagon madness of our day bears out his analysis.

So now my book leads, as did my search, to its final goal—another kind of path, strangely similar to don Juan's, as unique, as difficult in vastly different ways, with an even more daring goal. I believe it is a path with a heart—though I must recognize that it is only one of an infinite number of possible paths, and that no heavenly hierarchy sanctions it or gives it a final edge. This path hinges on analyzing the process by which paths function, and, as don Juan would say, by exercising the self-confidence to claim knowledge as power, seizing the tiller by which realities are made.

8

mythos and logos

The discoveries we make at the edge of our "clearing in the forest" are given shape by the nature of our looking. There is no way of looking at the forest except by the light of our own reason, and this light determines the particular kind of forest then seen.

The kind of looking we *can* do is itself determined by and limited to previous interactions between forest and clearing. We stand on ground that is the whole human venture. Having become subservient to our own technology, however, we see ourselves split off from our continuity leading *to* this technology. We misinterpret the nature of both clearing and forest and think our current ground newly discovered terrain having no relation to past clearings, rather than recognizing where we stand to be a metaphoric mutation of that ground. We interpret our mutations of this inherited web of concepts as discoveries of fixed absolutes "out there." Looking at our past only through our mutation of it, we seem isolated from it. On the other hand, we recognize the baggage we have had to bring with us to be the same old trunk. So we interpret ourselves as clever animals who, having found a hole in the zoo's fence, have wandered into alien territory. Unable to deny our physical inheritance from the past we have become overly fascinated with it, while denying and ignoring our psychological heritage which has been the real formative agent.

Our new historical research is thorough. We may know more about certain past eras than the participants of those periods themselves. Our relation to the past is not so important from the standpoint of mechanical developments contributing to science, however, as it is to the growth of a psyche, the emergence of a thinking earth that built up this network of concepts, now capable of almost infinite synthesis. To accept our physical mode of being as ancient and formative, and yet fail to grant the psychic mode the same status is to help split our world in half.

Archaic cultures had a skimpy history at best, but they possessed rich myths, traditions, and symbols, giving continuity, purpose, and meaning. Ancestors, for instance, played a vital role. Recitation of one's lineage gave a secure place in time, a sense of personal participation in a long drama. Genealogy, learned from memory and half-symbolic fantasy, often reached back to the very gods. Ancestor worship expressed an archetypal imagery indicating a cultural continuity with the whole scheme of life. One's forebears had not just "joined the god," but were, in effect, the gods themselves. Jesus' Fatherhood of God, Sonship of man, Father Abraham, and "before Abraham was, I am," indicate this shaping of a god by the whole history of man.

Interpreting history from a scientific rather than psychological viewpoint alienates us from Blake's "larger body of man," our true self. We can be integrated with ourselves, and understand our true position and potential, only by personally experiencing the full mode of our mind, which is a mind that shades into the past.

The average man cannot contemplate such things as deeper processes of mind so long as "those that know" deny their existence. And the ideologies presently strangling us *do* deny the peripheral areas of mind. The current vogue ignores mind and concentrates on biology. There is a kind of nihilistic fascination in pointing out that since we must ingest food, defecate, and copulate, we are only another animal. This constitutes massive denial of our true selves. It is a repetition of our old and chronic "failure of nerve." For we are larger than the sum total of the mechanisms of our form. There is no being but in a mode of being, and each thrust of life incorporates previously-developed forms of expression, but our form should not blind us to our content.

Language plays the dominant role in the shaping of our world view and world-to-view. We know now that language is not a mode of animal communication. Surely animals communicate. Recent studies of the higher apes compel such a conclusion. But language is far more than communication. Animals communicate without language and without symbols. Susanne Langer points out that language deals not just with some higher form of general animal function, but with a *new function* developed in the hominid brain. More than mentality is involved in language. Language is a function of such complexity that not one, "but many subhuman mental activities underlie it."

C. E. Bitterman, of Bryn Mawr, has offered a theory of *discontinuity* in the evolutionary growth of mind that substantiates Langer's quarrel with biogenetic psychology, and may well indicate a wider tendency in life. The old idea of evolution saw the growth of "cephalization," or *mind,* as an additive process, simply building up more complex patterns of a basic brain function. Bitterman shows, however, that new mental functions, found in widely variant steps in ascending species, are not just additive parts, basic replications of a mechanism. They are, instead, *radical discontinuities* introducing entirely new functions and possibilities.

Old functions might give hints of a direction for new possibility, but no quantitative manipulation of the old can produce the new. There is a qualitative addition. This addition is from that creative spark that leaps the logical gaps with naive ease. The development of a new life form follows, then, the same creative pattern found in the formation of the *Eureka!* illumination, the *metanoia,* the radical discovery experience. It is another expression of the same thrust.

Speech is radically discontinuous with those life forms leading up to it. Speech serves no adaptive purpose, no "pair-group" survival function, as the naive realists claim. Yet speech *was* developed by life, and its purpose can be understood from its real function, a function long championed by Langer and slowly being grasped by others. This purpose has been spelled out here in my book. It was part of the development of a system of logical choice, of value judgment, and of projected symbol-making, through which new possibilities for reality could be consciously directed. This was a radical step of universal significance, and life leaped the gap with a discontinuity between old and new.

The cause of the need is the cause of the fulfillment of the need, as Langer quotes Flüger. The passionate question created its own answer, or, as Tillich would say, the divine answer was shaped by the existential question. That a formative, creative force should evolve from an ape-like creature is no more puzzling than that the earliest automobiles were literally horseless-carriages. That man sits in the same vehicle does not mean that the internal-combustion engine is really just a horse.

This discontinuity in the growth of mind makes ridiculous our current attempts to equate man with the lower animals. Langer doubts that we can rely on any built-in behavior patterns. The range of our possible actions has been so enormously widened by our conceptual powers—imagination, conception, and speculation—that "no inherited repertoire could fit the contingencies" of our world. Skinner may have enjoyed his ping-pong-playing pigeons, but then to presume that the mind of *man* could be controlled by turning on the right lights, pushing the right buttons, is the most unrealistic of naive-realistic fantasies.

The failure of psychology rests squarely on its inability to deal with the *psyche* itself. Mental phenomena comprise the one area that has frustrated psychology. So for several generations now psychologists have busied themselves with something they *could* manipulate, the worm, the rat, the dog, the poor hairy ape. But the correspondences they have so laboriously made have proved thin material.

In recent years there has been a renewed attack on consciousness, declaring it nothing more than electrochemical discharges in a complex adaptive device. As a result, psychology has not only failed to grow as the other sciences, but has surely failed in its logical role of filling the vacuum left by religion.

Among other things, Langer blames the failure of psychology on its inability to allow the "heavy strains of bold, speculative hypothesis to be laid on it." Not only has psychology failed to provide us with the material for a new mythos, by which a truly modern culture could form, it has fed directly into the self-abrogation and denial on which such atavistic and destructive nonsense as the *Naked Ape* ideology has leeched out its obscene existence.

Langer writes that despite man's zoological status the gulf between the highest animal and the most primitive of humans is fundamental. This difference she attributes to the human brain and its use of symbols.

A culture, in Langer's terms, is the symbolic expression of developed habitual ways of experience as a whole. This symbolic expression takes on a mythical form. Jerome Bruner claims that personality imitates myth in as deep a sense as myth is an externalization of personality. Society patterns itself on "idealizing myths," and the individual man is only able to "bring order to his internal clamor of identities in terms of prevailing myth." Life, writes Bruner, produces myth and finally imitates it. This, I would note, suggests a kind of mirroring.

As a result, Bruner says, our standard of what is humanly possible is profoundly affected by our view of ourselves. We act ourselves into ways of believing and believe ourselves into ways of acting.

Our current views of human possibility set up contradicting and fragmenting paradoxes. We view ourselves ironically on the one hand, and assume boastful posturings on the other. We unleash forces and feel ourselves capable of unlocking secrets of the universe. At the same time we feel largely dissociated from and fated to our very actions.

Northrop Frye, in his *Four Essays,* writes of the *alazon,* the impostor who pretends to be more than he is, the *miles glorious.* On the other hand is the *eiron,* the man who deprecates himself. Our modern image plays the *alazon* in that we pretend to be unique from previous developments; superior, because of our science and gadgets, to all other cultures in spite of a lack of a cohesive culture of our own. And we play the *eiron* in that we deprecate ourselves—considering ourselves but a clever ape, able by some freak to catch on to a mechanism *a priori* and superior to us. Thus we suffer guilt and fear of reprisal over our manipulations of nature, and a sense of alienation from our continuum, our ecology, our fellows, and ourselves.

Langer points out, as did Jerome Bruner, that we live in a web of ideas, a fabric of our own making. "The activity of imagining reality is the center of experience," she claims. The average man, though, picks up his symbols and ideas for imagining from "those that know." He may never analytically understand the workings of the various disciplines that shape his time, but he senses the general frame of their reference, and becomes very much aware of the drift of their conclusions. He does not contemplate serious matters often. Abstract and logically developed ideas "seep into the untutored thought only as concrete, familiar models are found to picture them."

The concrete models by which he is able to picture the current view of himself are destructive to him, fated, and strip him of hope. As a bit of thinking protoplasm, caught on this cold cinder for his brief second, without rhyme or reason, what else to do but jostle for a bit of snatched hedonism, soon palling, before the time runs out? It is not just fortuitous that those promulgating the images of despair then capitalize *on* that despair.

We blithely accept the ideology of a Naked Ape viewpoint, while equally dismissing what should be at *least* the other side of the coin, Jung's archetypal imagery: those "primordial images (that) are the most ancient and the most universal 'thought-forms' of humanity." The reason for the dismissal is not hard to find. Blind urges, instincts, glandular responses that jerk us about as puppets on strings, are legitimate to the current tough-minded nihilisms. "You can't change human nature" is the favorite Pentagon rationale for murder. Thought-forms inherited from the past suggest that man is more than simply another animal. And power over, domination and control, feed best on deprecations of the human, hardly on granting him esteem and value. If thought is a force of its own, capable of being sustained as a cultural or racial continuity, though not too susceptible to analysis, small wonder the current nihilisms evade it as a viable and independent force in life.

Langer warns that the cultural losses to science should not be taken lightly. She does not see science likely to "beget a culture" unless and until a truly universal artistic imagination "catches fire from its torch and serves without deliberate intent to give shape to a new feeling," by which she means a new realm of tangible, commonly-shared experience. A scientific mentality capable of filling this new need would have to go beyond anything called by its name today. It would have to encompass mind, growth, language, history, and produce social concepts that have meaning for a humanity "which inhabits the whole earth and reaches for the other stars."

Such a new cultural concept would have to include all mental phenomena, all experiences of mind, and from a phenomenological standpoint, not from the conventional dogmas of laboratory duplication and control. The mind is more than that. It is an open system of synthesis, not a simple biological mechanism as small minds, unable to grapple with large issues, try to make it.

Langer defines mental experience as *feeling*—the generic basis of all mental experience, sensation, emotion, imagination, recollection, reasoning, and so on. She does not like the term *unconscious,* but speaks of "many cerebral acts that are not mental," though they may modify mental acts. She qualifies *mental acts* as those centering in the brain and that are *felt,* that have some psychic phase. A great deal of cerebration, she notes, goes on "below the limen of feeling, or experience."

Mistrusting *unconscious* also, I have used the term *autistic,* which is, of course, but jargon substitution, for this activity "below the limen of feeling." I have suggested that the function runs into a continuum beyond analysis, that it shades smoothly at some point into that organization of energy we call *matter*.

Langer feels that a psychology oriented by her concept

would run smoothly into physiology without losing its identity. I would like to urge an even more comprehensive and vigorous psychology, pursuing Langer's direction even further, an examination of mind that runs as smoothly into *physics* itself. Only then will we realize fully the activity of thought, and the rightful potential of man.

Life then becomes an integrated process of interdependent functions. Much of our problem is in a failure to recognize the unique roles of the different functions. To view ourselves only from the standpoint of the tangible mental acts, what I have termed reality-adjusted reason, if I read Langer correctly, is to seriously miss the capacity and meaning of mind, and thus, as Jung claimed, to miss the meaning and capacity of man.

Langer sounds akin to Teilhard when she writes of a "vast change in society, nothing less than a biological shift of functions to new structures." This shift has disrupted cultural patterns for which we have no replacement. What is lacking is a sufficiently large *mythos* to encompass our new capabilities.

Modern man needs a definite and adequately big "world-image," Langer writes, stating what we all surely recognize, that our "world-image has collapsed." Powerful concepts are needed to cope with the welter of new conditions that beset us, she continues, and going "back to Kant, back to Plato," and so on, will not give us the abstract, powerful, and novel ideas needed for our time.

An adequately large image of man can never be less than one encompassing all aspects of man's mind, including that problematic and intangible level "below the limen of feeling." No concept will be powerful enough to cope with the welter of new conditions unless it takes into account the true nature of man's mind as a shaping force in reality, a force that has brought about the very reality needing the new concepts.

Teilhard de Chardin claimed that the central idea of the Christian Gospel was that the universe is *a creative process carried on by man's imagination, an operative power.* In Teilhard's view, the universe is "capable of becoming more supple, more fully animate."

Mircea Eliade saw the thrust of life culminating in Jesus as nothing less than *man's freedom to intervene in the ontological constitution of the universe.*

Now these are surely bold claims, bold enough to qualify for Langer's new needs. We are blocked from hearing the worth in them, however, by the milieu from which they arise. We have experienced such a nonsensical, paradoxical, and harmful parade of posturings from Christendom in the past that such notions as Teilhard's and Eliade's seem untenable. The very imagery in which such ideas arise blocks us from hearing them.

Christendom's long prate concerning the absolute division between God and Man, the unholy dangers of man's assuming godly proportion, has become fixed in our ears. The strident voice of the priest, warning us of the dragon before the Tree of Life, is archetypal. Though we now dismiss the metaphors involved, the notion is ingrained and has had its effect in producing an ideology of the *eiron.* The old notion is now projected onto pseudoscientific imagery. The new priest poses as the Naked Ape.

As our world-image has collapsed, our image of God has collapsed. Carl Jung felt that the "weight of history is unbearable without the idea of God." But he also noted that once metaphysical ideas have lost their capacity to recall and evoke the original experience, they have not only become useless "but prove to be actual impediments on the road to wider development." Jesus' fury over the Pharisees was that they "stood at the gate and would not let others through." The symbol of God may have become esthetically and intellectually offensive. The enormous gap between representations of God by the preachers and theologians and the actualities of life presents a paradox that modern man will simply not tolerate.

Jung considered the God-image a complex of ideas, of an archetypal nature necessarily regarded as representing a certain sum of energy which appears as a projection—that is, is seen as something "out there" and absolutely-other when it is really an inward condition that is unconscious, or, as Langer would say, "below the limen of feeling." And so, before dismissing the projection called God, it would be fruitful to examine closely the inward situation that triggers the projection.

In this book I have used the metaphors *forest* and *clearing* for our reality and its potential, or for reality-adjusted thinking and that continuum of possible synthesis triggered by passionate desire. I have claimed that the correspondences and boundaries between the functions are and always will be obscure. Obscure because conscious looking is a search for verification of the notions that impel the search, and always has a circular, mirroring element in it.

Imagination nevertheless opens to syntheses larger than the sum total of reason. Something from the dark forest seems to be added to or encompassed by the creative vision from our clearing. The new structures "found" in the forest always reflect the expanding light from the clearing, but are always more than logical synthesis can produce. There is a form of *radical discontinuity* in every truly creative idea or discovery. And so *projection,* while no doubt the case, is not the whole case. It involves *more than* the logical mode of thinking that does the projecting.

The clearing in the forest, our reality-adjusted thinking, hinges on a common bond of objective agreement. The threshold between this kind of thinking and the forest itself I have called the *autistic* mode. Reality-thinking, autistic thinking, and that logically necessary empty category, the unconscious continuum, are all of a piece. You cannot have one without the other. Each implies the other; none are the other; none can *be* except by or in the other. The process of reality is an interaction between the three. They are not discontinuous. They merge slowly and imperceptibly into each other.

To speak of nature or reality as though such a category exists independently of the categorizing function that *speaks* of it is every bit as one-sided and presumptuous as to suppose that no nature exists except as a categorizing function of mind, or to presume that a function of mind could operate outside the matrix of a nature. We can only explore how our categorizing influences the categories that we find ourselves in. The meshing of these components I have called the mirror-to-mirror function, realizing that the simplistic one-to-one correspondence implied has to be sharply and constantly qualified. An element of randomness writes a question mark over all our efforts.

By now I think I have laid some groundwork for a defense of that saying by Jesus that "what we loose on earth is loosed in heaven," and I believe we have the materials for updating and reinterpreting the ontological insights afforded us by that genius's metaphor "heaven." If the religious metaphors prove archaic and stand in the way, they should be thrown out. But save the *function* toward which they point. Perhaps we cannot re-bottle that new wine of his; the old skins into which it was immediately put, in spite of his pleas, have probably soured it beyond redemption. But within his postulates might reside the formula by which we can make some new wine for our new, if empty, bottles.

This function of mirroring is found in the trance state in a simple, direct, but limited way. It is found in the transference procedure in general. It underlies the question-answer process, the formation of postulates, the discoveries of science, the workings of the creative imagination, and all those "radical discontinuities" of life.

By now we should be able to see that the thinking we call God and the thinking we call man are all of a piece. The differences are functional. The process cannot work well so long as the differences are misunderstood, projected rather than stood under and accepted.

The autistic mode is equally everything, the way by which "all things are in all places at the same time," as suggested by Whitehead. Physics sees the relation through its own prism—and there is no other way to see—recognizing that the farthest thing in the universe influences the closest. The metaphors for interpretation are endless, but each metaphor shapes the reality then experienced as the function.

This open capacity of synthesis has no value judgment since to judge as value is to choose, limit, and close in on a specific, that is, to become that chosen. In order to choose and limit *consciously*, and still openly synthesize, another process of thinking has evolved—*man*. The evolutionary development of this new function may well have been trial and error, random chance, or purposive, as Teilhard believed. To presume one or the other is equally arbitrary though reality influencing. Nevertheless, life *has* created the means for a conscious directing of potential and *we* are the means, aware of it or not, liking it or not.

This new procedure attempted by life, that of creating a system of logical selection from an open capacity, is ornate and complex, beset with problems and subject to enormous variations and breakdowns. No small part of the problem is the vehicle itself, this "hominid creature," carrying within him eons of triggered responses. The simple mirroring model I have drawn is qualified by our inheritance—from the simplest energy forms on up. The infinite contingency of nature makes the problem of structuring an open system ornately complex.

Carington believed that any idea expresses itself unless inhibited by other ideas. In an infinitely contingent universe, operating by profusion, ideas expressed must of necessity be at least partially compatible and mutually non-inhibiting. Everything tends to strike a balance, with all forms tending to perpetuate themselves. As Bohm pointed out, such balances are only temporary, the very forces bringing about a balance working equally to change. The slow breakdown of such forms, and creation of others, makes no difference to an autistic, non-judging, criteria-free system that is "equally all things."

The development of self-consciousness, necessary for value and conscious directing of potential, poses a multitude of problems. To be self-conscious is to be aware of the dissolution. Further, each person then has the capability of organizing a unique reality picture, as exemplified, for instance, in don Juan. (The problem of stress this creates at early adolescence is fascinating, but must await a further work.) Chaos is the underlying threat of the open system become self-conscious. Thus the self-modification demanded by a common agreement, necessary for a common world view and a society, is also a natural source of conflict. Organizing a common reality seems to be bought at the price of individuality. Ideally the flexible personality could enter into such common agreements without loss of self. Underlying the ultra-conservative's paranoia is his *inability* to enter into sub-sets of reality play other than his own. Once he has modified to a world view he is frozen into it. Alien views become threats to his very universe.

Even this brief attempt to touch on the problem of form and content starts branching exponentially, like a tree at every tip, and must be ignored now to get back to the subject at hand. And that point is the need of a modern *mythos* sufficient to give a cultural symbol for organization—one that will not be bought at too great a price of potential.

Such a mythos must be psychological, based on the ramifications of personality and thought, not on media, technology, or any of our products. We are infinitely more than our things. It is our capacity of production, not our products, that is the key.

Parapsychology failed also to materialize as an opening through which our position might have clarified. Like the figures of don Juan and Jesus, though, it gives indications of the overall picture. Jule Eisenbud gives amusing accounts, as did William James three-quarters of a century ago, of the resistance of colleagues to any suggestion of a parapsychological element in man. Eisenbud pinpoints part of the reason. Psychical data suggests that man has within him untapped powers and any data offering evidence of man's being more than a naked ape is met with powerful negation. Within a generation after James's death, the tough-minded were attributing to fraud all the extraordinary events he tried to get his fellow-professors to witness. One thinks of Galileo and his telescope. Recognition of James's and Eisenbud's phenomena would lead to every bit as upsetting a crack in the egg as Galileo's, an occurrence that will not be tolerated by current priesthoods.

Eisenbud agrees with Jung and the depth psychologists that the culprit is the split of consciousness from unconsciousness, the "Fall" in mythological terms. The split is widening, too, Eisenbud claims. Man has tended to project farther and farther from himself his responsibility for the evil that goes on around him. Modern times may have really begun, writes Eisenbud, when man could project his own will for the death of others onto some "out there" power and say: "I didn't do it, he did."

Eisenbud points out that the conspiracy of denial and rejection followed by science, concerning that "below the limen of feeling," is bred into its very marrow. All potential not funneled through their peculiar view of fate is dismissed as not even happening, as occult, delusion, *folie à deux,* mass hallucination. Avis Dry turned out a very scholarly study of the "schizophrenia" of Carl Jung.

We tend to think of the Golden Age of Greece, that short half-century of magnificence five hundred years before Jesus' birth, as the Greek part of our Greco-Hebraic heritage. It was the post-Platonic Greece of the Stoics that molded our western history, however, that same "failure-of-nerve" thinking to which Singer attributed the death of early science. Some scholars attributed to Greece the breaking with the archetypal cyclic world view, introducing the objective mode of thinking leading to science. But, as Polanyi and others point out, the Greeks destroyed only the *unity* of man and his world, while leaving intact that *world* as a cyclic unit. In the resulting Greek representation of reality, man is a passive and helpless bit of protoplasm caught in the grindstones of fated cosmic forces. This was the very view that crushed Jesus' new ideas, and used his imagery as expression of this very fate.

At root is the age-old battle, whether to recognize the mind as a whole unit encompassing its reality or to split the mind from its wholeness. Religion and science too often prove blood brothers beneath their different vestments, and man proves the victim of their civil war.

Clear lines of demarcation between cyclic and historical thinking are not easily drawn. More to the point is that both attitudes are ever-present in varied ways. What depth psychologists fail to understand or point out is that the split of mind between conscious and unconscious thinking is a necessity for the mind to achieve objectivity.

In order to become aware of the function of reality, the mind has somehow to stand outside itself, which it apparently can do only by projection. To attribute to some absolutely-other thing or symbol a process of our own thinking entails a split of mind which splits the reality. But objective thinking necessarily involves projection. It is a form of empty-categorizing that fills itself, a form of myth-making and realization, the way by which life bounds forward.

The projection device is not so easily replaced. I am not sure that new content can structure without forms of it. Surely projection of absolutes "out there" played a decisive role in the development of science. The problem is that the projection turns on the projector and becomes a fixed concept controlling the direction of new projections. The physicist projects his imaginary particle or wave, which, because it appears utterly remote from anything human, is thought to be the ultimate reality.

Blake anticipated Eisenbud's appreciation of this kind of madness, two hundred years ago. Blake saw that the inversion of Stoic thinking led to the deadness of the stone as the only real, while the enormous capacity of life, the imagination of man, is considered the most unreal.

Piaget's stages of logical development enter the picture. To be more than an infant in the ecological womb, man has to dissociate himself from the process which he is. To develop your mind to the point where the faith of a grain of mustard seed *can* move mountains, you have to dissociate yourself from the very function by which mountains can so move. By the time you develop *to* that point of conceptual ability, your very process of logical development will have split your mind so thoroughly that the idea of moving mountains cannot be entertained unambiguously. This is why *metanoia*—that adult transformation of world view—is the only apparent way around the dilemma.

Perhaps life will discover a way by which the paradox can be overcome. That is, a way in which the development of logic will not destroy the autistic openness. Hilgard's studies indicate partial accomplishment of this. The intriguing figure of Mozart comes to mind. His reality adjustment was rather poor, granted, but he apparently displayed almost from the beginning a complete openness to creative synthesis, operating beautifully within the strict confines of a disciplined structure.

Paul Tillich understood that logical thinking could only develop by splitting personal, ego-centered thinking from the whole mind. He failed to carry through on Jesus as a symbol for the bridge *between* the modes of mind, however, and in the last analysis surrendered at least in part to the very Stoic view he saw as Jesus' rival. Tillich presumed that ambiguous thinking was the fare of man, leaving us only with the hope that God would bridge the gap. This still leaves us subject to fate, and is in itself a projection.

The hero has always been the one who could somehow re-enter his autistic state with his objective mind, and bring some boon back to man. As Joseph Campbell states, that message, in its many guises, has always been that the God-state so entered was the true nature and real being of man. This implies though that man is responsible for his reality, and the Greco-Hebraic backlash to Jesus' proposal is not hard to understand. Projection gives a world of absolutes "out there," and places responsibility elsewhere—even as it sets up a psychological need for heroes that show a crack in the egg so created.

There was a small but passionate impact from Carlos' don Juan, similar to the perpetual, if covert, attraction found in Jesus. Perhaps many interpretations will be made of don Juan; cults may spring up in the shadow of the book; seekers may ascend the Mexican hills in search of the old sorcerer. For there is an underlying desperation in us, unstated and inchoate, that is nothing less than a split mind's intolerable realization of its split world. We long for a way out—a way down and out—from this current structure that is, as Ronald Laing put it, rather an obscene madness.

Our current psychosis is no more or less than that of all ages. The same power structures maneuver man as he has always been maneuvered. The eternal knaves feed on the eternal fools now as always, fattening them up far better, in our rich and rare corner of the world, since needing fatter fools.

There is a difference today, though, and it is neither just in the barrage of brainwash designed to convince us that we really *do* have the kingdom right here—within the grasp of one more round of installments—nor that we are told daily that this is the best of all worlds. It is that we are told that this world is the *only* one, that this is all there is. It is that we are told not only that man *can* live by bread alone, but that he damned well *better* since bread is all there is.

All gods are jealous—and the one in the saddle now, selling all that bread, has a winning thing for sure, a power and success unknown in history. The man in the streets has no choice but to believe "those who know about these things," and the scientific-technological mind convinces man that those channels controlled by their various, if competing, priesthoods are the only channels available. God, if he is acknowledged by this clique, is the god of a Warren Weaver—made to fit the needs of the scientific-technician world view, shutting the door on the hope of man as thoroughly as the most rabid atheism. Meanwhile the split of psyche grows apace, reaching for a point of nihilistic self-doubt that can finally destroy itself as the only reasonable solution.

Recently a little book called *The Cross and the Switchblade* sold over sixteen million copies. It has been called the "most phenomenal *hidden* best seller in history" (my italics). Perhaps it sold so well because in it a man told a believable story of a psychic activity of an extrasensory kind, apparently operating outside the control of that university-scientific-political-industrial-military complex that denigrates and denies such modes of mind. The book's coauthor, David Wilkerson, claimed that this psychic activity moved into, changed, and specifically directed his life along new and larger lines. He became the totally unpredictable, guided by a formative kind of synthesis that moved only in the context of his complete openness to the instant moment. The little book smacked of the crack in the egg.

By and large, those who hate the world and long for a way out have no place to go. The only published underground is apparently run by the opposition, leading back into the sterility from which escape is sought. The church, by and large, rests on good, solid successful citizens. In return for support, the church gives sanction for the good life. The National Association of Manufacturers carried on a lively courtship for years under the byline: Church and Industry—Together on the Current Scene. And this cozy togetherness was not at all misplaced. Not inconsiderable in the censure of James Pike was his casualness concerning the financial holdings of his diocese, holdings jeopardized by Pike's stand on race. The Trinity could look after itself but a bishop's first duty was to the solvency of his diocese.

In any generation few people really believe there can be something like a crack in the cosmic egg, a way down and out. Even fewer look for it. Rarely indeed has anyone ever gotten through it. But the crack is there and must be used. It must play a part in any viable mythos for our current predicament. In my next chapter I will defend and try to explain briefly the crack as represented in don Juan's twilight between the worlds, and Jesus' Narrow Gate.

I am not so naive that I think Jesus' *Way* could be revived, though I know that archetypal energy is still potent. I am aware that his "new being" was aborted almost from its beginning, killed off by that Stoic "failure of nerve." Neither do I claim any social value in don Juan's *Way of Knowledge* (though surely there is energy there, too, as Carlos found out). My contention is that in these figures we find historical cracks that should be explored to give understanding of the crack itself. It is not only a time for bold hypothesis, but for bold analysis.

No decent scientist would ignore such an intriguing riddle as a *quasar*. He would leap into the puzzle with glee. There is something cowardly in that the preacher and the cultist so thoroughly intimidate psychology that it shuns great examples of the crack. Psychology could open to the most exciting venture of our history, the role it should have rightfully assumed, by a new openness of mind. And it is *adventure* that we need, that we must have. Not just the vicarious adventure shared with rare heroes exploring the planets, admirable as they are. Every man needs the personal adventure of finding the true depths of himself. Every man needs a way out from being only a cipher in a computer, a subservient cog in the machine. If our cultural confusion is to find its mythos sufficiently large to orient us into a unity, hero-archetypes, and the crack they represent, must play a part.

At any rate, cracks in the cosmic egg can always be created, and our culture needs one very badly. I recall a conversation several years ago with an Air Force Colonel, a man of education, good breeding, impeccable manners. He was a frustrated man, though, for he had recognized the dangers to our country and knew quite well the immediate steps which had to be taken were our nation to be saved. What he advocated was the "taking out" of the eastern hemisphere of this green earth. We have the capability, he pointed out. We *can* do it. Unless we remove *them* they will remove *us*, and the time is now. It was the only expediency and his logic was clear. His approach was calm, with a dispassionate objectivity, a certain dignified regret, mixed with icy practicality.

He spoke in Kahn-like reasoned statistics on probable survivors, rebound capability, and so on. When I mentioned that "taking out" a hemisphere meant taking out families like mine he said I exemplified the real threat to America. It was the weak man who could not operate by sane rational thought, but who reacted according to emotions, that caused the grave danger of our time. If only the unemotional, the practical men, the Pentagonians, could just rule, he said, the problems could be met squarely, bravely, and *solved*.

I think of the 800 billion dollars in appropriations the Pentagon can anticipate as of my present writing here, and the new levels of energy being imaged up by brilliant minds in fantastic university laboratories sponsored by all that powerful Pentagon money. I think of Teilhard de Chardin's dream of man "seizing the tiller of the world," reaching for that energy beyond all atomic and molecular affinities, that mainspring of the universe. I think of David Bohm and his 10^{38} ergs—not available yet, but, as he mused, when conditions change . . . And I think on the frustrated Colonel who would "take out" one lobe of this thinking globe's brain. And I wonder how long before conditions change, and the Pentagon comes into its own, and that strange surgery might work its final lobotomy on this living sphere.

And I think on that little bit of planet, Ceres, and all its exploded parts lying in neat, Bode's Law orbit. Did Ceres, too, reach for that mainspring of the universe, only to have the thrust seized by "practical men" solving social problems by removing others? And so I wonder as Ceres' fragmentations, Pentagons, Colonels, 10^{38} ergs, and takings-out of hemispheres echo like insomniac questions of the night.

Back in the mid-thirties a German told Tom Wolfe that Germany was caught on a fast train with a madman at the throttle. To jump off seemed suicide, to stay on even worse. The metaphor holds for today as severely and more universally. We, too, are caught on a train, a supercharged one, rolling madly downhill, faster and faster. Though we chart our increases of tempo with fascinated awe, neither our giddy success nor our new "freedoms" can cover our underlying alarm.

For there is *no engineer to our train,* not even a madman. And there is no brakeman. For there is no steering mechanism, and there are no brakes. And the terrible rumor from the front of the train is true: there are no tracks out there ahead. The mad machine throws its own down as it thunders murderously along.

Who can say—perhaps the brave new optimists are right. Perhaps the hill *will* last forever, with no sudden curves or precipices along the way. Perhaps it *could* happen that way. It just never has before.

The German was right. To stay on the train is madness, to leap from it suicide. But there is still a Way—a narrow, hard Way, a difficult crack between the worlds where, losing your life, you can find it. Therein might lie the only hope for the train itself, improbable as the notion sounds.

9

don Juan and Jesus

All logical systems, East-West, scientific-religious, cyclic or linear, originate in an analysis of the way reality is structured. Then, by various techniques, the system develops as an attempt to use the analysis to obtain some particular product from the process analyzed.

The idea of eschewing products, and seizing the very process by which reality *organizes* is the radical departure found in don Juan's Way of Knowledge, and in Jesus' Way of Truth. Don Juan and Jesus consider the world to be an arbitrary construct, not an illusion as in the East or a fated absolute as in the West. Since the world is an arbitrary construct, the means of construction, not a particular construct, or the products of a construct, are the focal point of attention.

Don Juan and Jesus believe the materials of the world to be subject to dramatic alteration and reorganization by an activity of the mind. Both systems work to lower the threshold between reality-adjusted thinking and autistic thinking, and without loss of identity. Both systems have analyzed the way by which reality events shape, and have then dared to dissolve the structure of a common domain, the selective world agreed upon in ordinary social thinking. Such a dissolution would ordinarily threaten the ego-personality which has been centered and formed *by* the common domain, and this is a risk assumed.

Both don Juan and Jesus have as a goal the seizure of the ontological function itself and both attempts hinge on a complete surrender *to* the function. Through a sacrifice of self and absolute obedience to the *way* of the system, union with the process of reality is achieved. There is a single underlying way by which all reality forms and "union" with this procedure is possible. However, the system or means of achieving such union determines the *kind* of reality then shaping as experience for the person involved. There is a single unitary core of reality-functioning, but it is not available in a "pure form." It *is*, in actuality, according to the method of *actualizing* it. The subject's approach to the function determines his realization of it.

Don Juan recognizes the ordinary world to be but one of an endless number of possible constructs. The man of courage and daring in his culture will explore as many possibilities of this as he can, simply because the possibilities are there and that is what life is about. Man can restructure reality in freely-synthesized ways. Though death is the final victor, to live a strong, hard life, in which reality opens its endless possibility, is the mark of a warrior, a man of knowledge, and the only conceivable way to live.

Jesus aims to restructure particular events *within* the world. He aims toward a special consensus concerning the ordinary reality. Non-ordinary reality is used only for the sake of the ordinary world. Achieving a new and different "editorial hierarchy of mind" the follower of the *Way* serves as catalyst for new syntheses when our fated and autonomous blindnesses, split from our whole mind as they are, lead us into inescapable dilemmas.

Don Juan seized the ontological process to construct paths of "breathless wonder." Jesus seizes the process to bridge the modes of mind. Don Juan is in love with eternity. He is a kind of hedonist of the psyche. Jesus is in love with time. He is a pragmatic Hebrew, concerned over his fellow man. The esthetic differences of goals, of techniques and disciplines, give dramatically different results. But the process of attainment is similar.

Eastern thought viewed the world as a fated illusion and yearned for the *real* world. This is a proposition denied by both don Juan and Jesus, who know the world to be perfectly real. Greek-Stoic thought viewed the world as a fixed mechanical unit, distinct from the mind of man. This, too, is denied by don Juan and Jesus, who see the world as a matrix for continual resynthesis. Both recognize the world as an agreed upon and practiced construct in a continuum of possible constructs. Both recognize this as true with any and all possible worlds.

Don Juan created private but equally-real worlds for personal adventure, and accepted as a natural part of his path the isolation within his created point of view. Carlos experienced this as "the aloneness of a single person on a journey." Jesus recognized that no communicable, shared reality is possible except by agreement between the participants of that world. So his system was to carry don Juan's open synthesis *into* the ordinary world. Jesus will break with the world of common agreement, but only under special circumstances and for special goals.

The crack in the egg is sought by Jesus to restructure some specific problem area in ordinary reality. His system works only in relationships between people. His non-ordinary states are created as *shared* states by the constant focus on the needs of the other. No isolation is engendered. Two or three can gather together and reach a non-ordinary consensus, a point of agreement different from that of the ordinary world. Group agreement gives a mutual feedback of verification, sustaining the non-ordinary even in the ordinary. Carlos might call feeding the five thousand a special consensus of non-ordinary reality, or healing the man with a withered arm a special consensus about ordinary reality. In all cases, filling some need is Jesus' motivation and this proves to be the only way his particular crack is sustained.

Don Juan spoke of learning by doing as the only way to knowledge. There was no act of grace suddenly bestowing the goal. And yet there was the ally, a helper available once the subject had proved himself and learned to open to and control the technique of bringing about states of special reality.

Jesus' knowing, too, could only be obtained by doing, a course of action and thinking as rigorous as don Juan's. In conjunction with reality-adjusted thinking went an unambiguous single-minded organization similar to

Bruner's "thinking for the left hand." Once this kind of thinking was practiced the world no longer split against itself, and there was freedom to "intervene in the ontological constitution of the universe," as Eliade put it, since conscious thought then had ready access to that point in the continuum where there was no judgment, no distinction between kinds of organization.

Neither don Juan nor Jesus could offer intellectual procedures or explanations of their way, since logic and reason are only the surface part of mind, the part splitting a total awareness. Both deny absoluteness of "sanctity" to any particular system, and, eschewing the products of systems, they are equally offensive to all systems. The only thing sacred to don Juan and Jesus is the way in which systems are built. Allegiance can only be given the *process* if balance of mind is to be achieved and sustained. Unbending intent is don Juan's requirement, a passionate concern. Idolatry, Jesus would say, is considering as absolute or true any *product* of the reality process. The *process* is the only truth, the only absolute, and the way to freedom.

Don Juan would have but one apprentice in his life, as his own benefactor had had but one. Many might be called to Jesus, but few would be chosen. Few would ever find the Narrow Gate. Both systems were esoteric, difficult to attain, and harder to sustain. Both demanded a risk of life—the world turns and rends its heroes—and, more seriously, a risk of soul or mind.

Growth within the way was not automatic or assured. The continuing response of the person gave the context for growth. Peter could be either the Keys to the Kingdom, or Satan, depending on his use of all his faculties and openness to the guide.

In his evaluation procedures, don Juan had set the expectancies shaping Carlos' future experiences. He did this by strong negative and positive reactions to the contents of Carlos' preliminary ventures. Jesus, too, reacted with quick negatives and positives to his follower's responses, questioning and probing their reactions, attempting to determine their expectancies associated with the Way.

Both systems required "frugality" or conservation of energy. Every aspect of life had to be reserved for the path. This implies no nonsense of a limited or fixed quantity of "libido" in a Freudian sense, but ultimacy of commitment and unambiguous intent. Extraordinary effort was needed to break with the broad stream that makes up the self-mirroring world of the ordinary. The activity of restructuring in the face of the strength of statistical reality called for extremes of energy and determination in Jesus' Way. And restructuring in the wake of psychedelic dissolution called for the same commitment and strength in don Juan's Way.

Shelter, nourishment, companionship, and so on, are the needs ruling the split man. They are the products by which short-circuited demonic power is wielded by one man over another. All these products of the broad way must be ruthlessly cut out, boldly denied. Fasting played a role in both systems. One became a "eunuch" for the sake of the Kingdom. Don Juan kept telling Carlos that he thought about himself too much. Self had to be forgotten. Only the path was important.

Both don Juan and Jesus were figures for transference, and both provided the clues for the initiating of the way. Both promised a helper or ally who would come and open one to ever-greater levels of growth and power. Power, an automatic result in both systems, was a crucial point of danger. The Temptations in the Wilderness graphically typified the main categories of misuse of power and loss of the Way. In don Juan's system any power once attained was never lost. Unless voluntarily surrendered, however, and given over only for the furtherance of more knowledge, the power became immediately demonic and blocked all further possibility of growth. Double the talents, Jesus promised, and you would be given twice that many more—for more doubling. If *invested*. Otherwise all were taken away.

Any attempt to use power for personal ends destroyed the Way in Jesus' system as well as don Juan's, and a practical, functional reason, not a "spiritually moral" one, was the cause. Desire for freedom from the tensions of reality as found in mystical systems or desire to use the potentials of the whole mind for ego-interests are out-of-balance maneuvers; the point of rapport with the whole mind is simply lost. In the mystical experience the self is dissolved, if only temporarily, into the continuum. In desires of the ego, the imbalance is toward self, breaking the rapport with the whole mind, and further trapping the person in the fixed products of the ordinary world.

In Jesus' system concern *for* others on the one hand, and total allegiance to the autistic "spirit" on the other, achieved the otherwise impossible balance. Clarity of mind, a clear understanding of one's own motivations, was necessary in both systems. Single-vision, or non-ambiguity, was the prime criterion. The path had to be chosen freely, as ultimately desirable, having counted the costs of following it.

There was no free directing of the path itself, however. Personal responsibility was for a surrender to the peculiar qualities of the path. A cultural hierarchy of values helped give the guidelines for action. A continually-renewed commitment was necessary, though, for the only known goal was the process of movement along the path itself. The path was an open structure forming only as one moved along it. The "obligatory acts" in Jesus' system were much more dependent on the context of the moment than were don Juan's.

Death was a contingency in both systems. In Jesus' system death was the ultimate demonic, accepted and assumed as an unavoidable property of the split mind but not of the integrated one. The demonic was controlled by denying absoluteness to those aspects of life over which the demonic has power. The soul never "sinning," never granting allegiance to the products of a system, and allying only with the function of systems-building itself, would never die. Only when concern for the path was greater than concern for self could the self achieve security.

In don Juan the capacity for exertion of extraordinary energy had to be effective, quite literally, for survival. Non-survival had to be accepted, however, as the mark of profound belief. No goal could be entertained by mind except the goal of the path itself. And this path was its own end.

Don Juan had no prospect of survival. Death was the final victor.

With Jesus, agreement, if only among two or three, could establish a non-ordinary reality by consensus within the group. This kind of autistic bridge between people is found in don Juan, who brought about non-ordinary events shared, unhappily, by Carlos in non-hallucinogenic ways. It was, in fact, this conscious restructuring by don Juan of ordinary events, right out in the light of day, that finally defeated Carlos by their sheer horror.

Fear had to be accepted, faced, admitted, and then gone beyond. Until one recognized the reason for fear he was not fully aware of the qualitative distinction between his new Way and the world's Way. The follower was then still double-minded and divided in intent. The real onslaught of fear arose at recognition that the events of ordinary reality were arbitrary. Langer's fear of "collapse into chaos should our ideation fail" is strong. We are a built-in function of delineation, defining, delimiting, constructing by ordinary consensus a tight little island in a sea of apparent randomness. This is genetically, psychologically, and inherently, the strongest motivation we have, the skeleton of our minds, egos, ways of being. To threaten it is worse than death. The crack in the egg is no small threat.

Don Juan exerted all his dramatic abilities and knowledge to maneuver Carlos into just the position where his *certainty* that the reality of everyday life is implicitly "real" *would* be undermined. Only the complete collapse of that certainty could remove the last barrier to accepting the existence of separate but equal realities, those realities of "special consensus." The component elements of ordinary reality could be denied and thus open to restructuring. Carlos sensed in this that there was then no guarantee that he could "provide himself indefinitely with consensus," and this abyss of apparent chaos drove him back into the broad stream.

The break with ordinary consensus is thus profoundly serious. This is what Jesus meant when he said that we must give up our life to find greater life, and that while the animals had a definite place, the Son of Man had none. Such cures for psychic ills are strong medicine, no matter how sick the patient.

Jesus could exert great sway in an event of the moment, but was frustrated that the import of his maneuvers faded from his followers' awareness. His followers centered their faith in his personality, while *his* constant aim was to center their faith in the function of faith itself. His problem was similar to that of transference in psychoanalysis. As a transference-agent he could catch his followers up in the restructuring of an event, but they could not see the transference function as itself the crack in the egg. They made the common error of idolatry—making Jesus into the source of magic. And it was the function of reality formation toward which Jesus pointed, toward which he tried to be "transparent."

No line can be drawn between what don Juan was, what he taught, and what his Way of Knowledge was. But *he* was not the end product; he considered himself impersonally in respect to his path. Similarly, only by making himself the focus of attention could Jesus reorganize the concept-percept structure of his followers and open them to the crack. Function and man appear synonymous because the function can only be pointed toward by *being* the function. There is no being except in a mode of being.

In Chapter VI I mentioned the psychology professor walking the fire by holding the fakir's hand. Without the fakir as trigger, without seeing him actually walk, it is difficult to see how the professor could have been so seized. But the fakir was neither the reason for the phenomenon nor the bearer of magic. The restructuring ability was innately within the professor all along, a part of the very mechanism of his being.

Leonard Feinberg came away from Ceylon convinced that somehow the god Kataragama was an operative and real force within the accepted fourteen-mile radius of his temple. The dramatic events of the ceremonies were capped by peculiarly synchronous after-effects that disturbed Feinberg's western point of view as much as the fire-walking. The tough-minded scholar and the classical Christian react to this sort of thing with equal scorn, appropriate to their belief's esthetics. The scholar's contempt will be that a fortuitous congruence of events should be interpreted superstitiously, which means outside the acceptances of the scholar's own path. The Christian's scorn will be that an efficacious god could be a viable fact within a twenty-eight mile circle. Both scholar and Christian are functioning in identical ways, just under different metaphor, and both are evading the mechanics of being.

Carlos never resolved his half-suspicion, half-conviction, that the god Mescalito was somehow synonymous with the peyote plant itself; that the unique quality of Mescalito was within the properties of the hallucinogen in some independent way. He knew the hallucinogen of itself led nowhere. Aldous Huxley's experiences with mescalin, the synthetic of peyote, bore not the faintest resemblance to Carlo's experience. Carlos recognized the handiwork of don Juan; but Mescalito's person and total experience were not dismissible as just hallucination.

Those with ears to hear would understand. Jesus spoke of his "Kingdom" as like a leavening, the kind the housewife puts in her flour to give life to the inert ingredients. Only a tiny bit of leavening is needed to work and raise large quantities of flour. Beware, though, Jesus warned, of the leavening of the Pharisee, the world of legalistic split-thinking and rationale; and beware the leavening of Herod, the world of power battening on the brother's blood, the final demonic, the forces of death. Beware because *all* leavenings work, all raise the flour, and equally well. Leavening is ontological, neutral, impersonal, natural. Jesus said that his "Father" judges not. God is the function of leavening, not the capacity for choosing types of leavening. Judgment is given to the "Son." Man chooses, God responds automatically. That is the way the process works. Don Juan said there was an infinite number of paths, and that we should choose our paths with care.

It is not just fortuitous that the metaphors Jesus used to describe both the way to and the resulting state of his "Kingdom" show remarkable similarity to Hilgard's outline for hypnotic transfer. Reality-adjusted thinking was Jesus' point of departure. He did not break with logic or "law," the reasoning functions of mind. He spoke of perfecting logic in order to go beyond it. His child-metaphors have meaning only against an adult background. The first demand he makes is that the ego-centered, reality-thinking personality must be surrendered. Unless you hate your life you cannot follow where he goes—not just because ambiguity would result from trying to hold two orientations at once; more, unless you are willing to give up your world view structured from infancy, those concepts directing your percepts cannot be restructured.

An indeterminately-wide capacity for resynthesis is incorporated in the structure of our minds. This capacity is blocked, though, by the very system of logic which *must* be developed to structure the mind to the point where resynthesis is then possible. Paralleling Piaget and Hilgard makes this clear. No resynthesis is possible to us until an initial synthesis gives a ground on which to stand.

It is not just fortuitous that somewhere around age twelve logical development begins to firm up, and that this is the age of the archaic transformation rites. Neither is it fortuitous that this is the age when our educational system breaks down most seriously, (try teaching in a junior high school,) or that mythological overlay gave this as the setting for Jesus' first manifestations of seizure, and so on.

The materials of the common domain, the clearing in the forest eons in process, must be the materials for synthesis, for there are no other materials. If a kingdom of heaven is desired, it must be synthesized from the available stuff. The world is no trivial illusion blocking a pure soul's vision of heavenly vistas. The world is the matrix from which all things must operate. To be realized, made real, is to be born into the world. In order to be in the world, one's world view must shape according to the shape of that world. The logical process of structuring the mind into a modified relation with the world of man may be arbitrary, but it brings about the only reality available. Any restructuring is then equally arbitrary, a matter of choice and commitment, but it is a restructuring.

There are many forms of trance-thinking, and every

system or discipline incorporates some aspect of it. Sometimes this state is only a temporary lowering of the threshold of the logical mind to incorporate a new experience not available to logic. Recall Hans Selye's observation that every great scientific postulate-illumination had *happened* to the scientist in a hypnagogic state. With don Juan, the new states created were entered into for adventure, becoming as valid as the ordinary reality, little by little firming up into tangible structures, each building on the other. Don Juan's process imitated the way by which The Creation itself is brought about. The flaw in his system, and the probable reason for its obsolescence, was the ego-isolation within the construct. It gave only a private world.

With Jesus the same function is used, but only as a shared venture. Creating only *interventions* in the common domain, one remained *in* the world, the "larger body of man" was kept intact. His "interventions in the ontological constitution of the universe" were on two levels. The first was when the logical process broke down, as in conflicting personal relations, or when logical choice had created insoluble problems, and the crack was opened as a way down and out. This was "forgiveness." No problem was "solved" as such, in some brilliant logical analysis. Rather, the situation was simply restructured, giving a clean slate, a new possibility for synthesis. The procedure could be repeated infinitely, there was no heavenly hierarchy of value judgment determining its granting. The only criterion was that the materials had to be surrendered *for* the resynthesis. Since no logical prestructuring was possible, it was an unknown venture each time, a kind of "little death" as Blake called it.

The second category of intervention was in the ordinary cause-effect mechanisms of reality. Without fire burning, charcoal-broiled steaks are not possible, nor the joy of the hearth. There are times of ultimate concern, though, when a way down and out from this universal mechanism is needed. When the ordinary mechanics break or lead to destructive results, disease, disaster, and so on, the crack is needed to restructure events. Since the ordinary mechanics are infinitely contingent, accident is inevitable. But the crack opens to that mode of thinking itself infinitely contingent, and capable of infinite synthesis. The way down and out is an instantaneous restructuring of some isolated, specific point of relation, a carrying of the non-ordinary to the ordinary, and an equally instantaneous establishment of the ordinary mechanics. Hypnotic anaesthesia is a minor case in point. Blood circulation and nerve response are vital mechanisms —else the whole house of cards tumbles down—but in certain instances can be suspended as needed.

The end goal of don Juan's way was adventure. The end goal of Jesus' way was solving problems of individual and society in the shared adventure of group life. Interventions are made only to correct, alleviate, fill out the inevitable shortcomings of a system limiting an infinite openness to specific actualities. The crack in the egg was utilized only for the good of the egg, never for self. But since the self is also the egg at some point, the self was taken care of peripherally and automatically by caring for the egg. "Man, if you know what you are doing," (when you use the crack,) "you are blest."

It would have been a neat system. It could have achieved the unity of man in the only practical way—attainment of desire for every man. It would have been rather a universal mutual-back scratch, through which all our itches, beyond personal reach, could be tended. It would have been a massive *power for,* rather than our current demonic and fragmenting *power against.*

Cracks in the egg cannot be built into a cosmic egg. They can only come about when the embryonic form expands and needs room beyond its genesis. The crack is found by the time-tested technique found in all systems, of necessity, the only one that works: a repeating of the initial process of world view formation. A surrender is made as a "child" to a father-figure who gives sureness and confidence that one *can* give over his life, his conceptual frame-work, to the image and receive it back enlarged.

In all education, *metanoia,* or change of concept, there is some form of duplication of this world view structuring. Those whose initial experiences, of entry into fantasy and return to reality with their parents, were rewarding may have an edge here. Perhaps we can see why education fails so sadly; why there are at best mostly technicians and too few physicists; why "hardness of heart" may be built in from infancy.

It is not fortuitous that Jesus used the father-figure as his symbol for transference, neither is it just an echo of Old Testament archaisms—which it very soundly is, in spite of Harvey Cox, and for good reason. Nor is it at all just coincidence that Jesus used the child-metaphor for the subject making the transference.

The symbol of transference determines the nature of the resulting hierarchy of mind. Sadly, I will never know don Juan and so can never experience his Path of breathless wonder. When Jesus said "no man comes to the Father but through me" he was simply stating this very case. His "Father" is a very specialized and carefully-delineated symbol of transference, designed to give that "loosing on earth" that we want "loosed in heaven."

Both the systems of don Juan and Jesus were end products of ancient cultural drifts. Don Juan's was so completely developed that no innovations were possible within it. Don Juan was the remnant of an ancient though disappearing culture. Jesus was the culmination of a long-building synthesis, incorporating his own culture and even beyond. "Before Abraham was, I am," indicates an "inflation of the psyche" seized by an archetypal imagery long in building. He was the *Eureka!* illumination of a long process of synthesis brought to fruition through extremes of cultural crisis. He was the focal point of a passionate quest centuries in building, and the translator of the answer into the common domain.

In our day we tend to dismiss suggestions of "unconscious" cultural forces, since we deny properties of mind other than those of an electrochemical, biological nature. This notion makes it difficult for us to understand culture in general. Only recently have anthropologists broken from this narrow and pedantic error. An unconscious exchange is apparent between Carlos and don Juan, and the suggestive force of that exchange went far *beyond* the person of don Juan. This contributed to Carlos' perplexity about the reality of Mescalito. Recall Cohen's observation that under LSD the Freudian patient immediately reflected and thus verified the analyst's assumptions. An indeterminably ancient set of archetypal assumptions and "sets of expectancy" underlay don Juan's Way of Knowledge. As with Jesus, Carlos sowed a wind—and reaped a whirlwind.

A cultural hierarchy, represented as the Two Brothers, directed the contents of the aboriginal Dream-Time. No syntheses outside the cultural set of expectancies ever resulted; there was no antisocial behaviour. A cultural hierarchy directed the Balinese in their seizures. The material for the restructurings had been automatically absorbed as part of the overall cultural conditioning. A strict protocol controlled the content of the seizures. The trance state never led to antisocial behaviour.

A cultural synthesis was the "hierarchy" in Jesus' *metanoia.* His "father-symbol" was the sum total of the human venture. As Bruner said, life creates myth and finally imitates it. Jesus, seized by the catalytic synthesis of the long quest, translated the answer in flesh and blood, giving a concrete symbol of the new cultural synthesis. He set up the expectancies for new possibility and gave the pattern for the best representation we could make of life for the best mirroring response. He used dramatic restructurings of ordinary reality as examples of the possibilities—whenever he could find a person willing to suspend an ordinary world view and enter into a subset with him. He used these restructurings as don Juan did with Carlos, to try to show the arbitrary character of ordinary reality, and the equality of other possibilities. He emphasized a decorum and respect for the world, while yet giving a criterion for deciding when you should "hate" this world and break with its statistics and employ the non-statistical openness.

Don Juan was contemptuous of those who would try hallucinogens without the proper disciplines. In the same way, the logical processes of mind, the disciplines, "law or judgment" in the terms of his day, were never evaded by Jesus. Unless your "righteousness exceeded that of the Pharisees and lawyers," you would never get through to the crack in the egg. Dissolution of ordinary consciousness, or isolation in non-ordinary states, plays no part in Jesus' system since the entire concentration of "obligatory acts" is on one's fellow man. This kept the follower *in* the world, while hopefully not *of* the world.

A new hierarchy of concept, such as don Juan's or Jesus', organizes the new kind of reality event, but only on the spot, so to speak, out of the materials given from the ordinary context of reality. There is small probability of finding out what the new reality is like *first* and then deciding to try a switch of allegiance. The forest shapes according to the light of the clearing. In scheming out the possibility of an "after life," Jesus realized there could be no such thing *a priori* to his actions. He would have to go and "prepare a place" in that "house of many mansions," the open possibility of synthesis.

The systems of don Juan, Jesus, and other cracks in the egg produce unique events not available to the non-committed person. Fire-walking can be observed by others, but the walking itself is another matter. With don Juan, becoming the process was the only way to discover what it was about. The same holds for Jesus. The rewards of the system could not be displayed to a non-believer to convince him that the plunge was worth the risk. A person had to *enter into* the creation of the state in order to share in it. That is why healing stood a good chance of being a bridge over the gap in Jesus' time. There were simply not many rivals. And that is why healing stands far less chance of bridging the gap today. *Agreement* between two or three on what is being done is the key. Agreement is freedom from ambiguity. Double-mindedness fragments.

Ignored to this day by Christian orthodoxy is that Jesus was *helpless* to create non-ordinary events unless his hearers surrendered their hierarchy of mind to him, at least for the moment and at least in regard to the problem at hand. Jesus could trigger a "special consensus" about reality, and so change events, among those who had *nothing to lose,* those country dwellers and city poor, those crippled and diseased without hope, those whose world was terrible enough to make the risk of suspension of ordinary criteria, with its overtones of a "collapse into chaos," the lesser of evils. Things were different indeed with the clever intellectuals, the people in power, the "doctors of law." "Hardness of heart" is as much indicative of success within an established system as it is some sort of moral failure. No one abandons a game which he is winning. Jesus pities the rich young ruler unable to grasp the new reality because he could not let go of the old.

The empty category can be filled, but it must first be created. Long centuries of sacrifice by hook-swinging took place in India before broken by that believer seized by the notion that he really *was* the temporary incarnation of the god, as the priests had represented for centuries. Once that notion had been realized, dramatically concretized and made real, no bodily harm ever came again to the "victim." The mythos leads the logos.

Don Juan had entered a firmly-established path through a long and hard apprenticeship to his own benefactor. No such system was handed Jesus. His illumination was probably symbolic, of necessity, as was Kekule's hypnagogic imagery giving rise to the benzene ring hypothesis, for instance. The genius of the man was called into play to translate the experience into reality. A high degree of improvisation and innovation is found in Jesus' sayings and actions. Hugh Schonfield brilliantly portrayed this venture in his *Passover Plot,* though in another work I have contended with him on several points.

The common materials of common reality had to be Jesus' materials for translation since the common world was his focus of concern and since there *was* no other material. The Greek-Stoic perversion of Jesus' imagery has projected his magnificent display of courage and genius onto an "out there" Olympus. To translate the imagery of his *Eureka!* into a communicable form, however, Jesus had to *be* that imagery, act it out, give it flesh-and-blood reality, fill the empty category with the only material available, himself, knowing that the average man can grasp concepts only as a concrete, workable image is given him.

Recognizing that "what we loose on earth is loosed in

heaven," Jesus tried to give the *kind* of loosing we should do, the kind of representation we *should* make of God, or life, if we want the non-judging mirroring process of reality to work to our best advantage. It was a purely practical, pragmatic venture. He set up a pattern of representation, an image of transference, a pivot for restructuring, by which we can, "becoming as little children," achieve a new hierarchy of mind, a way down and out to freedom from fate.

On the other hand, he recognized and warned that *any* representation of God or life was *true* insofar as believed in. Any leavening fills the flour. Kataragama is as true and real as his Hindu followers. He works. Science works. Carlos found Mescalito a functional fact.

The unknown continuum of potential, the dark forest with its circles *ad infinitum,* the large category of the unknown, rains on just and unjust alike. This function "judges not." Any question asked with ultimate seriousness merges into this unjudging ultimacy and tends to express itself. Any sowing enters this contingency and tends to set up its own reaping. Any world view organizes a world-to-view. Any representation of God produces accordingly. Understanding and accepting responsibility for this function can make us free.

The whole character of don Juan's or Jesus' system was interlocking. The only way by which the ally could be brought about in the mind was by surrender and commitment to the initial transference figure, who was also the content of imagery by which the synthesis could organize. Recall how P. W. Martin's *Experiment in Depth,* carried its own materials for synthesis. The same self-verifying procedure takes place in physics.

Fasting entered into Jesus' Way as it does in all non-ordinary systems. His forty-day fast in the wilderness, duplicated in our day from necessity by marooned travelers, was the way of breaking with the world of necessities and statistics. Fasting bypasses the logical blocks. Jesus refused food, saying he had nourishment his followers knew nothing about. Don Juan commented casually that food would not be needed for their several days' trip to the mountains where they would be guests of the god

Mescalito. The ways of the world would not be essentials when one had opened to the ways of the god. Don Juan never made an issue of the two- and three-day fasts that preceded new steps along his path, such was simply a natural part of the tradition.

To move against the certainties and energies of "the world" calls for an equally sure conviction and a concentration on balance of mind. To center all the forces on the restructuring of an ordinary event in a non-ordinary way called for exceptional organization of self.

Jesus *sighs heavily* as he goes to raise Lazarus. In his growing and reckless confidence, he delayed two days, not only to make sure Lazarus would be dead but to gather the forces of mind necessary to illustrate this extreme example of the "glory of God," the open-ended potential of being. Jesus *sighs heavily* as he moves to heal the deaf man. The fire-walker *sighs heavily* as he walks to the pit of fire. There is a childlike quality in bringing the dream state through the crack to fruition. Such an inner state is balanced by a tough and resilient clarity of mind in the outer self. One is like a lamb to the inner spirit but like a fox to the outer world. This is the balance of mind.

As with don Juan's "ally," Jesus' "Holy Spirit" would instruct in the "right way to live." This "instruction" was only a synthesis of the instant moment itself, however, not any sort of foreknowing. The "ally" is only a catalyst acting on all parts of the immediate context. In Jesus' move-for-the-world this means all those other persons who are also the autistic, also the "father son"; they also contain the kingdom of heaven within them. To prestructure, or "take thought of the morrow," would set up logical blocks of expectancy preventing free synthesis. The synthesis would of necessity have to include the instant moment of, and move for, all parts of the context equally, since all parts are equally the context to the non-judging autistic.

Eternity is still in love with time. The desires arising out of time are the organizing nucleus for whatever "eternity" might be. In every case of Carlos' meeting with Mescalito, the god could only ask: "What do you want?"

Jesus promised his followers: "Whatever you ask in my name will be given you."

"What do you want?" is the only question eternity can ask of time, and it is our divine gift to answer by asking our own question. Desire, passion, curiosity, longing, novelty, daring, creativity, productivity, lust for life, ecstasy, joy, adventure, all these are the highest thrusts of life, the most divine of attributes, the most sacred of possessions. And all these have been the attributes *mistrusted* and *condemned* by that dark priesthood probing for control, domination, and battening on the brother's blood. Without these seeds from time, however, without these vital gametes from the larger body of man, the womb of eternity is barren.

In another study I have attempted a defense of Jesus as a genius with radically new ideas, an evolutionary *Eureka!* development by which life tried to develop a new aspect of potential. I have tried to outline how completely the massive "failure of nerve" of that period, epitomized in Stoicism, and seen by Singer to have destroyed early science, was the victor in the struggle for man's mind. This same failure of nerve is the very psychological contradiction dominant today, the perennial cause of the split mind. This frozen logic of Stoicism not only triumphed but then incorporated the imagery of Jesus, inverting and negating his entire thrust. Thus was the "rushing torrent of the river of God" turned into a "broad but feeble stream" called Christendom, to use Edwin Hatch's metaphor.

One or two comments by Augustine, that final death-knell of Jesus' Way, indicate how the symbols of the Way had been absorbed into Greek logic until indistinguishable. Writing of the Stoic Seneca for instance, Augustine exclaimed: "What more could a Christian say than this Pagan has said?" Concerning the Platonists, Augustine stated that "the sole fundamental truth they lacked was the doctrine of the Incarnation." Since this "doctrine" was itself purely Greek, foreign to a Hebraic background and undetectable in the ideas, sayings, or actions of Jesus, we see how the new wine had long since been put in old skins.

Considering the world an immovable fated cycle, and man a tragic incidental on its surface, with God an abstract "pure essence" off in his ninth circle or wherever, the Greeks were unable to ask or hear a Job-like ultimate question. To the Greeks nothing could ever happen to the cosmic egg, only to incidental man. And to the Greeks, boxed in by their own logic, no answer came.

Stoicism rewrote Jesus' crack in the egg as a mythological once-for-all happening. Their projection placed the Way out of bounds for man. Thus man was really no longer responsible for his world, but only responsible to the priesthood organizing the dogma. The open-potential catalyst is completely unpredictable, and the forces of social control, feeding on predictability, quickly shut it out.

The "Will of God" shaped as the new metaphor for the old Greek Fate. The "Son of God" was no longer rational man; the "Father" no longer the logos-shaping mythos, the symbol of transference; the "Spirit" no longer the threshold of mind; "God" no longer that divine-demonic, non-judging, amoral, raining on just and unjust alike, the hard taskmaster reaping where he sows not, doubling the talents, any talents, mirroring any desire, and crying "More! More! Less than all will never satisfy." By the Greek perversion these became Olympian figures rather than psychological symbols of ontology. They were abstracted from all reality. Jesus' Way, the greatest of human *Eureka!* ventures, became a fairy tale, a maudling, ridiculous, pious fraud.

Actually, none of the accounts of Jesus' "non-ordinary" reality maneuvers need be discounted. A miracle is a non-ordinary state in the don Juan, fire-walker sense, rather than in the Greek mythological fire-from-Olympus sense. Christendom has largely ignored Jesus' insistence that acts greater than his would be a product of his system. Based on Greek logic as it is, rather than on the non-structured and open Way, theology never understood or really believed in those happenings. Since miracles represented cracks in the egg beyond all probability, the self-styled guardians of the egg, determined to protect man *from* himself, projected those cracks into the nethermost regions of inaccessibility.

The "interventions in the ontological construct" attributed to Jesus and promised for his followers are as logical within *his* premise and system as are different reality states in don Juan's, fire-walking in the Hindu's, or atom bombs in the scientist's.

And surely, from the evidence I have tried to bring together in this book, it should be obvious why Hugh Schonfield's thesis of Jesus' taking a drug to simulate death so seriously misses the point, and places Schonfield, in spite of his remarkable work, squarely in the camp of those theologians he challenges. Such a notion of trickery on Jesus' part, double-mindedness of the first rank, would have automatically fragmented the very state of mind that was the *only* weapon Jesus had.

The technique, improbable as it sounds, by which one might open to this Way even today has been outlined in this book. The Laski-Wallas-Bruner outline of creative thought (Chapter IV) is easily traced in Jesus' own seizure and translation, and was clearly established as the pattern for his followers. The reason for the similarity is simple—there is no other way for newness to come about. We are dealing with the ontological way of all things, not heavenly mysteries or occult secrets.

Surely the obstacles to any crack are many and formidable. The scientific allegiances are no more powerful checks than the theologians—those standing at the gate preventing others from going through.

Greatest of the several tragedies of the Stoic inversion of Jesus, culminating in Christendom and still operative under various guises, was *representing God as reason,* considering God to be *rational.* Again, it is a case of projection. Reason and logic are the qualities of limitation and definition produced by man's conscious thinking. We are, to use religious imagery, "made in the likeness of God" in that non-logical, autistic mode of mind, the mode we cannot get at directly and manipulate, but which is closer than our very consciousness, the breath of life making all things real. God became only an extension of *man* through this classical view. This inverted view trusts only its own logic and mistrusts God's unruly and unpredictable characteristics which then are considered Satanic. The Classical view, as Blake and Northrop Frye point out, inverts the true situation and mistakes reality-thinking for the *autistic,* which is, ironically enough, claiming man to be God, the *very error* theologians have been most strident in condemning. Down through the centuries they have been yapping at their own image in the mirror.

Man is the imaginative tool or technique by which life "thinks" in a rational, value-giving and limited way, selecting that which might be real. We have received only a mirroring of our own limitations, and have thus seen ourselves fated, by the Classical view. Calling God "Nature" has not changed the resulting fate. A change of metaphor will not make a bad idea good. To attribute human qualities to God is to have mirrored back *just this quality* of limitation, trapping us in our own logic.

The man who challenges: "if there *is* a God, why doesn't he do something about things?" must grasp that the part of mind thinking in this "why" kind of way is the rational mode of life, reasoning man. The closest thing there will ever be to a God responsible for the question is the *asker* of that question. The capacity to fill empty categories is not selective, or the breeder of categories. "God's mode" for thinking selectively is *man.*

There is no magician up there pulling strings if his whim and fancy can just be tickled by the right words. There is no Moral Governor of the Universe, no oriental tyrant able to grant amnesty if we can but find flattering enough incantation. There is no divine mind with beautiful blueprints. There is no super-computer behind the scenes able to out-figure the statistics if we could but hit on the right combination to trigger the mechanism.

The formative process of life is non-ambiguous since it is equally all possibilities. Any non-ambiguous idea becomes an organizing point for realization in this process. Ordinary logical thinking is ambiguous and enters only indirectly as one of an infinite number of random contingencies which may or may not be decisive. Non-ambiguous impressions and notions are generally "below the limen of feeling," and so appear to happen as fate when becoming points for formative realization. Fear, for instance, takes on an ultimate, non-ambiguous nature and tends to create that which is feared. Hatred is the same, trapping the hater in his own hell. A conscious, passionate, singleminded intensity tends to dampen out ambiguity and achieve a realization. Ultimate ideas in that "secret place of mind," the rock-bottom of real belief, shape one's ground of being.

We *must* become aware of the force of mind and develop a balance between the modes of thinking. The materials for achieving this wholeness have been in the common domain for two millenia now, though continuously evaded by our failure of nerve. The current dilemma allows no further evasion. Langer's "boldness of hypothesis" is not just desirable but crucial for survival.

Surely we see each nation groping for protection in this present nightmare, and each further developing the capacity to obliterate all life. But this is merely making outward and evident an inner condition previously projected "out there" as fate. We are finally confronting the mirror of our true selves—we are that fate. We are in our own hands.

Our leaders, placed in positions of power, immediately succumb *to* that power and speak of "dealing from positions of strength," which translates into power *over* and *against*—a desire to be God. The great hopefulness exhibited by that long-gone America of the Marshall Plan and the young United Nations, moving for others as the best protection for ourselves, has been eclipsed in a mirroring of our adversary's paranoia. Now we find that it is we ourselves, not that perpetual enemy, who are considered the "nightmare of the world," as Toynbee plainly called us.

We could have risked our lives to serve and been saved. Inflated with power we have succumbed to don Juan's first stumbling block. We have undergone a temptation in the wilderness, hideously failed, and ironically claimed divine sanction for our folly. What will we do about total power, for soon we will all have it—not just the "most powerful and richest nation on earth," but even these tiny and backward nations whose faces we have ground in the dust of our concupiscence and lust. Soon they, too, will hold the trigger to our mutual demise. What then? Having cast our bread on the waters it will surely be returned. Sowing, we must surely reap. Nothing can mitigate the mirroring we subject ourselves to—nothing but turning from this path that has no heart, this path that can only kill.

Invested in a furtherance of life's thrust toward awareness and expansion of potential, our power could lead to stars and all the "joys and pleasures" in them if we so desired. Used against ourselves to prove our "leadership," to prove that we cannot be pushed around, all development will cease. Power will become ultimately demonic, and this little venture into awareness, in this little corner of infinity, will simply cease to be. Don Juan and Jesus understood this—stood under and responsibly accepted—within their own framework of imagery and representation. And we need their understanding.

We face new situations—but new techniques are arising. Through these current ventures, briefly mentioned in this book, we are creating pieces for this new puzzle, and we will yet fit them together into an even larger image of man. The picture must encompass those pieces already created, however, for it is only by placing one foot firmly in the past that we have firm ground for a step into the future. Our emerging picture will find its true dimension in that frame of continuity encompassing our total heritage. Our next step will hinge on opening to the total process of mind and that means that shadowy area encompassing the whole development of psyche. In Jesus, and even don Juan, we find such symbols for the larger body of man. Triggered through such imagery of the total man, the *autistic* process can synthesize from that enormously rich trial and error understanding reaching through the whole thinking phylum of our living earth.

Do you not see why balance of mind and the non-ambiguous process can only be utilized by passionately holding to some symbol of *wholeness,* a symbol that stands equally for *all* parts of the process itself—which means the absolutely other to us, the neighbor? Do you not see why anything *less* fragments us and isolates us in our surface limitations?

Do you not see how logical thinking, in order to even function, must limit to a specific, and that this specific is then the only apparent reality—and how this fragmented form of thinking then orients quite naturally around the notion of *scarcity,* the idea that in order to *have* we must take from and deprive others, since only a limited amount can be seen? Do you not see that fragmented thinking turns all others into potential enemies, until we live, as Northrop Frye said, as armed crustaceans, damned to a perpetual alarm and crisis, where life itself is a threat to life? Can you not see that opening to the whole mind must open to a constant yield always sufficient, always ample? The cause of the need is the cause of the fulfillment of the need. The empty category is an ontological function. Stepping out into nothingness is impossible—though nothing can be seen, something always forms underfoot. Our universe is not a fixed and frozen machine grinding out in entropy. It can always be what we have need of it to be. The eternal mental life of God and Man has enough to go around—eternally round and round—by moving for and not against.

The new directions outlined here in my book can be seen as harbingers of a new and larger season in our own cycle, and we will manage, I do believe, to hold through this winter of confused discontent. Leonard Hall, Carlos Castaneda, Lévi-Strauss, Polanyi, Hilgarde, Bruner, Langer, and all the rest—these tend toward recognition of the arbitrary character of reality. There is a growing acceptance of Carl Jung's understanding of mind, though his insights are adopted under different imagery, and his genius not credited as the source. The impressive impact of Teilhard de Chardin may well resist attempts by cyclic thinkers to warp his illumination into their deadly circles. Parapsychology suggested a direction, but a more tangible and "scientific" approach will probably be the key, since this is the path already taken. The scientific tool may well prove the bridge, but even so there will come a time when such intermediary devices and projection techniques are obsolete. Such a transition will be gradual and natural; one stage will fuse easily into the other. We may always be simply "discovering Nature's Laws."

In Berkeley, California, for instance, the Carnegie Institute has pioneered a program for developing a kind of free intuitive creativity in young children. The young child is presented with problem-filled adventure readings, situations *without* formal, logical conclusions, where no prestructured logical "answer" exists, even in the minds of the creators of the system. The child has to create a "solution" freely in order to continue the adventure, and the self-motivated technique avoids those arbitrary absolutes which act as constricting, goal-oriented motivations in ordinary education. With no *a priori* answer, and no outside criteria, the child develops a trust and confidence in an inner, open logic too often stifled by formal schooling. Developing this free-synthesis capacity has led, in turn, to impressive leaps of the intelligence quotient itself—that questionable gauge of reality-thinking.

The whole experiment is a gesture toward bridging the modes of mind, and the results could reach beyond science fiction. We may yet see the day when the tragedy of school is overcome.

Prophetic, in a Teilhardian way, was Arthur C. Clarke's little mythos-fantasy, *Childhood's End.* Here science and all intermediate mechanisms of projection had finally given way to a direct "intervention in the ontological constitution of the universe." There was an absorption and loss of individuality implied in Clarke's little dream, reminiscent of a problem never solved by Teilhard. But there was also an odd, if strained, similarity between Clarke's extrapolation and that "coming again in glory" of Jesus' misplaced and misunderstood Apocalypse.

For now the kind of non-ambiguous thinking demanded by a don Juan or a Jesus seems highly improbable.

Too many priesthoods have too tight a control and domination over our fragmented minds. That *Childhood's End* where in we might "level this lift to rise and go beyond" will have to encompass, perfect, and make obsolete a vast number of brilliant but restricting disciplines. We will have to become more righteous than a host of Pharisees, but we will get around these stumbling blocks by the only creative method—which is "agreeing quickly with your adversary," the way to use stumbling blocks as stepping stones.

As for myself, however, today is the day, and I dare not wait for some slow cultural drift finally to pave the way that I might easily float into some nebulous social salvation. I cannot depend on "them" "out there" to order into coherency this small sphere of my only present now. And I find, fortunately, that the process of reality remains unchanged. Ultimate allegiance to a symbol of openness really does open things. The search for the proper materials, the passionate intensity, the decorum and respect, the willingness to be dominated by that desired, leads now as always to the needed synthesis. The fusion still arcs across the gap—the crack surely follows.

If some single, lonely reader is desperate enough, and "hates" an obscenely mad world sufficiently to give it up and open his mind to a restructuring for love *of* that world, things can be different for him, even now. And if he could find two or three to gather with him and agree on what was mutually needed, in this highly-specialized form of agreement even more things could be different. That—strangely—is the way, and the only way by which the broad social drift itself will ever be changed for the better.

So I would urge you to remember, when the forces of despair and destruction hedge you round about, that you need not succumb to their dark statistics. The non-statistical is even here—closer than your very self, and it is yours, and it works. The relation of mind and reality has been but dimly grasped—surely only hinted at in these pages of mine—but even these brief glimpses are blinding. As Whitman said "I am ever shutting sunrise out of me, lest sunrise should kill me." And surely we must channel with care, and take our waking slow, for even in these tentative gestures of ours, outlined here, even in this our infancy of awareness—people *do* walk fire. We *are* an open possibility.

10

vision and reflection

When Carlos started down the mountain with the bags of Mescalito, he found them impossibly heavy and suffered cruelly carrying them. Don Juan warned him not to let the bags touch ground lest the god be lost to Carlos permanently. After a grueling time the bags suddenly became "light and spongy," and Carlos ran down the mountain and caught up with don Juan. The god is never obtained cheaply, but he wears easily and well.

In mythology every Tree of Life is guarded by a dragon, a monster hideous and deadly to behold. The priest in us brands this monster the great evil and warns us away for the safety of our souls. William Blake claimed that this dragon grows only in the human brain—as does the priest himself. When the bravest of heroes ignore all warnings and throw their lives to the winds to reach the goal, they find the dragon a phantom spun out of their own fear and doubt. They push the flimsy image aside, and enter their kingdom.

Perfection, Northrop Frye claims, is the full development of one's imagination. The timid reflective thinker sees perfection as a quality abstracted from a real thing, and thus the sole property of an abstracted and unreal god. Perfection is the utilizing of all the modes of mind, finding that the Trees of Life and Knowledge are twins from the same taproot. Perfection is daring to embrace the universe itself as our true dimension, daring to steal the fire of the gods, to walk on water or fire unafraid, to heal, to claim plenty in time of dearth, to behold boldly that desired and become what we have need to be.

There have always been two predominant and rival views of man and his position or predicament. Tough- and tender-minded come to mind, as do cyclic and linear, hawk and dove. Blake saw our ambivalence in terms of biblical *vision* and Greek *reflection. Reflection,* relying on material things, ends in the dead inertia of the rock as the only real, the mind as the unreal. *Vision* is creative imagination using the eyes as windows to see *with* actively and not *through* passively.

Vision sees life as an "eternal existence in one divine man." Reflection sees life as a series of cycles in nature. Northrop Frye says we vacillate our life away between the two notions, never fully conscious of either. Reflection is Blake's *Diabolos,* the nihilistic impulse of self-doubt reminding us of our helpless frailty and increasing our dependence on the current priesthoods. If the fire-walker listened to this side of his nature, he would never walk fire. As Blake said, "If the sun and moon should doubt, they would immediately go out."

The victory of the cyclic theory becomes the view of a fallen, deadlocked world, a mechanical horror. In Eastern terms this world is a cosmic error to be overcome, from which to escape back into an undifferentiated continuum. In Western terms the universe is a monstrous *necessity,* grinding itself out in a great entropic road to folly and nothingness. Frye points out that we are incapable of accepting this view as objective fact. The moral and emotional implications of it become mental cancers breeding cynical indifference, short-range vision, selfish pursuit of expediency, and "all the other diseases of selfhood."

Reflection inverts the "eternal mental life of God and Man, the Wheel of Life," into a dead cycle. Wonder, joy, imagination, ecstasy, even love, are smugly diagnosed by these cyclic destroyers, who test the blood count, analyze the temperature, the oxygen content, the background of the subjects, and learnedly dismiss as aberrations the highest capacities life has yet produced. All free actions are held in ridicule, only reactions are left. The belly and groin are made supreme, the only point of realness, and the strings by which the vulture-priests think to make the Naked Ape dance to their grindings. But the ape is not controlled thereby, he merely goes mad and dies or destroys.

Saturation with images of violence creates violence, and saturation with ideologies of reflective thinking creates suicidal despair. We need an image, a mythos, representing a way upward and outward where creative longing can be released and not denied. But reflective thinking seizes the insight given by vision and turns it into a dogma that makes for reliably ineffective, lifeless supporters of the world, *in* that world and hopelessly *of* it.

The cyclic religious view loves to speak of "God's plan" for mankind. We are a theatrical group, they say, our roles preordained according to some shadowy script. As free actors we do not follow the prescribed actions, as interpreted by the ruling hierarchy of those who know. Or there is "God's great *symphony*" spread out for all to play, if we would just follow the notes properly and watch the beat of that great-baton-up-yonder, a pulse which synchronizes strangely with the heartbeat of the current powers that feast on fools.

Science has only a small shift to turn this preordaining god into an inflexible and other-to-us Nature, with all the universe laid out on a grand economy of laws. To discover these laws is the Promethean goal, the religious duty in new vestments. And cultures are crushed, the young gods are condemned to years of a madness-producing attempt at *metanoia* called education, and whole civilizations are whipped into line to serve the new god.

We are not involved with a preset script on a preset stage. We are a magnificent and terrible improvisation in which we must be spontaneous playwrights, actors, critics, and audiences. There is no orchestral score up there with every note assigned and waiting. We are, at best, an aleatoric performance. Cacophony and discord are inevitable, yet infinite combinations await us. We err and are bound to err in this open system, yet we are never bound to our errors, as an infinite ability to correct these errors is built in.

We long for an ultimate and our longing is itself the ultimate. Our need is the universal, that with which we satisfy is the particular and never sacrosanct. There is no absolute "out there" of logic, reason, love, goodness, or perfection. Nature is amoral, indifferent, operating by profusion. Needing these things we can only become them by boldly holding them as our rightful due. Life creates myth and then strives to fill it by imitation.

Susanne Langer warned that our losses to science should not be taken lightly. And what we have lost is our psyche, our very soul. Mass psychosis, sickness of soul, is the price we are paying for letting a product become our absolute, letting a tool become master. The young rebel lashes out blindly at this living death to which he is condemned and which he must support, for which he must fight. The tragedy is that by the time he senses a deadly trap he has become, by the very process of reality formation, that against which he instinctively rebels. The only logical tools with which he can fight create the very situation he hates. As don Juan said, "When you find the path you are on has no heart, and try to leave that path, it is ready to kill you." Very few men, he observed, can stop to deliberate at that point, and leave the path.

Any path we choose is arbitrary, but in our choice we shape the world as it is for us. Cohen felt that whatever reality is, we will never know it. I have claimed that reality is what we *do* know, that the world as it is for us is one we represent to ourselves for our own response. So it is with nature, God, "ultimate matter," and so on. We can never get at these as such. Everything we say about them, our sciences, dogmas and creeds, are only representations we seem fated to make and to which we are fated to respond. God, as surely as "Nature," is a concept shot through and through with the mind of man.

And yet, who for a minute believes that nature is *only* a projection of man's mind? Nature is something of which I am a part, and which I must represent to myself. But it is also something which I am not. My thinking and that nature thought about create an event, but they are not identical. Man is not God or nature because he projects gods and natures for his life. Projection is not the whole mechanism even though it shapes the ground on which we stand. There is always more than this.

Teilhard projects his longing onto a great *Omega-Point* "out there." But even there we would find some super-shell, and we would itch to find its crack. In a peculiarly prophetic vision a century and a half ago, Walt Whitman asked, looking up at the vast universe of stars: "When we have encompassed all those orbs, and know the joys and pleasures in them, will we be satisfied then?" No, he realized, "we but level that lift to rise and go beyond."

Without man there is no leveling to rise and go beyond. We give the direction and meaning to the process of becoming. It is time to see man in his true perspective, as Whitman did when he wrote: ". . . in the faces of men and women I see God, and in my own face in the glass, I find letters from God dropt in the street, and every one is sign'd by God's name."

Blake put it in this quatrain:

God appears and God is light
To those poor souls who dwell in Night,
But does a Human form Display
to those who Dwell in Realms of Day.

And yet, how easily Blake assumed as *given* that light that gave his Realms their Day, that light by which his Human Form could *be* displayed. Whitman writes, "I am ever shutting sunrise out of me lest sunrise kill me." This is the given premise on which the function rests, that which we can shape into a level to lift, that toward which we can rise to go beyond—a light of which I cannot speak except to those who would know already of what might then be said—beyond our words, where speech itself is superfluous, a knowing beyond the clouds of all unknowing, an answer beyond all questioning.

For here is the catalyst that shapes *Eureka!s* and gives syntheses beyond our mind's wild reach. Here is the catalyst that acts when it has something to catalyze, and always remains unchanged in so doing. Here is the unattainable, that I cannot will or think into my being, falling into my life even as itself, fleetingly, unbelievably, outside all structured thoughts, strivings, systems, and games. Here all paths are opened and synthesized, our freedoms underwritten and assured within.

Here in this universal swirl is found the knowing of all the nameless griefs and joys, the dregs of all our bitter cups, our agonies, our questions why, our rages, our impotences and despairs. Here, too, is that long, hard dying, held in arms helpless to sustain a fragile breath. Here are both lover and loved split by that Liebestod that tears one's universe asunder.

But here is More! More! Here is our need and the fulfilment of all need. Here is the balm for the unbearable, the arc across the unbridgeable. Here is the ongoing of loser and lost.

So I find that my concern and love for life, my longing and desire, have sowed a wind within this orb of skull, and here in this spiraled fire I reap the whirlwind of all the worlds.

guide to the reference and bibliography system

Source credits, references, explanatory notes, and bibliography are listed in the following pages. They are not indicated in context but are easily found in the reference section. For example, if you are on page 7 of Chapter 1, and find reference to Michael Polanyi's observation that education is a form of conversion, you will find in the reference section the following:

CHAPTER 1 CIRCLES AND LINES

7 Polanyi: *education = conversion.* (79) p. 151.

Under Chapter 1, page 7, is Polanyi's name; the key-words *education = conversion;* the bibliographical source number corresponding to Polanyi's book in parentheses (79), *i.e.,* number 79 of the bibliography; and the page number in Polanyi's work, p. 151, from which the reference is taken. Commentary, if any, is included after the key-words.

references and notes

Chapter 1 Circles and Lines

PAGE

1 Bruner: *direct-touch.* (9) p. 130.
2 Bruner: *concepts-percepts.* (9) p. 6.
4 Bruner: *social fabric.* (9) p. 130.
4 Sapir: *illusion.* (36) p. 87.
7 Polanyi: *education = conversion.* (79) p. 151.
8 *fire-walking.* (see chapter 6).
8 Lévi-Strauss: *semantic universe.* (61) p. 268.
9 Bohm: *zero-point energy.* (see chapter 5).
9 Jesus: *mountain-removal.* (72) Matthew 17:20, Mark 12:22, John 14:12.
10 G. Feinberg: *tachyons.* (26) p. 42, 43.
11 Polanyi: *indwelling.* This is Polanyi's principal thesis running throughout his work. (79, 80, 81).
11 Whitehead: *value = limitation.* (103) p. 95.
14 Jung: *inner-contradiction.* (45) p. 71.
14 Lévi-Strauss: *archaic intellect.* (61) p. 268.
15 Teilhard: *destiny.* (92) p. 47.
16 *innate ideas versus realism.* Two views of the old argument from one issue of *Synthese.* (15, 33).
18 *Codex Bezae.* This story fits in with Jesus' entire attitude toward logical thinking (law) and is probably genuine. (66) p. 50.
18 *loose on earth.* The term was a legal one in current usage. Jesus' use of it encompasses its mundane sense in a larger ontological framework. (72) Matthew 16:20, 18:18, Mark 4:24–25.

PAGE

19 Bruner: *left-hand.* (9).

19 Polanyi: *tacit-primary.* (81) p. 12, 13, 26, etc.

20 *autistic.* The word has a variety of uses but Peter McKellar's explanation led me to its adoption for the "shadow side" of thinking. It has negative connotations, but not so many as the term "unconscious."

20 Polanyi: *child-thinking.* (81) p. 19.

24 Selye: *hypnagogic.* (85) p. 47.

25 Polanyi: *beauty + discovery.* (81) p. 37, 38.

26 Tillich: *hidden content.* (97) p. 267.

30 Laing. (56) p. 114, 115.

30 Smythies. (16) p. 70.

31 Whitehead: *foolishness.* (103) p. 49.

31 Piaget: *autistic = magic.* (76) p. 152, 168. (77) p. 204, 244. (78) p. 302, 303.

32 *Ars Antiqua-Nova.* 14th century artists called themselves the New Artists, and the preceding period the *Antique* artists.

33 Hoffer-Osmond. (41) p. 108. *Also see:* Tart's book, *Altered States of Consciousness,* is a work of considerable importance, but one I found too late for inclusion. (91).

33 Cohen: *LSD and intent of investigators.* Creativity can be sponsored by psychedelics, but is dependent, as all such activity, on the intent of all concerned. As Harman, *et al.,* report, the expectations and intent determine the characteristics of the experience. Therapeutic concerns breed personal problems as the center of the experience. "Kick-seeking" breeds euphoria and visions. Creative problem solving can likewise be induced by programming the experience around elimination of distractions, attention to detail, confidence in abilities, and lack of hypercriticisms. (16) p. 84. *Also see:* (91) p. 446–447.

34 Bruner: *colors.* (10).

35 Solley-Murphy: *sea of data.* (88) p. 178.

PAGE

35 Huxley: *valves.* (43) p. 22, 23.

36 Sherwood: *universal percept.* (16) p. 97. *Also see:* Joe Kamiya's studies on sponsoring alpha-wave production in subjects. (91) p. 507. Kasamatsu and Kirai's studies of Zen meditation. (97) chapter 33.

36 Cohen: *unsanity.* If awareness turns back on the fundamental electrochemical activity that constitutes perception and thinking, a basic-unity experience would be inevitable (Cohen's argument). On the other hand, the "undoing" of the psychic structure (deautomization) permits increased detail and sensation, possibly giving awareness of new dimensions of the total stimulus array. (16) p. 97. *Also see:* Deikman's arguments, pro and con. (91) p. 39.

36 Carington: *field of consciousness.* (13) p. 175, 176, 179, 202, etc.

37 Whitehead: *no simple location.* (103) p. 74.

37 Bruner: *sensory deprivation.* (10). *Also see:* Zubek's anthology of research on sensory deprivation, an exhaustive survey that points up how overdrawn and possibly atypical my example was (107). However, all the phenomena of my example are common, though not often occurring completely at one time. Above all, as Rossi points out, *the manner in which the research questions are formulated* influences the design of the research and the interpretation of the results. This observation verifies the central thesis of my entire book. (107) p. 42. Among conclusions of research so far, are: a lack of variability of sensory data is compensated for by internal syntheses to give variety of sensory experience. Deprivation of one sensory mode will be compensated for by the other sensory modes (a certain level of synesthesia, mixing of sensory modes, is always present). (107) p. 201. Schultz (1965) refers to *sensoristasis,* the organism's attempt to maintain an optimal range of sensory variation; restriction of sensory intake lowers sensory thresholds and the system tries to maintain its norm or balance of senses. (107) p. 242.

38 McKellar: *no mental experience.* (64) p. 73.

42 Vasilieve: *mustard plaster*. The Russians have also done extensive research on "non-visual" seeing, first detected in work with the blind, and now apparently being fostered and developed along startling lines. (100).

42 Jung: *sun-phallus*. (46) p. 152.

43 Stace: *Koestler*. (90) chapter 9.

46 Livingston: *commitment*. (62).

Chapter 3 Blueprints and Viewpoints

49 *feral children.* (32). *Also see:* "Wolf Children of India," *American Journal of Psychology*, XXXVIII, 1927; "More about Wolf Children of India," *American Journal of Psychology*, XLII, 1931.

50 Jung: *Tabula-rasa*. (48) p. 267.

50 Jung: *peeling the unconscious.* (46) p. 152.

51 Langer: *miscarry of language*. (57) p. 110.

51 Bruner: *transformation*. (11) p. 109.

52 Smythies: *child-world hallucination.* (16) p. 70. *Also see:* Deikman writes that the studies of Werner, von Senden and Shapiro suggest that development from infancy to adulthood is bought at the price of some stimuli and stimulus qualities and exclusion of others. Reversal of this process, regression, thus might release aspects of reality otherwise unavailable (a point dwelt on later in my book). (91) p. 39.

52 Bracken: *German theory*. See Phillipp Lersch on "levels of the mind." (8) p. 212.

53 James Old: *rats*. Stimulus of this area of the human brain underlies much of the research reported on by Tart (91), and has more recently been successfully produced non-psychedelically by Drs. Masters and Houston (*The New York Times*, August 26, 1970, p. 35). (73).

54 Blake: *poem*. Auguries of Innocence. (5).

PAGE

54 Blake: *garden = mind.* Marginalia to Reynolds. (5) p. 453.
54 Gesell: *recovery by Kamala.* Chronology. (32) p. 103–7.
54 Gesell: *mold.* (32) p. 67.
55 Erickson. (69) p. 71, 72.
55 Levy Bruhl. (44) p. 16.
55 Jensen. (44) p. 14.
56 Whorf: *agreement.* (104) p. 213–214.
57 Langer: *speech not survival.* (57) p. 106, 113.
57 Bruner: *father to man.* (9) p. 7.
58 Hall: *roots of culture.* (36) p. 177.
58 Whitehead: *fundamental assumptions.* (103) p. 49.
58 Carington: *fact not law.* (13) p. 198.
59 Gibson: *visual field.* (36) p. 62.
59 Hall: *synthetic vision.* (36) p. 65
59 Hall: *culture = world.* (36) p. 65.
59 Cohen: *world not as seen.* (16) p. 45.
60 Bruner: *senses not one-way street.* (9) p. 6.
61 Hall: *vision = transaction.* (36) p. 75.

Chapter 4 Questions and Answers

63 de Bono. (21) p. 20f.
64 Polanyi: *Paul.* (80) p. 44.
64 Russell. (83) p. 180.
64 Hamilton: *quaternions.* (60) p. 332, 335.
65 Toynbee. (60) p. 114.
65 Einstein: *illumination.* (1) p. 236.
66 Kazantzakis. Introduction. (50).
67 Augustine. (60) p. 326, 327
67 Wesley. (60) p. 327.
69 Teilhard: *take apart.* (94) p. 110.
70 Piaget. (76) p. 204.
71 James: *overbelief.* (60) p. 327.
71 Poincaré: *hooked atoms.* References to Poincaré's insights occur continually throughout all studies of the creative act. (64) p. 116.
72 Bruner: *categorizing.* (9) p. 20.

72 Bruner: *outline of creativity.* (9) p. 23, 25.
73 Eliade: *Yoga.* (24) p. 10.
74 Hunt: *occult.* (42) p. 55.
75 *Kekule's imagery.* Selye, Langer, and many others have referred to this intriguing case. (64) p. 121.
77 Cohen: *analysts.* (16) p. 182.
77 Kline: *hypnotism.* (51). *Also see:* Kline's collection of reports concerning the "Bridey Murphy" hoax. And throughout Tart's study, the interaction of subject and hypnotist is clearly established; and, in the case of mutual hypnosis this unconscious rapport takes on profound dimensions. (91).
78 Yeats: *automatic writing.* (25) p. 220.
78 Laski: *Martin.* The remarks concerning Martin are in no way to be considered disparaging. That his work is a clear example of overbelief construction and *metanoia* doesn't diminish its impressive quality and deep possibility. (60) p. 328. *Also see:* Martin's own work. (59).
81 Laski: *"who can doubt."* (60) p. 330.

Chapter 5 Mirror to Mirror

84 Singer: *fluid frontiers.* (86) p. 392.
84 Singer: *mind-nature.* (86) p. 336.
84 Bruner: *science not discovery.* (10) p. 7.
84 Weaver: *human enterprise.* (101) p. 44.
84 Bronowski: *science as art.* (94) p. 249.
84 Teilhard: *discovery-creation.* (94) p. 249.
86 *kidney transplant.* Address over WAMC (Albany Medical College), Eastern Education Radio.
86 Popper: *episteme is gone.* (101) p. 51.
87 Weaver: *foundations.* (101) p. 51.
87 Whitehead: *science = rational of God.* (103) p. 13–16.
87 Whitehead: *basic stuff.* (103) p. 17.
88 Whitehead: *simple locations.* (103) p. 52–57.
89 McKellar: *certainty systems.* (64) p. 168.

PAGE

89 Boring: *ego in controversy.* (7) p. 6.

89 McKellar: *concepts = things.* (64) p. 176.

90 Bruner: *engineered tinkering.* (9) p. 162.

90 Polanyi: *metanoia.* (79) p. 151.

90 Polanyi: *no systematic.* (79) p. 159.

90 Polanyi: *self-modifying.* (79) p. 151.

91 *hardness of heart.* (72) Mark 6:5, 6. Matthew 13:58.

91 Polanyi: *intellectual passions.* (79) p. 159.

91 Bernard: *ideas given form.* (41) p. 6.

92 Bruner: *empty categories.* This list could be extended to book form. (10) p. 14.

93 *Bode's Law.* (86) p. 238.

93 Bohm: *experience = observation.* (6) p. 98.

93 Pauli: *intuition and attention.* (75) p. 15.

93 Polanyi: *discovery is irreversible.* (79) p. 123.

94 G. Feinberg: *Maxwell and Einstein.* (27).

95 Ladriere: *mysterious connection.* (54) p. 74.

95 Pauli: *percept and concept.* (75) p. 152.

95 Bohm: *no eternal forms.* (6) p. 156.

95 Bohm: *necessary relations.* (6) p. 156.

96 Teilhard: *change of state.* (94) p. 180.

96 Bohm: *history.* (6) p. 99.

96 *atomic idea.* In his section on Greek philosophy, Will Durant gave a splendid description of the atomic notion and suggests an even greater antiquity for it (*Life of Greece,* 1939). (86) p. 99.

97 Bohm: *evidence for atoms.* (6) p. 99.

97 Conant: *better theory.* (85) p. 280.

98 Bohm: *universe not based on atoms.* (6) p. 164.

98 G. Feinberg: *basic stuff is known.* (27).

98 Bohm: *sub quantum.* (6) p. 156.

99 Teilhard: *ultimate energy.* (94) p. 250.

99 Bohm: *new sources.* (6) p. 164.

100 Planck: *contradiction = progress.* (85) p. 280.

101 Teilhard: *radical energies.* (94) p. 250.

101 Teilhard: *thought perfects.* (94) p. 176.

102 Teilhard: *psyche-soma.* (94) p. 176.

CHAPTER 6 FIRE-BURN

PAGE

104 L. Feinberg. (28).

106 Grosvenors: *Ceylon.* (34).

108 *Greek walkers.* Dr. Krechmal writes of the *sighing of* the trance state, a typical characteristic. (53).

109 *hook-swingers.* (52).

110 *Manasseh.* (17) p. 441.

112 Neumann: *precedence of inner.* (71) p. 294.

112 *Jesus—hate world.* (72) Mark 12:26.

113 *hand to plow.* (72) Luke 9:62, Mark 6:48, 49.

113 Jung: *rational, irrational.* (47) p. 48.

113 Bruner: *fate.* (9) p. 160.

114 Tillich: *ground of being.* As well as underlying thesis in all of his work. (97) p. 156. (96) p. 297–299.

CHAPTER 7 BEHOLD AND BECOME

116 Hilgard. (40).

116 Jung: *hypnotized patient.* (48) p. 219.

118 Hilgard: *fantasy play.* (40) p. 382.

119 Hilgard: *flexible role.* (40) p. 382.

120 Belo: *trance.* (2).

120 Hilgard: *trance and child.* (40) p. 388.

120 Belo: *child trance dancers.* (2) p. 4.

121 Hilgard: *parent role of hypnotist.* (40) p. 24, 25.

121 Hilgard: *loss of hypnotic susceptibility.* The mystery is not why some people can achieve deep trance but why most people are not able to do so. Hilgard has made strides toward this problem. (40) p. 382. *Also see:* Ronald Shor on hypnosis and reality-orientation. (91) p. 233–250.

122 Hilgard: *transference.* (40) p. 386.

123 *Meares—tooth extraction. Medical Journal of Australia,* McKay, June 1963. (40) p. 126, 127.

124 Hilgard: *role-playing.* More on this in reference to don Juan. (40) p. 391. *Also see:* Tart explores mu-

tual hypnosis which expands the possibilities of the state far beyond anything to date. (91) p. 293.

125 *Aborigine.* (3) p. 29, 43, 57, 64, 66, etc.

127 Lévi-Strauss: *intellectual.* (61) p. 89, 268.

127 Lévi-Strauss: *aborigine isolation* (61) p. 89.

128 Murdock: *stupidity and primitive.* (68) p. 26, 41. *Also see:* Spencer and Gillen offer an exhaustive study of central Australian natives, but view their subjects from a 19th century white man's chauvinism. Again we have, "The idea of making any kind of clothing . . . appears (not to have) entered the native mind." (89) p. 16.

128 *16,000 years of aborigine development.* (70).

129 Berndt: *impressed-surprised.* (3) p. 6. *Also see:* Spencer and Gillen devote a large segment of their study to the ceremonies and rituals of the Arunta, since these constitute a major portion of the native culture. (89).

129 Berndt: *aborigine genius.* (3) p. 6.

130 *camel—needle's eye.* (72) Matthew 19:24.

132 *don Juan and Carlos.* (14).

136 *early American cultures.* (59, 67, 74).

139 *don Juan—looking breathlessly.* (14) p. 137. *Also see:* Tart's work in mutual hypnosis has created non-ordinary reality states every bit as strong and unique as the Mescalito ones, and, since shared, offer an exciting possibility. (91).

139 *don Juan—paths can kill.* (14) p. 118.

Chapter 8 Mythos and Logos

143 Langer: *new function.* (58) p. 30.

143 Bitterman. (4).

144 Langer: *Flüger.* (58) p. 105.

145 Langer: *failure of psychology.* My too late discovery of Dr. Charles Tart's remarkable anthology (91) must enter as this belated qualification to my complaint about psychology. Some extremely important and exciting work is surely emerging, and

PAGE

there are simply no limits in sight for the possibilities. (58) p. 5.

145 Langer: *zoological status.* (58) p. 111.

145 Langer: *culture-symbol.* (58) p. 98.

145 Bruner: *personality-myth.* (9) p. 36.

145 Bruner: *clamor of identity.* (9) p. 38.

145 Bruner: *human possibility.* (9) p. 150.

145 Bruner: *acting-believing.* (9) p. 132.

145 Frye: *alazon-eiron.* (31) p. 39, 40.

146 Langer: *web of ideas.* (58) p. 147.

146 Langer: *imagining reality.* (58) p. 150.

146 Jung: *archetypal imagery.* (45) p. 10.

147 Langer: *loss to science.* (58) p. 107.

147 Langer: *science-culture.* (58) p. 107.

147 Langer: *feeling-experience.* (58) p. 11.

147 Langer: *below the limen.* (58) p. 14.

147 Langer: *mental acts.* (58) p. 21.

147 Langer: *psychology and physiology.* (58) p. 11.

148 Langer: *vast change.* (58) p. 140.

148 Langer: *world image.* (58) p. 167.

148 Langer: *novel ideas.* (58) p. 182.

148 Teilhard: *creative imagination.* (92) p. 115.

149 Eliade: *freedom to intervene.* (23) p. 160.

149 *priest before tree.* (12) p. 92.

149 Jung: *unbearable history.* See section, "The Self." (45).

149 Jung: *God image and projection.* (52) p. 56.

153 Eisenbud: *parapsychology.* My references to Eisenbud are only general, summarizing from the last section of his study. It may be that Eisenbud's own emotional and psychological needs suspended his critical judgment, and that he was duped by Serios, as critics claim. I find the evidence of this inconclusive, and know enough parallel phenomena to make the Serios venture feasible and probable. At any rate, Eisenbud's insights concerning our "failure of nerve" are surely valid. (22).

154 *scholars on Greek objectivity.* Polanyi outlines the paradox of the ordinary assumptions concerning Greek rationale. (80). Harvey Cox sees the Greek

PAGE

development as giving historical rather than spatial perspective. (19). Henri-Charles Puech's *Eranos-Jahrbuch* states that the Greeks held motion and becoming as inferior degrees of reality (Zurich, 1951, Vol. XX, p. 60, 61). Arthur Koestler saw Plato's *Republic* as more horrible than Orwell's *1984* since Plato desired that which Orwell recognized as nightmare. Eliade sees Plato's doctrine of Ideas the final version of archetypal and static concepts. (23) p. 123. Plato can be regarded as the philosopher of "primitive mentality" giving currency and validity to the modes of life and behavior of archaic humanity. (23) p. 34. It was just this concept of eternal repetition which Christian thought attempted to transcend. (23) p. 137.

156 Tillich: *ambiguousness is our fate.* One of Tillich's greatest insights, and the one most irritating to his Stoic-oriented brothers, was that God was not a "divine mind," but constituted a mode fundamentally different from rational thought. (99).

156 Campbell: *hero archetypes.* (12) p. 39, 93.

156 Laing: *obscene madness.* (56) p. 55–59.

157 Weaver: *God.* (101) p. 110, 111.

Chapter 9 Don Juan and Jesus

Note: No specific page references to don Juan are given here. My use of Carlos' material involves a synthesis of the structural analysis concluding his work, combined with the accounts themselves.

164 *group agreement.* (72) Matthew 18:19.

165 *interventions.* (72) Mark 12:22–23, Matthew 17:20.

165 *sole allegiance.* (72) Matthew 25:33.

165 Tillich: *idolatry.* (97) p. 13.

165 *Narrow Gate.* (72) Matthew 7:13, 21.

165 *Peter also Satan.* (72) Matthew 16:20, immediately followed by Matthew 16:23.

166 *double the talents.* (72) Matthew 25:14–30.
167 *no directing of path.* (72) John 3:8.
168 *agreement.* (72) Matthew 18:19, 20.
168 *lose life.* (72) Matthew 16:25.
169 *fading of import.* (72) Mark 8:14–21, Matthew 15:15–17, Matthew 16:9–12.
169 *idolatry—Jesus as magic.* (72) Mark 10:18.
170 *kingdom as leavening, also as mustard seed.* (72) Matthew 13:33, Matthew 16:5, Mark 4:31, 32.
170 *on judgment or logic.* (72) John 5:22.
171 *"hate" your life.* (72) Matthew 10:37, for instance.
171 *age 12 and transformation (mythical overlay).* As Bruce Metzger points out, Mark is the most "realistic" of accounts, Luke the final product of "softening" or mythical overlay. (72) Luke 2:41–52.
172 *forgiveness as unlimited openness.* (72) Matthew 18:21, 22.
173 *child metaphor in metanoia.* (72) John 3:3, Matthew 10:15, Mark 8:35, Mark 10:15, Matthew 18:1–4, etc.
174 *no man . . . but through me.* (72) John 14:6.
174 *before Abraham.* (72) John 8:58.
175 *don Juan's archetypal background.* A full grasp of the achievements of the mound-builders is alone enough to dispel all notions of "primitive stupidity" of earlier cultures on our continent. To mention but a small segment of the new material concerning the antiquity of American culture, see (55, 59, 63, 67, 74).
176 *helpless to create.* (72) Mark 6:5, Matthew 13:58.
178 *any ultimate produces its response.* (72) Matthew 21:21.
179 *sighed heavily.* Krechmal notes the "sighing" of the fire-walkers. (53). (72) John 11:33, 38.
180 *ask in my name.* (72) Matthew 18:19.
180 Tillich: *ecstasy-creativity.* (99) p. 24.
180 *desire, fruitfulness.* There is a strong "Dionysian" element in the Jesus of John's Gospel. And this fourth Gospel is, according to Cornfeld, in many of its sections the *oldest* Gospel material, contrary to

ordinary assumptions. Surely a strong overlay of Greek philosophy is found there also, but Cornfeld points out unmistakable ties to the Qumran community—according to recent semantic research. (18).

181 *remoteness of God by Plato.* (20) p. 375, 376, 378. (38) p. 241.

181 *Stoic perversion of Jesus' Way* ". . . such has been Christianity . . ." (102) p. 60. Bishop Butler is "pure Stoicism almost." And Butler is the most powerful, clear statement of Christendom you can find. (102) p. 154. Ramm surveys the various spokesmen of "natural religion." William Blake had no love of this dark and destructive way of thinking. Crombie, Wenley, Hatch, and others, give insight into the destruction of Jesus' postulate by Greek logic. But since "theology" cannot be found in the Gospels, but rather in Greek philosophy, theologians have systematically ignored all such insights and have continued to grind their dead dust undisturbed. (82).

181 Polanyi: *Augustine on the relation of faith and reason.* Polanyi briefly touches on an aspect of Augustine's genius which is relevant in its own way, but because of overall context (Stoic rather than of the Way) still misses the mark. (80) p. 27.

181 Tillich: *spirit as threshold of mind.* (99) p. 21.

181 *"acts even greater."* (72) Mark 9:23, Mark 12:22, 23, 24, John 14:12, 13, 14.

182 *blocking Narrow Gate.* (72) Matthew 23:13.

183 *inverting Jesus.* (30) p. 53, 149, etc.

183 *man as reason.* (98) p. 13.

183 *no divine mind.* (99) p. 22.

187 Tart: *"new directions" in current research.* Tart's collection of readings on current research is the most significant and hopeful sign I have yet found. Almost any of the studies he includes are more important than the few listed in my context. Surely the opening to the whole mind will take place by these

scientists and their explorations, and I have to re-evaluate my criticisms of the "narrowness" of psychologists. Things are happening, and fast. (91).

Chapter 10 Vision and Reflection

190 *dragons and trees.* (12) p. 92, 93. (30) p. 137, 149. (23) p. 69.
190 *perfection.* (30) p. 37.
191 *one divine man.* (30) p. 383, 384.
191 *Diabolos.* (30) p. 135.
191 *diseases of selfhood.* (30) p. 384.
191 *reactions only.* Blake claims Satan is a "reactor." He never acts, but only reacts. He never sees, but has to be shown. (30) p. 401.

bibliography

1. "Adventures of the Mind" from the *Saturday Evening Post,* New York, Vintage Books, 1960.
2. Belo, Jane *Trance in Bali,* New York, Columbia University Press, 1960.
3. Berndt, *et al. Australian Aboriginal Art,* New York, Macmillan, 1964.
4. Bitterman, M. E. "The Evolution of Intelligence," *Scientific American,* Vol. 212, Jan. 1965.
5. Blake, William *Selected Poetry and Prose,* New York, Random House, 1958.
6. Bohm, David *Causality and Chance in Modern Physics,* New York, Van Nostrand, 1957.
7. Boring, Edwin G. "The Present Status of Parapsychology," *American Scientist,* Vol. XLII, Jan. 1955.
8. Bracken, Helmut von, and David, Henry P. *Perspectives in Personality Theory,* New York, Basic Books, 1957.
9. Bruner, Jerome S. *On Knowing, Essays for the left hand,* Cambridge, Belknap Press, 1962.
10. Bruner, Jerome S. *A Study of Thinking* (with Goodnow & Austin), New York, Science Editions, 1962.
11. Bruner, Jerome S. *Toward a Theory of Instruction,* Cambridge, Belknap Press, 1966.
12. Campbell, Joseph *The Hero with a Thousand Faces,* New York, Pantheon, Bollingen Series, XVII, 1949.

13. Carington, Whately *Matter, Mind and Meaning,* New Haven, Conn., Yale University Press, 1949.
14. Castaneda, Carlos *The Teachings of don Juan, A Yaqui way of knowledge,* Berkeley, University of California Press, 1968.
15. Chomsky, Noam "Recent Contributions to the Theory of Innate Ideas," *Synthese,* Dordrecht, Holland, D. Reidel Pub., Vol. 17, 1967.
16. Cohen, Sidney *The Beyond Within,* New York, Atheneum, 1965.
17. Cornfeld, Gaalyhu *Adam to Daniel, An illustrated guide to the Old Testament and its background,* New York, Macmillan, 1961.
18. Cornfeld, Gaalyhu *Daniel to Paul,* New York, Macmillan, 1962.
19. Cox, Harvey *The Secular City,* New York, Macmillan, 1965.
20. Crombie, I. M. *An Examination of Plato's Doctrines,* London, Routledge & Kegan Paul, 1962, New York, Humanities.
21. de Bono, Edward "Lateral and Vertical Thinking," *Today's Education,* The Journal of the NEA, Vol. 58, #8, 1970.
22. Eisenbud, Jule *The World of Ted Serios,* New York, Wm. Morrow, 1967.
23. Eliade, Mircea *Cosmos and History, The myth of the eternal return,* New York, Harper Torchbooks, 1959.
24. Eliade, Mircea *Yoga: Immortality and freedom,* New York, Pantheon, Bollingen Series, LVI, 1958.
25. Elman, Richard *Yeats, The man and the masks,* New York, Dutton, 1958.
26. Feinberg, Gerald "Exceeding the Speed Limit," *Time Magazine,* Feb. 14, 1969, p. 42.
27. Feinberg, Gerald "Ordinary Matter," *Scientific American,* Vol. 216, #5, May 1967, p. 126.
28. Feinberg, Leonard "Fire-walking in Ceylon," *The Atlantic Monthly,* May 1959, 203:73–6.
29. Ferm, Vergilius *Ancient Religions,* New York, Philosophical Library, 1950.

30. Frye, Northrop *Fearful Symmetry, A study of William Blake,* Princeton, N.J., Princeton University Press, 1947.
31. Frye, Northrop *Anatomy of Criticism, Four essays,* Princeton, N.J., Princeton University Press, 1957.
32. Gesell, Arnold *Wolf Child and Human Child,* New York, Harper & Row, 1940.
33. Gibson, James J. "New Reasons for Realism," *Synthese,* Vol. 17, Dordrecht, Holland, Reidel, 1967.
34. Grosvernor, Donna and Gilbert "Ceylon," *The National Geographic Magazine,* Vol. 129, #4, April 1966.
35. Guthrie, W. K. C. *Orpheus and Greek Religion,* London, Metheun, 1952.
36. Hall, Edward T. *The Hidden Dimension,* Garden City, New York, Doubleday, 1966.
37. Halverson & Cohen *A Handbook of Christian Theology,* New York, Meridian, 1958.
38. Hatch, Edwin *The Influence of Greek Ideas and Usages upon the Christian Church,* London, Williams and Norgate, 1892.
39. Hatch, Edwin *The Organization of the Early Christian Churches,* London, Longmans, Green, 1901.
40. Hilgard, Ernest R. *Hypnotic Susceptibility,* New York, Harcourt Brace & World, 1965.
41. Hoffer & Osmond *The Chemical Basis of Clinical Psychiatry,* Springfield, Ill., Charles C. Thomas, 1960.
42. Hunt, Douglas *Exploring the Occult,* New York, Ballantine, 1965.
43. Huxley, Aldous *The Doors of Perception,* New York, Harper & Row, 1954.
44. Jensen, Adolf E. *Myth and Cult among Primitive Peoples,* Chicago, University of Chicago Press, 1963.
45. Jung, Carl G. *Aion,* New York, Pantheon, Bollingen Series, ii.

46. Jung, Carl G. *The Structure and Dynamics of the Psyche,* New York, Pantheon, Bollingen Series, Vol. VIII.
47. Jung, Carl G. *Two Essays on Analytical Psychology,* New York, Pantheon, Bollingen Series, Vol. VII.
48. Jung, Carl G. *The Archetypes and the Collective Unconscious,* New York, Pantheon, Bollingen Series, Vol. IX, #I
49. Jung, Carl G. *Symbols of Transformation,* New York, Pantheon, Bollingen Series, Vol. V.
50. Kazantzakis, Nikos *The Odyssey, A modern sequel,* New York, Simon & Schuster, 1958.
51. Kline, Milton V. *Hypnodynamic Psychology,* New York, Julian, 1964.
52. Kosambi, D. D. "Living Prehistory in India," *Scientific American,* Vol. 216, #2, Feb. 1967, p. 104.
53. Krechmal, Arnold "Fire-walkers of Greece," *Travel,* October 1957, 108:46–7.
54. Ladriere, Jean "Faith and the Technician Mentality," *Christians in a Technological Era,* New York, Seabury, 1964.
55. Laing, Ronald *Interpersonal Perception,* (with Phillipson and Lee) London, Tavistock, New York, Springer, 1966.
56. Laing, Ronald *The Politics of Experience,* New York, Ballantine, 1967.
57. Langer, Susanne K. *Philosophy in a New Key,* Cambridge, Mass., Harvard University Press, 1942.
58. Langer, Susanne K. *Philosophical Sketches,* Baltimore, Md., The Johns Hopkins Press, 1962.
59. Lanning & Patterson "Early Man in South America," *Scientific American,* Vol. 127, #5, 1967.
60. Laski, Marghanita *Ecstasy, A study of some secular and religious experiences,* Bloomington, Ind., Indiana University Press, 1962.
61. Lévi-Strauss, Claude *The Savage Mind,* Chicago, University of Chicago Press, 1966.
62. Livingston, A. R. "Perception and Commitment," *Bulletin of Atomic Science,* Vol. 19, Feb. 1963.

63. Martin, Percival Wm. *An Experiment in Depth,* New York, Pantheon, 1955.
64. McKellar, Peter *Imagination and Thinking, A psychological analysis,* New York, Basic Books, 1957.
65. Metzger, Bruce *The New Testament, Its background, growth and content,* New York, Abingdon, 1965.
66. Metzger, Bruce *The Text of the New Testament, Its transmission, corruption, and restoration,* London, Oxford at the Clarendon Press, 1964.
67. Miller, Rene "Teotihuacan" (Mexico), *Scientific American,* Vol. 216, #6, June 1967.
68. Murdock, George Peter *Our Primitive Contemporaries,* New York, Macmillan, 1934.
69. Montagu, Ashley *The Concept of the Primitive,* New York, Free Press, 1968.
70. Mulvaney, D. J. "The Pre-History of the Australian Aborigine," *Scientific American,* Vol. 214, #3, March 1966.
71. Neumann, Erich *The Origins and History of Consciousness,* Vol. II, New York, Harper Torchbook, 1962.
72. New Testament *The New English Bible,* Oxford University Press and Cambridge University Press, 1961. Revised Standard Version, New York, American Bible Society, 1952.
73. Old, James "Self-Stimulation of the Brain," *Science,* Vol. 127, #3294, Feb. 14, 1958.
74. Parson & Denevan "Pre-Columbian Ridged Fields," *Scientific American,* Vol. 217, #1, July 1967.
75. Pauli, W. *The Influence of Archetypal Ideas on the Scientific Theories of Kepler,* New York, Pantheon, Bollingen Series, 1955.
76. Piaget, Jean *The Child's Conception of Physical Causality,* London, Routledge & Kegan Paul, 1930.
77. Piaget, Jean *The Child's Conception of the World,* New York, Humanities, 1951.
78. Piaget, Jean *Judgment and Reasoning in the Child,* New York, Humanities, 1952.

79. Polanyi, Michael *Personal Knowledge,* Chicago, University of Chicago Press, 1958.
80. Polanyi, Michael *Christians in a Technological Era,* New York, Seabury, 1964.
81. Polanyi, Michael *The Study of Man,* Chicago, University of Chicago Press, 1959.
82. Ramn, Bernard *Varieties of Christian Apologetics, Part II, Systems Stressing Natural Theology,* Grand Rapids, Iowa, Baker Book House, 1965.
83. Russell, Bertrand *Religion and Science,* London, Oxford University Press, 1935.
84. Schonfield, Hugh J. *The Passover Plot, new light on the history of Jesus,* New York, Random House, 1965.
85. Selye, Hans *From Dream to Discovery, On being a scientist,* New York, McGraw-Hill, 1964.
86. Singer, Charles *A Short History of Science,* London, Oxford at the Clarendon Press, 1941.
87. Smythies, J. R. *Analysis of Perception,* New York, Humanities, 1956.
88. Solley, Charles M. and Murphy, Gardner *Development of the Perceptual World,* New York, Basic Books, 1960.
89. Spencer, Baldwin and Gillen, F. J. *The Native Tribes of Central Australia,* New York, Dover, 1968.
90. Stace, Walter *The Teachings of the Mystics,* New York, New American Library, 1960.
91. Tart, Charles R. editor *Altered States of Consciousness, A book of readings,* New York, John Wiley & Sons, 1969.
92. Teilhard de Chardin *The Divine Milieu,* New York, Harper & Row, 1960.
93. Teilhard de Chardin *The Future of Man,* New York, Harper & Row, 1964.
94. Teilhard de Chardin *The Phenomenon of Man,* New York, Harper & Row, 1961.
95. Tillich, Paul *Dynamics of Faith,* New York, Harper & Row, 1957.
96. Tillich, Paul from *Four Existential Theologians,* ed. Will Herberg, New York, Doubleday, 1958.

97. Tillich, Paul *Systematic Theology,* Vol. I, Chicago, University of Chicago Press, 1951.
98. Tillich, Paul *Systematic Theology,* Vol. II, Chicago, University of Chicago Press, 1957.
99. Tillich, Paul *Systematic Theology,* Vol. III, Chicago, University of Chicago Press, 1960.
100. Vasiliev, L. L. *Mysterious Phenomena of the Human Psyche,* New Hyde Park, N.Y., University Books, 1965.
101. Weaver, Warren *Science and Imagination, Selected papers,* New York, Basic Books, 1967.
102. Wenley, R. M. *Stoicism and its Influence,* New York, Cooper Square, 1963.
103. Whitehead, Alfred N. *Science and the Modern World,* New York, Macmillan, 1925.
104. Whorf, Benjamin Lee *Language, Thought, and Reality,* New York, John Wiley & Sons, and the M.I.T. Technology Press, 1956.
105. Wilkerson, David *The Cross and the Switchblade,* New York, Bernard Geis Associates, 1963.
106. Wolinsky, Gloria F. "Jean Piaget's Theory of Perception," *Science Education,* Vol. 48, #1, Feb. 1964.
107. Zubek, John P. ed. *Sensory Deprivation, 15 years of research,* New York, Appleton-Century-Crofts, 1969.